VIEW OF HAVERHILL, MASS.

The
History of Haverhill
Massachusetts

by

Benjamin L. Mirick

There was a time when red men climbed these hills,
And wandered by these glades, these plains, and rills;
Or rowed the light canoe along yon river,—
Or rushed to conflict, armed with bow and quiver,—
Or 'neath the forest leaves that o'er them hung,
They council held, or loud their war-notes sung.
— *MS. Poem*

HERITAGE BOOKS
2019

HERITAGE BOOKS
AN IMPRINT OF HERITAGE BOOKS, INC.

Books, CDs, and more—Worldwide

For our listing of thousands of titles see our website
at
www.HeritageBooks.com

A Facsimile Reprint
Published 2019 by
HERITAGE BOOKS, INC.
Publishing Division
5810 Ruatan Street
Berwyn Heights, Md. 20740

Copyright © 1991 Heritage Books, Inc.

Originally published
Haverhill:
Printed and Published by A. W. Thayer
1832

— Publisher's Notice —

In reprints such as this, it is often not possible to remove blemishes from the original. We feel the contents of this book warrant its reissue despite these blemishes and hope you will agree and read it with pleasure.

Please note that the volume used to produce this reprint had a few words of text missing from the bottom of page 82.

International Standard Book Numbers
Paperbound: 978-1-55613-497-5
Clothbound: 978-0-7884-6962-6

INTRODUCTION.

In the early history of almost every town, there is a great variety of incidents which are well worth preserving. However trifling some of them may appear to strangers, still they carry a deep and abiding interest to a native. No one can heedlessly listen to a narrative of the customs and manners of his fathers—to a recital of the deeds they accomplished, and the dangers they surmounted. Every valley and hill has its history—the ancient tree that stretches its long branches to the breeze—the flowers that spring up and blossom in our pathway—and the glassy stream that bursts from the green hillside, rippling in the shade of the thick forest, or winding slowly among the open and cultivated fields;—and it cannot but interest those who are now seeking pleasure or profit among them, when they reflect that, on the same places, their fathers reared their thatched cottages, defended themselves against the attacks of prowling beasts, and grappled with the fierce savages.

The depredations of the Indians form a prominent feature in the following pages. Haverhill was a frontier town for more than seventy years, and about thirty years it suffered all the horrors which accompanied savage warfare. The history of the dangers and hardships endured by some of the inhabitants, in the latter period, appears, in many instances, like some fabulous story; and, perhaps, we should so consider it, were it not derived from respectable and authentic sources. Scarcely a year passed, but more or less of them were slain, or captivated by their treacherous enemy,—an enemy, who spared not the old man, nor the infant, neither the strong man, nor feeble and helpless woman—all were alike the objects of their hatred and revenge. Many writers have ascribed to this revengeful race, pure and lofty virtue, high and delicate principles of honor, and firm and devoted friendship to those who have granted them favors. To these assertions I am not prepared to subscribe. If valor be a virtue, then some of them surely possessed it; but even these were few, for the courage of a great majority only prompted them to murder women and children, and attack men unawares, or while asleep. We have discovered none of their devoted friendships, nor their high principles of honor, in their intercourse, either in peace or in war, with the early inhabitants of this town. Nothing can justify their treacherous conduct—no plea can be urged in their behalf sufficient to palliate their diabolical cruelties.

The advancement of the American Colonies in population, riches and power, is unparalleled in the annals of history. The mammoth nations that have long since been swept from the field of existence, whose armies encircled mountains, and covered vallies; whose armaments triumphantly rode the great deep, and made the rock-built cities of warlike nations tremble at their appearance—these can boast, at no period, of a progress so elevated, so rapid as our own. Their early strength was like the infant's; as that will extend its arms to surrounding objects for support, so they leaned on contiguous nations for protection, until prosperity began to flow through their internal channels, till their limbs were indued with vigor, and they could gird on the sword, handle the spear, and go forth alone and fearlessly to conquer. Century after century came and passed; revolutions, attended with terrific gloom, horror, conflagration and bloodshed, were effected; and kingdoms tottered, crumbled and fell, before they attained the zenith of their power.

But it was not so with the Colonies. A few years only elapsed, when flourishing villages sprung up, as if by magic, from the gloomy wilderness, teeming with a hardy and fearless population. Scarcely a century and a half had revolved, when they arose in their strength, and shook the chains of monarchy from their limbs. The spirit of Liberty was an early and beloved inmate of the bosoms of our Fathers. It was a native of the soil on which they trod. It roamed upon the mountain that lifts its bleak brow to the clouds, as wild, as proud, and free, as the grey bird that builds her eyry on its loftiest cliff; sometimes it rested in its sunny places, or in the shadow of its tall trees; sometimes it basked on its sky-peaked rocks, or travelled with the winds over its wild recesses. It descended into the vallies and sate beneath the green chestnut, the sycamore, or cedar; or slept in the night-time among their sweetest flowers. At noon-day it drank from the cool fountains that burst from the silent caverns of the hills, and gently flowed through the shady woods. It was in every hill, glen, tree and stream, and readily infused itself into the bosoms of our fathers, where it was a welcome and cherished guest. At last, when it was chafed with the iron hand of oppression, it broke from its retreat, and defied the veteran armies and the multiplied armaments of the mightiest nation of Europe. Its voice was then like the sound of a terrible earthquake, or the roll of midnight thunders; and it rang, not only among our own White and Apalachian hills, but among the snow-clad cliffs of the Dofrafield, and through the land of palms and cypresses.

1*

That spirit of liberty,—that earnest longing for independence which animates the breast of man, is not to be spoken of—it is not to be written, analyzed nor criticised; but to be mused upon—to be felt—and to be acted in the field, or in the hall of legislation. It may be crushed, but never destroyed; it may nearly wither beneath the hot breath of monarchy, but it will never die. We might as well think of handling the lightning, or of changing the course of the thunder-bolt, as to destroy it. It is unfathomable—indescribable—unknown, but to him who feels it. The roar of conflicting armies, the crackling of a conflagration, the clanking of chains, the horrors of a dungeon—nothing will appal the heart which it animates.

In the long and arduous struggle of the Colonies for independence, Haverhill bore its share of the losses, both in men and treasure; perhaps none, of the same wealth and population, did more. Most of the inhabitants were ready, at any period, to sacrifice their fortunes, and even their lives, to support the government of their choice. Their taxes were frequently enormous, but they were cheerfully borne. Though darkness and gloom often hung like a pall over the struggling nation, still they were not dispirited, but clung to hope, like men who had determined to die, rather than see their beloved country groaning in slavery.

But few of these revolutionary worthies are now living. The most of them have been gathered to the harvest of death, and the venerable remnant that now remains, will quickly pass away. Their voices will be silent—their hoary heads will be no longer among us—they will be crumbling in the earth with their fathers. But the story of their achievement shall not be forgotten. Their swords and their sheaths shall be hung up in the halls of their children, as silent but intelligible witnesses of their deeds. Their glory shall never pass from their names; but, in whatever land the banner of freedom is unfurled, there will their memories be cherished, and their praises sung.

Though the interest created by a history of this kind is principally local, still no pains or expense has been spared to make it what it should be. When I began to collect my materials, the names of the first settlers were not known, and even the year in which the town was said to be settled, was, by many disputed. Many accounts have been published of the heroic deed of Mrs. Hannah Dustin; but the most of them which I have examined are very imperfect, and some of them inconsistent. To this, and the memorable attack by the French and Indians on the 29th August, 1708, I have paid particular attention; and believe that I have collected all the attending circumstances worthy of being preserved; many of which have not hitherto been generally known. I have collected the names of many persons who lived here at an early period; the names of those who were slain by the Indians, the day on which they fell, and in many cases the incidents connected with them. The reader will also find short biographical sketches of some of the prominent men who were an honor to the town.

In my researches I found many ancient manuscripts in private families, some of which were written nearly one hundred and fifty years ago, but were laid aside with waste papers, and considered of no value. I have likewise discovered many almanacks, more than a century old, on which the owners kept a journal of remarkable events. The late Hon. Bailey Bartlett, just before his decease, copied from his almanacks, a journal kept by himself and his father, from 1732 to 1830. From this I have extracted many interesting facts. The Town Records are another source from which I have derived information. The first regular meeting held by the town was in 1643; and the book in which were recorded the doings of that and a few succeeding years, is in a very tattered condition. Some of its pages can scarcely be decyphered. It seems that the Indians, in one of their attacks, obtained possession of it; but it was found soon after in the westerly part of the town, now Methuen, in a very damaged state. I have inserted some things which were handed down by tradition; but have, in most cases, given them as such, and have admitted none but those which seemed probable, or were derived from respectable sources.

These are a few of the numerous authorities from which I have drawn my information. It cannot be expected, in such a variety of facts and dates, as is contained in the following pages, that all will be perfectly correct; though great pains have been taken to have them so. To those persons who have assisted me in collecting materials, and have taken an interest in the publication of this work, I offer the fervent expressions of my gratitude; and I am particularly indebted to Charles White, Esq. and Charles Minot, Esq. of Haverhill; Mr. Benjamin Greenleaf, Preceptor of Bradford Academy; John Farmer, Esq., of Concord, N.H.; William Gibbs, Esq., of Salem; and Mr. Joshua Coffin, of Newbury, whose manuscript history of his native town, will, I understand, soon be presented to the public.

HISTORY OF HAVERHILL.

1640.

THE first intimation of the settling of Pentucket, now Haverhill, which we have been able to discover, is contained in the following letter from Giles Firmin to Gov. Winthrop, dated 26th Dec. 1639.

" *Much honoured and dear Sir:*
But that I thinke it needlesse (God havinge more than ordinarye fitted you for such trials) my letter might tell you with what griefe of spirit I received the news of that sad affliction which is lately happened to your worship, by means of that unfaithful wretch; I hope God will find a shoulder to helpe you beare so great a burthen. But the little time there is allotted me to write, I must spend in requesting your worships counsel and favour. My father in law Ward, since his sonne came over, is varey desirous that wee might sett down together, and so that he might leave us together if God should remove him from hence. Because that cant be accomplished in this town, is verey desirous to get mee to remove with him to a new plantation. After much perswasion used, consideringe my want of accommodations here (the ground the town having given mee lying 5 miles from mee or more) and that the gains of physick will not finde mee in bread, but, besides apprehendinge that it might bee a way to free him from some temptations, and make him more cheerful and more serviceable to the country or church, have yeelded to him. *Herein, as I desire your counsel, so do I humbly request your favour, that you would be pleased to give us the libertye of choosinge a plantation; wee thinke it will bee at Pentuckett or Quichichchek [Cochichawich] by Shawshin:* so soon as the season will give us leave to goe, we shall inform your worship which wee desire: And if that, by the court of election, wee cannot gather a company to begine it, wee will let it fall. We desire you will not graunt any of them to any before wee have seene them. If your worship have heard any relation of the places, wee should remaine

thankful to you, if you would be pleased to counsel us to any of them. Further, I would entreate for advise in this : The towne gave mee the ground (100 acres) upon this condition, that I should stay in the towne 3 yeares, or else I could not sell it : Now my father supposes it being my first heritage (my father having none in the land) that it is more than they canne doe to hinder mee thus, when as others have no business, but range from place to place, on purpose to live upon the countrey. I would entreate your counsel whither or noe I canne sell it. Further: I am strongly sett upon to studye divinitie, my studyes else must be lost; for physick is but a meene helpe. In these cases I humbly referre to your worship, as my father, for your counsel, and so in much haste, with my best services presented to your worship, wishinge you a strong support in your affliction, and a good and comfortable issue, I rest your worships in what he canne to his power. GYLES FYRMIN.
IPSWICH, 26, 10th, 1639.
Wee humbly entreate your secrecye in our desires."

Firmin soon after went to England, where he became a celebrated non-conformist minister. He was the author of a work called the "Real Christian," and probably few books of that description have been more read or oftener reprinted.

Soon after, Mr. John Ward, together with some of the inhabitants of Newbury, petitioned the General Court for liberty to settle at Pentucket, or Cochichawich, as appears by the following:

"At a General Courte held at Boston the 13th of 3d month 1640 [13th May 1640,] the desires of Mr. [John] Ward, and Newbury men, is committed to the Governor, Deputy Governor, and Mr. Winthrop, sen. to consider of Pentuckett and of Cochichawich, and to grant it to them, provided they return answer within three weeks from the 21st present, and that they build there before the next Courte."

After some little consideration, Mr. Ward and his companions selected Pentucket ; and allowing them three weeks to come to a decision and return their answer, the settlement must have commenced between the 11th of June and the 7th of October following, the day on which the next Court was holden.

The following are the names of those persons who accompanied Mr. Ward, and struck the first blow towards erecting a settlement in the wild woods of Pentucket. Those in Italics were from Newbury. *William White, Samuel Gile, James Davis, Henry Palmer, John Robinson,* Abraham Tyler, Daniel Ladd, Joseph Merrie,

Christopher Hussey, Job Clement, *John Williams* and *Richard Littlehale*.

At a General Court holden at Boston, 7th October, 1640, "Mr. Edward Woodman, Mr. Paine, and Mr. Nelson, were appointed to view the bounds between Colchester [Salisbury] and *Mr. Ward's plantation.*"

By these extracts, taken from the records of the General Court, it is evident that the settlement of Pentucket was commenced in the summer of 1640, under the conduct of the venerable Ward. Cotton Mather says that Mr. Ward "settled in Haverhill in 1641;" but he certainly mistakes, for the express conditions granted to the petitioners, were, that "they should return answer within three weeks from the 21st May, 1640, and build before the next Court," which was on the 7th of October following. Soon after its settlement it was called HAVERHILL, in compliment to Mr. Ward, who was born in Haverhill, Essex County, England, and was the fearless and hardy pioneer of civilization into the gloomy and unbroken wilderness. The first house was erected near the old burying ground, one fourth of a mile east of Haverhill Bridge; but in the course of two years, a house was built near Mr. Ezekiel Hale's Factory.

On undertaking important enterprises, our pious ancestors generally associated with them ministers of the gospel; but in the settlement of Haverhill, a clergyman was the projector and leader. No tongue could more faithfully portray their moral character and religious feelings—no language could speak more powerfully their elevated sentiments. Where the sound of the woodman's axe echoed amid the forest solitudes—where the thatched hut was reared, and the blue smoke issued from its wooden chimney, and curled far upward among the thick branches—*there* was heard the sound of prayer, and devout hearts spake of Jesus, of Calvary, and the sepulchre. Beneath the shadow of the kingly oak, the hardy settler and his children, with their rugged and sunburnt visages, could gather in the deepening twilight, while their teacher stood among them, and taught them from the book of God. If their babes looked up to the sky, when the summer's sun had gone down in its glory, and asked who gave it such beauty, they were answered, God; if they looked up in the depth of midnight, and saw the stars, and extended their puny hands as they would take them in their grasp—if they gathered flowers in their pathway—or if they gazed upon the tempest-cloud, and concealed themselves, and wept for fear;—their teacher told them that all these were the works of God; that they could kneel in the forest, by the fountain, and the river, and He would be among them.

Before the town was settled, it was covered with an immense, and in some places, almost impenetrable forest, except the lowlands or meadows. These were cleared by the Indians, perhaps centuries before the discovery of America; and they were covered with a heavy growth of grass, which grew so exceedingly thick, and so very high, that it was impossible to discover man or beast at a distance of five rods. They resembled the celebrated prairies of the West in every thing except extent. Every autumn the Indians set the dried grass on fire, so that they might more easily kill the deer which came to feed on it, the next spring. On account of the grass, they were prized above all other lands by the first settlers, for there they procured hay for their flocks; and they were divided into small lots, and distributed among them. The forest was filled with various kinds of small birds. Innumerable flocks of ducks resorted to the ponds, and the timid loon was seen sailing majestically on their waters. The wild deer reposed in the shady groves, or bounded over the hills, followed by the eager hunter. The loud bark of the raccoon was heard, and the wily fox was often seen leaping through the woods. But the worst enemy, of the beast kind, to the infant settlement, was the cruel and voracious wolf. They sometimes roamed the woods in droves, trotting like dogs, and in some of their excursions destroyed large numbers of sheep. At one period they had become so bold and troublesome, that a large plat of ground was enclosed near the common, and used as a pasture for the sheep. Shepherds were likewise appointed to protect them, and at night they were collected into a close fold, or pen. Hardly a day passed in which depredations were not made; and almost every night their dismal howlings broke upon its solitude.

Haverhill was sold by two Sachems, or Chiefs, Passaquoi and Saggahew; and the tribe which inhabited it was under their jurisdiction. They were not, however, entirely independent; but acknowledged allegiance to a higher power, invested in Passaconnamy,* who was the great powah, or priest, of all the tribes in this quarter. No expedition of moment, or action of importance, was commenced without his consent. He gained this power over his brethren by the aid of religion, their notions of which are thus described by Lewis: "They believed that after death they should go to the region whence came the pleasant south-west wind, where dwelt their great and benevolent God, Cautontowit, and where they should enjoy perpetual pleasures, and hunting and fishing without weariness. They endured the most acute pains without a murmur, never laughed loud, and their words and deeds were seldom strangers." Their principal village was on the banks of Little River, near its mouth; and the house of Thomas R. Appleton stands on what was once their burial ground. When that cellar was excavated, a number of skeletons were dug up in a very good state of preservation. Heads of arrows have frequently been found in that quarter, stone mortars in which they pounded their corn, and other utensils of a warlike and culinary kind. The arrow-head was a flat stone, about two inches in length, gradually sloping to a sharp point at one end. This was fastened to an oak stick about twenty inches in length, and when thrown with a strong, elastic bow, often gave a deadly wound. The mortar was a soft stone, of considerable dimensions, in which they scooped a hollow place, varying in depth and diameter, according to the size of the family.

Their women performed all the drudgery of their households, and were likewise the tillers of the soil; the men deeming it debasing to engage in any thing but hunting, fishing and war. They were not destitute of music, for they were accustomed to sing songs while

---

* This name in the Deed is spelt, *Passaconnaway.*

engaged in almost every occupation. When they launched their birchen canoes on the smooth waters of the Merrimack,* to proceed on any expedition, they sung a song, intermixed with low and gutteral sounds, while the rowers marked time with their oars. When they went to war with their neighbors, returned from thence, or impaled the victims they had taken, they sung their terrific war-songs, accompanied with dances, when they screamed and hallooed to the extent of their voices, and threw their bodies into almost every position. When they buried a warrior, the deeds he had done in battle, the courage he had displayed, and the scalps he had taken, were all recounted in song. When the mother wished to pacify her restless child, she sung to it a song as gentle and tender as the rudeness of her language would permit, which corresponded in effect with the English lullaby; and she could display her affections to her offspring with those peculiar tones, looks and manners, known only to mothers, though they might appear to us, harsh and ungraceful. The white mother cannot boast of deeper and stronger affections for her babe, than the red mother could for hers, whose home was in the forest, but whose heart was unacquainted with the gentleness, which is thought, by some, to be generated by civilization.

They also had their different kinds of food. Doubtless all have heard, and perhaps eaten, of samp, succatash and hominy. These names are of Indian origin, and designated their kinds of dishes. Samp was made of corn boiled in the kernel, and when it was parched and pounded for journies, it was called nokehike.† Succatash was made of corn in the kernel, after it was shelled from the cob, and shelled-beans, boiled together. Their hominy was also made of corn, pounded in their mortars and boiled. This last dish is very much admired at the present day; and soon as the corn has sufficiently ripened, the New-England farmer selects a portion purposely for a "mess of hominy."

The Indians were the first proprietors of the soil. May it be asked, where they are? have they been cru-

---

* The Indians called it more frequently Monomack, which signifies in English, a Sturgeon. † Lewis.

elly exterminated—were they plundered of their lands, with the aid of the sword—were their wigwams stained with their blood, and with that of their children?—No; our fathers came among them peaceably; the whistle of the bullet, armed with death for the red-man, was not heard till they began a war of extermination with the infant settlement, and put in practice their horrid system of cruelty towards their unfortunate captives. As civilization advanced around and among them—as its footsteps were planted where their dwellings were reared, they seem to have withered before its breath, and sunk silently into the graves of their fathers.

If we contemplate the rapid growth of our cities and pleasant villages—if we gaze on the tall spires as they are brilliantly flashing in the sun-light—if we look before us, and behind, and see the cultivated fields stretching far onward, interspersed here and there with beautiful dwellings—we find in them a subject of gratulation to the proud-hearted and enlightened freeman. But, as the mind looks backward into the years registered in eternity, and inquires for the nations that were once numerous and mighty—for the kings who went forth, with their people, to battle—for the warriors who bent their bows on the mountain-cliffs, and in the vallies,—then the heart grows sad over the memory of those that have been; it bleeds over the tombs of the nations made desolate; a sadness is mingled with our joy, and our rejoicings end with a tear.

1641.

At a General Court of Elections, holden at Boston on the 2d of June, "Mr. John Woodbridge, Matthew Bayse, John Crosse and George Giddings, they four, or any three of them, are appointed to set out the bounds of Salisbury and Pentucket, alias Haverhill; they are to determine the bounds which Mr. Ward and his company are to enjoy as a towne or village, if they have *six*

houses up by the next General Courte in the 8th month."
[October.]

By the above it appears, that not so many as six houses were built prior to June; but probably the required number was erected by the 7th of October following.

The first birth recorded, was that of a son of John Robinson, who lived but three weeks. The second was likewise a son of his, who also died within a week after his birth.

In September the Governor received letters from Connecticut and other places, informing him that the Indians through the country had combined to destroy the English. The time appointed was soon after the harvest. They were to separate themselves into small parties, visit the houses of the principal men for the professed purpose of trading, while others concealed themselves in the vicinity. Those who were in the houses, while partaking the hospitality of their owners, were expected to fall upon them unawares, slay them, and seize their weapons, while the party concealed were to rush suddenly in and prosecute the massacre.

Upon this intelligence it was thought advisable, by the Governor and Council, to disarm the Indians within their jurisdiction. Forty men were accordingly sent with instructions to disarm Passaconnamy, who "lived by Merrimack." The alarm was so great that the company started on the Sabbath; but on that and the succeeding days, a heavy rain had fallen, which made the paths so intolerably bad that they were unable to reach his wigwam. They, however, came to his son's, and took him, a squaw and her child, the wife and son of Passaconnamy, prisoners. On their return, fearing that the son would escape, they led him with a line; but this was not a sufficient security, for he soon slipped it and ran into the woods, when one of the company fired at him, but without effect.

Soon as the Governor and Council heard of these unwarrantable proceedings, they feared the resentment of Passaconnamy; and immediately sent Cutshamakin,[‡] the Sachem at Braintree, who had been before disarmed and imprisoned for the like suspicions, to inform him that the imprisonment of his relatives was without their order, and to tell him the reasons why they disarmed the Indians within their jurisdiction. He was told at the same time, that, if they were found innocent of their suspicions, their arms should be immediately restored. "He returned answer that he knew not what was become of his son and his squas (for one of them was ran into the woods and came not again for ten days after and the other was still in custody) if he had them safe again then he would come to us, accordingly about a fortnight after he sent his eldest son to us, who delivered up his guns, &c." *

No massacre of this kind was perpetrated; but it was afterwards ascertained that such a plot had existed, headed by Miantonamoh, Chief of the Naragansetts, which was developed by three or four of its members. It was discovered to Mr. Haines of Connecticut, by one of them, who, "by some special circumstances, viz: that being much hurt by a cart (which usually there are drawn by oxen) sent for Mr. Haines and told him that Englishmen's God was angry with him and sent Englishmen's cow (meaning the oxen in the cart or wain) to kill him, because he had concealed such a plot against the English." †

Passaconnamy was rather friendly to the English than otherwise. He soon after went to Penacook, where he extended his dominion over the Agawams, Naamkeeks, Pascataquas, Accomentas, and others. We can learn the name of only one son, Wonolanset, who succeeded him as Sachem at Penacook, and always refused to fight the English. ‡

1642.

Though the town was settled and houses were erected in 1640, the grantees had no title from the Indians, the original proprietors, until this year, when they nego-

---

* Winthrop, page 258. † Hubbard.
‡ Rev. Nathaniel Bouton's Sermons, in commemoration of the organizing of the first church at Concord, N. H.

tiated with their Sachems, and obtained the following deed, which is a correct copy from the original. *

"Know all men by these presents, that wee Passaquo and SaggaHew wth ye consent of Passaconnaway: have sold unto ye inhabitants of Pentuckett all ye lands wee have in Pentuckett; that is eyght myles in length from ye little Rivver in Pentuckett Westward: Six myles in length from ye aforesaid Rivver northward: And six myles in length from ye foresaid Rivver Eastward, wth ye Ileand and ye rivver that ye ileand stand in as far in length as ye land lyes by as formerly expressed: that is, fourteene myles in length: And wee ye said Passaquo and SaggaHew wth ye consent of Passaconnaway, have sold unto ye said inhabitants all ye right that wee or any of us have in ye said ground and Ileand and Rivver: And wee warrant it against all or any other Indeans whatsoever unto ye said Inhabitants of Pentuckett, and to their heires and assignes forever Dated ye fifteenth day of november Ann Dom 1642.

Witnes our hands and seales to this bargayne of sale ye day and year above written (in ye presents of us.) wee y^e said Passaquo & SaggaHew have received in hand, for & in consideration of y^e same three pounds & ten shillings.

John Ward

Robert Clements   PASSAQUO

Tristram Coffyn

Hugh Sherratt

William White

y^e signe of (!)

Thomas Davis

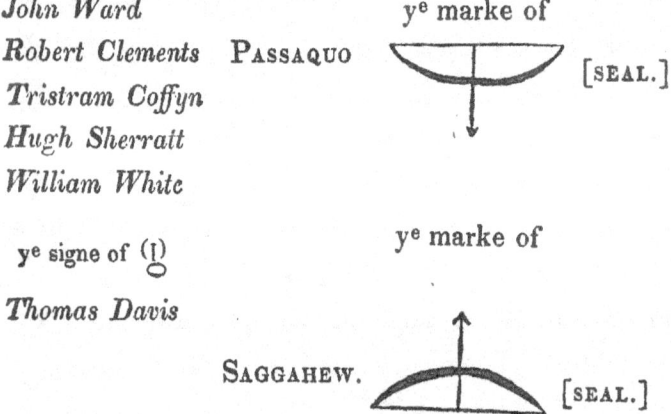

y^e marke of

[SEAL.]

y^e marke of

SAGGAHEW.

[SEAL.]

On the side of it the following is written:—" Entered and recorded in y^e County Records for Norfolk (lib. 2d, pa. 209) y^e 29th day of April 1671 As attest Tho. Bradbury Recorder.

Recorded ye first of Aprill 1681 among ye records of Lands for Essex at Ipswich: As attest Robert Lord Recorder."

---

* This curious manuscript, which is nearly two centuries old, is now in the possession of Charles White, Esq.

On the outside it is endorsed, "The purchase from the Indians by Haverhill men, Recorded."

In 1680, the deed was copied into the Town Records, and the following testimony was taken by Nathaniel Saltonstall, which is written on the succeeding page.

"The Rev. Teacher of ye church & towne of Haverhill, Mr. John Ward; & William White and Tho. Davis do testifie that Haverhill towneship or lands then by ye Indians called Pentuckett, was purchased of ye Indians as is mentioned in ye deed in this paper contained, w^c is entered upon record and that wee were then inhabitants at Haverhill and present wth ye Indians Passaquoi and Saggahew (who were ye apparent owners of ye land & so accounted) did signe and confirme ye same; and that then, wee, (with others now dead) did signe our names to ye deed, which land wee have ever since enjoyed peaceably without any Indian molestation from the grantors or their heirs. Taken upon Febuary ye 4th 1680 before Nath. Saltonstall. Assist."

John Ward, the minister, settled in the vicinity of the grave-yard, and on the 29th of September he had sixteen acres of land laid out to him for a home-lot, "with all accommodations thereunto belonging."* He was born in Haverhill, England, 5th Nov. 1606. He married Alice Edmunds, and had two children, Elizabeth and Mary; his wife died 24th March, 1680, and he followed 27th Dec. 1693.†

Robert Clement came from England early in the year, to Salisbury, and sometime in the summer removed to Haverhill. He was a cooper by trade, and was the first in town. In 1652, he married Elizabeth Fane, and had eleven children. He settled at first, a few rods east of the burial-ground, and in the following year removed to the Rocks' Village, where he improved "ye land in ye planting of corne."

Tristram Coffin came from Devonshire, England, with his mother, wife, and five children, in the ship with Robert Clement, and landed at Salisbury. He seems to have settled near Robert Clement, and tradition says

* No account can be found of any lands laid out prior to 1643, except Mr. Ward's, which is just mentioned in a note in the Town Records, at the bottom of the page, under the year 1643; and no record of the lands laid out to the other settlers of 1640, is preserved.

† A further account will be found of Mr. Ward, in the year 1693.

that he was the first person who ploughed land in Haverhill. In the following year he settled at the Rocks; and in 1645 he was licensed to keep an "ordinary," or tavern—hence the name of "Coffin's ordinary." Soon after, his wife, Dionis, was presented for "selling beere at 3d a quarte," contrary to law, which required four bushels of malt to the hogshead, and that it should be sold at 2d. per quart. Mrs. Coffin, however, made it appear that she put *six* bushels into a hogshead, and the Court acquitted her. Two of his children died in this town, and two were born, Mary and John. Joan, his mother, died in Boston, 1661, aged 77. Mr. Wilson preached her funeral sermon, and, as it was then said, embalmed her memory.* In 1649 he removed to Newbury, thence to Salisbury, where he projected the settlement of Nantucket, purchased, with his family, four tenths of the Island, and removed there with four of his children in 1662. Mary, who was born in this town, married Nathaniel Starbuck, at Nantucket, and all accounts agree in representing her as an extraordinary woman. In the language of John Richardson, an early writer, "the Islanders esteemed her as a Judge among them, for little of moment was done without her." It was her custom to attend their town meetings, where she took an active part in the debates, usually commencing her address with "my husband thinks" so and so; but Richardson says, that "she so far exceeded him in soundness of judgment, clearness of understanding, and an elegant way of expressing herself, and that not in an affected strain, but very natural to her, that it tended to lessen the qualifications of her husband." In 1701 she became a Quakeress, took the spiritual concerns of the the whole Island under her special superintendance, was speaker in their religious meetings, wrote the quarterly epistles, and was distinguished in every relation in life. Respecting her domestic economy, the same author observes: "the order of the house was such in all the parts thereof as I had not seen the like before; the large and bright-rubbed room was set with suitable seats or chairs, [for a meeting] so that I did not see any thing

---

* Sewall's Diary.

wanting according to place, but something to stand on, for I was not free to set my feet upon the fine cane chair, lest I should break it." The descendants of Tristram Coffin are very numerous, and among them is the distinguished Admiral Sir Isaac Coffin; more than 12,000 of that name are now in the United States.

Hugh Sherrit is supposed to have come from Salisbury; he lived to the advanced age of one hundred, and died on the 5th of September, 1678.

William White, one of the first settlers, and whose name is attached to the deed, came from Newbury. His wife was Mary [blank]; he died 28th September, 1690, aged 80; his wife then removed to Ipswich, where she died in 1693. Mr. White settled on the farm now owned by Mr. William White, and we find that he owned a farm in Newbury in 1650. Soon after the church was gathered, he became a member, and was one of its firmest pillars; he had the honor of the town very much at heart, was esteemed by its citizens, and was frequently entrusted with its most important business. His descendants are exceedingly numerous, and are scattered in almost every direction over the United States. In his will, which is dated 2d January, 1683, he says: "I give to the Rev. Mr. Ward, my Teacher, in Haverhill, 10s. in silver; I give to the church of Haverhill, of which I am a member, the linen cloth which is on the communion table, and one of the pewter dishes which was mine, which was used at the sacrament, and to be kept for that use only so long as it may serve with decency for the common good of that society. My will is, that the girl which was given to me by the girl's mother to breed up, if my wife will keep her untill John White [his son] marry, let her keep it, otherwise John White to put her out to sum one who will bring her up in good nurtour; if afterward she live with John till she is 18 years of age, or day of marriage, the said White is to cloth her well and to give her five pounds. I give to Edward Brumidgo a cloth jacket, and britches, and a shurt, all of mine own wearing." The amount of his property taken after his decease, was £508, 10s.

Thomas Davis married Christian [blank], in England; he settled in Haverhill early in the spring. His descendants were formerly very numerous in the town, for we find that there were nineteen families of them before 1720.

1643.

This year the Colony was divided into four Counties, Essex, Middlesex, Suffolk, and Norfolk. The whole number of towns in the Colony was thirty. Norfolk was composed of Salisbury, Hampton, Haverhill, Exeter, Dover, and Strawberry Bank, [Portsmouth.] The Courts were holden at Hampton. Previous to this division, Haverhill belonged to Essex. It remained in Norfolk until 1679, when, by order of the King, Massachusetts recalled all commissions granted for governing that part of the New-Hampshire Province three miles north of Merrimack River.* Accordingly the General Court of Massachusetts, 4th February, 1679, ordered Haverhill and Salisbury to be again joined to Essex. In each County, there was one regiment of militia commanded by a Sergeant-Major.

27th March. A tract of land containing 600 acres was granted by the Colony, to Mr. Nathaniel Ward, father of John Ward, "near Pentuckett, or near as conveniently may be."

10th May. The Court granted to the town a parcel of meadow-land. The grant says that it was "a parcel of meadow-land about sixscore acres more or less, west of Haverhill about six miles."

The first lawful town-meeting was holden this year, on the 6th November; and it is remarkable that the first vote passed, was to prevent an unnecessary destruction of the timber. It will be recollected that the town was then covered with a thick and heavy growth of wood—that an untrodden, and seemingly an inexhaustible wilderness, stretched itself between here and Canada. In all that vast and unexplored tract, no smoke curled from the chimney of a white man—his voice was not

---

* Hutchinson.

heard amid its hills, nor were the prints of his footsteps seen in its vallies. What then should suggest to our fathers the idea of preserving the timber, when they could turn their eyes on neither side without beholding immense quantities of it? They probably expected that their descendants would rapidly increase—that the forest would fall before them like grain before the reaper—and that their dwellings would be reared on every hill and valley.

The following is a correct copy of the vote:—
"Voted that no man shall fall or cause to be fallen any timber upon the Comon but what he shall make use of within nine months next after it is fallen or otherwise it is and shall be forfieted." At the same meeting they voted, "that there shall bee three hundred acres laid out for houselotts and no more; and that he that was worth two hundred pounds should have twenty acres to his houselott, and none to exceed that number; and so every one under that sum, to have acres proportionable for his houselott, to gether with meadow, and Common, and planting ground, proportionably." This land was laid out east of Little River, where the village stands, and was called an "accommodation grant."

Richard Littlehale was chosen "clerk of the Writs," and "town Recorder." He continued in office till 1664. The Court of Writs was a small Court established in town to try such causes as did not exceed forty shillings. It was sometimes called the Court for "small causes;" and frequently the Clerk of the Writs and Town Recorder were filled by one person.

1644.

At a Town-meeting, holden the 6th of February, it was voted, "that all landholders shall pay all publique rates according to their number of acres that they hold to their houselotts; and if any man shall buy one acre of meadow, one acre and halfe of planting ground, or one acre of commonage to his houselott, he shall pay proportionably for evrey acre or commonage with the house lott."

It will be perceived that the landholders only paid the public taxes, and that each man was rated according to the number of acres in his "house-lot," and not according to the property he possessed.

18th Feb. It was "voated that Joseph Merrie should have foure acres of land to his house lott, with all accommodations of Common or meadow and planting ground proportionable." "Voated to Abraham Tylor foure acres of land for an house lott, with Common and meadow and planting land proportionable." "Voated that Hugh Sherratt should have two acres more added to his six acres, which he hath alreadie."

It appears by the last vote, that Hugh Sherrit had six acres granted to him before, but no record can be found which gives an account of it; nor is there any record of the lands laid out to the inhabitants prior to 1643, excepting Mr. Ward's. Their number was so small, they probably deemed it unnecessary to record them.

25th Feb. One acre more was added to the house-lot of Henry Savage.

27th Feb. "Voated that Job Clement should have a parcell of ground, not exceeding one quarter of an acre at the mill Brooke, being bounded forth by the Free-men to sett him up a *tann-house* and *tann-fatts* upon, to him and his heires forever."

Mill Brook, as it was then called, is now occupied by Colonel John Woodman, and the tannery was erected near the mouth of it. Job Clements was the first tanner in town, and was the brother of Robert, one of the signers of the deed.

19th Sept. "Two Churches," says Hubbard, "were appointed to be gathered, the one in Haverhill, the other at Andover (both upon Merrimack river.) They had given notice thereof to the magistrats and ministers of the neighboring Churches, as is the manner with them in New-England. The meeting of the Assembly was to be at that time at Rowley, (the forementioned plantations, being then but newly erected, were not capable to entertain them that were like to be gathered together on that occasion.) But when they assembled, most of those who were to join together in church fellowship at that time, refused to make the confession of their faith and repentance, because, as was said, they declared it openly before in other Churches, upon their admission into them. Whereupon the messengers of the Churches not being satisfied, the assembly brake, before they had accomplished what they intended. But in October, 1645, messengers of Churches met together again, on the same account, when such satisfaction was given, that Mr. John Ward was ordained pastor of the Church in Haverhill, on the north side of the said Merrimack, and Mr. John Woodbridge was ordained pastor of the Church of Andover, on the south side of the same."

The first marriage in town was that of Job Clement and Margaret Dummer, who were married on the 25th December.

Thomas Dudley was chosen to succeed Mr. Winthrop as Governor of the Colony. He came from Northampton, England, where he had been a Captain in Queen Elizabeth's army; and afterwards became a non-conformist to the Episcopal Church. On his arrival into this country he was appointed Major-General of all the militia in the Province. He died at Roxbury, 31st July, 1653, aged 77.

1645.

The singular manner in which many of the votes are recorded is quite amusing. The following is correctly copied.

14th March. "It was voted by the freemen and not to be disannulled wth out the consent of every freeman in ye plantation that every inhabitant may keep for every acre that he hath to his house lott, either an horse beast, ox, or cow, wth a foale or calfe wth a yeare old, a two yeare old and a three yeare old untill they shall be of the age of three yeares and an halfe, upon the Commons appointed by the greater part of the freemen and no more." What was then called the common, were such lands as were not granted to any individual.

This year, near as can be ascertained, there were thirty-two landholders. John Ward, Robert Clement, Job Clement, John Clement, Joseph Merrie, Abraham Tylor, Hugh Sherrit, Henry Savage, Christopher Hussey,* Daniel Hendrick,* John Williams,* Richard Littlehale,* William Butler, John Ayer, sen., John Ayer, jun., Joseph Peaslee,* William White,* John Robinson,* Henry Palmer,* Thomas Davis,* George Corliss, Nathaniel Wier,*† James Fiske, Thomas Hale,* James Davis, sen.,* James Davis, jun.,* John Eaton, Bartholomew Heath,* Tristram Coffin,* Daniel Ladd, Samuel Gile,* and John Davis.*

George Corliss settled on the land now owned by Ephraim Corliss, Esq., and the latter gentleman is of the sixth generation of his descendants who have lived on the same farm. John Robinson, in 1657, bought a house-lot in Exeter, and soon after moved to that place.

The plantation of Haverhill was incorporated into a Town.

The first church was gathered in the summer of this year; it consisted of fourteen members, eight males and six females; and Mr. John Ward was ordained their pastor. Johnson, an early writer, says :—"The Town of Haverhill was built much about this time, lying higher up than Salisbury upon the fair and large River of Merrimack : the people are wholly bent to improve their labor in tilling the earth and keeping of cattel, whose yearly increase encourages them to spend their days in those remote parts. The constant penetrating further into this Wilderness hath caused the wild and uncouth woods to be filled with frequented wayes, and the large rivers to be overlaid with Bridges passeable both for horse and foot; this Town is of a large extent, supposed to be ten miles in length, there being an overweaning desire in most men after Medow land, which hath caused many towns to grasp more into their hands than

---

* Those names which have an asterisk attached to them, were from Newbury.   † Uncertain about his being a landholder.

they could afterward possibly hold; the people are labourers in gaining the goods of this life, yet they are not unmindful also of the chiefend of their coming hither, namely, to be made partakers of the blessed Ordinances of Christ, that their souls might be refreshed by the continual income of his rich grace, to which end they gathered into a church-body and called to office the reverend Mr. Ward, son to the former named Mr. Ward, of Ipswitch.

> With mind resolved run out thy race at length,
> Young Ward, begin, whereas thy father left,
> Left hath he not, but breaths for further strength,
> Nor thou, nor he, are yet of hope bereft:
> Fruit of thy labours thou shalt see so much,
> The righteous shall hear of it, and rejoyce
> When Babel falls by Christ's almighty touch,
> All's folks shall praise him with a cheerful voice.
> They prosper shall that Zions building mend,
> Then Ward cease not with toyle the stones to lay,
> For great is he thee to this work assigned,
> Whose pleasure is, heavens Crown shall be thy pay."*

1646.

13th Jan. It was voted that the inhabitants should have liberty to make one hundred pipe-staves, on the common, for every acre which his house-lot contained; and, "that they should fall no timber within two miles of any of the house lotts." If a person fell a tree within the prescribed limits, he was to pay five shillings, which was to be appropriated for the benefit of the town; or, if he fell any more than was required to make his proportion of staves, he was to pay the same sum.

We have reason to venerate the character of our ancestors. They were not mercenary, or unprincipled; they were not warriors;—they came not with the sword, to exterminate the natives, nor to lay waste their green

---

* This Church was the twenty-sixth which was gathered in the Colony, and the Town was the twenty-third which was settled.— *Pemberton's MSS.*

and beautiful wilderness, and leave desolation in their path. A firm belief in the power and goodness of the Almighty seems to have governed their actions. This sustained their hearts, and nerved their arms—this made them resolute in trouble, and humble in prayer. In the midst of the wide and unbroken forest, their prayers arose, and their solemn songs were wafted on the same breeze that played on the mountain-top, and among the foliage of the lofty oak. They could kneel on the banks of the babbling brook, or in the deep shade of the trees, to worship.

It is pleasing to observe the respect and veneration which they showed to Mr. Ward, their Minister, or Teacher, as he was more frequently called. It speaks volumes for the christian virtues of the man, and the moral character of his people. On the 29th October, " all the freeholders being present," they voted that Mr. Ward's land should be "rate free" during his life, if he continued to be their minister. At the same meeting they voted him a salary of forty pounds to be paid in " wheat and indian," and his wood was to be brought to his door, "and cut and corded."

At this meeting the first selectmen were chosen; they were Thomas Hale, Henry Palmer, Thomas Davis, James Davis, and William White.

The following is a list of persons who settled in town as early as this year, and whose names are not before found. *Christopher Hughes*,* Stephen Kent,† Goodman Ormsbie,‡ George [blank,] John Page, Robert Swan, *William Holdrige*, John Chenarie, Matthias Button, James Pecker, Edward Clark, Peter Ayer, Richard Singletary,† George Brown, John Hutchins,† Henry Sawyer, Thomas Ayer, Robert Ayer, Theophilus Shatswell, *Goodman Perry*, Isaac Cousins, *John Woodin*, Robert Clement, jun.

Goodman was the common appellation among the men, excepting when they addressed their minister,

---

* Those in Italics were not landholders.

† Those names which have this mark after them were from Newbury.

‡ " Goodman" was not his given name, but is applied because that is not known.

magistrate, or any militia officer of a higher grade than Lieutenant; to whom they applied the title of *Mister* *Goodwife*, or *Goody*, were the terms applied to women, excepting when they addressed the wives of those before mentioned, whom they called *Madam;* and the appellation, *Mrs.* was placed before names of both married and unmarried women, when it was written.

Bartholomew Heath, Daniel Ladd, and Daniel Hendrick, were made freemen.

A stray mare was taken up by Robert Clement, sen., and the following is his description of her:—"She is a red sorrell with a little white star in her forhead and a few white haires on her left showlder; she is a mare wich hath bin riden."

There were four brothers by the name of Ayer; John, Robert, Thomas and Peter. The three former settled near the house now occupied by Capt. John Ayer, 2d; and the latter settled in the North-westerly part of the town, in the West Parish. Capt. John Ayer, 2d, is the sixth generation who has lived on the same spot. Their descendants are very numerous, and are scattered throughout every State of the Union. In 1700, it is supposed that nearly one third of the inhabitants in this town were of that name. They were a fearless, athletic race of men, and were mostly cultivators of the soil.

1647.

13th Feb. John Ayer, sen. and James Fiske, were fined for not attonding town meeting in season.

The inhabitants petitioned the General Court for a tract of land to enlarge the town. The following is the answer of the Court, which was holden at Boston, 27th October:—"In answer to the petition of Haverhill, y^o Courte concieving such vast grants to be greatly prejudicial to ye publick good, and little if at all advantageous to particular townships, apprehending 4 miles square, or such a proportion, will accommodate a sufficient tract of land; in such a case thinke meete a Committee be chosen to view the place and returne their apprehensions to ye next General Courte, to which end, with the petitioners consent, they have nominated Mr. Dummer, Mr. Carlton, John Osgood, and Ensign Howlet, or any two of them, provided Ensign Howlet be one to do it." *

At this Court a law was enacted, requiring each Town which contained fifty families to establish a free school; and those which contained one hundred, were ordered to keep a "Grammarschool."

At this early period the town was destitute of a bell; but to supply this defect they employed a queer substitute. It was voted that "Richard Littlehale should beat the drum on the Lord's day morning and evening, and on lecture days, for which, and also for writing public orders, he is to have 30 shillings; he is also to beat the drum for town meetings."

George Davis was presented " for unseemly conduct towards his first wife's daughter."

Richard Green was presented for " being drunk."

John Brown was fined 30s. for striking his wife.

The Town was presented for being destitute of a ferry.

This year the settlement began to extend northward. Grants of land were made to Henry Palmer and others, in the plain north of the Pond-meadow. A few houses had been built near the spot where Mr. Hale's Factory now stands; and George Corliss had erected a log house on his farm farther west.

Thomas Whittier, of Newbury, came into Town and brought a swarm of bees, which were probably the first in the place. They were willed to him by Henry Rolfe, of Newbury, who says: "I give to my kinsman, Thomas Whittier, my best swarm of bees."

Job Clement was made freeman.

---

* Richard Dummer, of Newbury; Edward Carlton, of Rowley; John Osgood, of Andover; and Ensign Thomas Howlet, of Ipswich

1648.

The population of the town had increased so rapidly, that it was thought expedient to erect a house for public worship. Previous to this, it is presumed that they assembled alternately in the different houses, for that purpose; and tradition says, that, on pleasant sabbaths, the inhabitants were wont to assemble beneath the branches of a large tree, which stood near the burial ground, to listen to their beloved preacher. On the 3d of March, the town voted that "the Meeting House shall stand on the lower knowle at the lower end of the Mill Lot."* The house was erected and finished according to the original design, in the succeeding autumn. It was twenty-six feet in length, twenty feet wide, one story high, and destitute of a gallery, or cupola.

A second division of pipestaves was granted, similar to that of 1646.

Thomas Hale, Henry Palmer, and Thomas Davis, were appointed to try "small causes," under forty shillings.

Hugh Sherrit was put under bonds for good behaviour.

At the March term of the Court, the town was again presented for being destitute of a ferry, and was ordered to provide a "suitable boat within six months, or pay a penalty of forty shillings." The town immediately appointed Thomas Hale to keep the ferry, and the price for ferrying was established at "one penny for a passenger, two pence for cattel under two yeares old, and four pence for such us were over that age;" it was at the place now called the ferryway. It appears that the inhabitants, before this, passed over the river at the same place, but no regular ferryman was appointed until this year.

---

* What was then called the Mill Lot, is the present burial ground, and the adjoining lot, owned by Col. John Woodman. Why it was called by that name, is not positively known; but it is probable that a mill was erected on that stream very soon after the settlement of the town, of which there is no account—and hence the name.

13th Nov. John Ayer and Job Clement were chosen grand jurymen.

"Y^e Courte being informed that the shoulders of Haverill are destitute of any officer to exercise them, it is therefore ordered by this court that all ye inhabitants, who have a right to vote in ye election of officers, to meete and choose sum mete person for the place of sargent to exercise them." This is the first notice we have of a military character; but it cannot be positively ascertained that the order of the Court was put into execution; and, from various circumstances, we are inclined to think that it was not.

1649.

The town was ordered by the Court to erect a watch-house, a pound, and stocks, immediately.*

6th April. The first Constable chosen, was James Fiske, and in the succeeding autumn, he was fined 6s. 8d. by the Court, for not returning "the warrants for jurymen in season."

18th Feb. A part of sour-meadow, so called, was granted to James Davis, sen. and James Davis, jun.

This year, that part of Rowley called Merrimack, was settled by John and Robert Haseltine, and William Wild, who had peculiar privileges and immunities. It was incorporated by the name of Bradford, in 1673. What is now Boxford, was then called "Rowley village."†

---

* We have never been able to find any vote in the Town-Records relating to the stocks, or whipping-post; perhaps our fathers were ashamed of them, as well they might be. But that such abominable means for inflicting punishment, were erected, and often made use of, is indisputable—for many of our elderly citizens can remember when they stood beside the present Congregational Meeting-house, a terror to the despiser of their "blue laws," and a monument of disgrace.

† Coffin's MSS.

1650.

About this time two orchards were planted, one by John Clement, and the other by Stephen Kent. As near as can be ascertained, the former was situated a few rods north of the grave-yard, and the latter near the house where Mr. Samuel W. Ayer now lives.

Two barns were built on the land now called the "Common," by Bartholomew Heath and Joseph Peaslee.

22d May. The bounds between Haverhill and Salisbury, were ordered to be laid out by the Court, at the request of the inhabitants of Haverhill; and in December following, Thomas Hale, John Clement, and John Davis, were appointed to "meet the men from Salisbury and lay out the bounds between that town and this."

14th Oct. The Court passed a law against the "intolerable excess and bravery" of dress. No person whose estate did not exceed £200 was permitted to wear any gold or silver lace or buttons, great boots, silk hoods, ribbons or scarfs, under a penalty of ten shillings.

20th Dec. It was voted that the name of every freeholder should be kept in the Town's book, and that he be compelled to attend town meetings, when lawfully warned;—"and having lawful warning he is to come within half an hour after the meeting is begun, and continue till sunset if the meeting hold so long, under the penalty of halfe a bushel of Indian corn or the value of it."

Considerable land was granted to individuals west of Little River, on the Merrimack; and Hugh Sherrit, Bartholomew Heath, James Fiske, and John Chenarie, had liberty to lay down their land in the plain, "and have it laid out over Little River, westward."

Three fourths of an acre and the "clay pitts" were granted to John Hoit, a brick-maker, if he would become an inhabitant of the town. This is the first notice we have of the clay pits; they are situated in the West Parish, near Ephraim Corliss, Esqr's. and are now known by that name. It appears that the pits were dug, and that bricks were made some years before; but the name of the person who carried on the business cannot be ascertained.

This year there were forty freemen in town, and nineteen who had taken the oath of fidelity.

1651.

22d Sept. George Brown and Daniel Hendrick were appointed to lay out the highway between this town and Salisbury.

21st Nov. Theophilus Shatswell was appointed to join the men from Rowley, and lay out a road between that town and this. This road was approved of by the Court, at Ipswich, in 1686.

1st Dec. Isaac Cousins, and others, petitioned the town for liberty to build a saw-mill. Their petition was granted; but they were restricted from using any timber within three miles of the meeting-house, on the common lands, except pine and hemlock; they were to pay every twelve-hundreth board "to the use of the town in General;" and the town also reserved to itself the privilege of purchasing merchantable planks, and boards, at three shillings per hundred. This mill was erected upon Little River, near the spot occupied by Mr. Ezekiel Hale's Factory; and after that, the stream was known by the name of Sawmill Brook; and is so called by many aged people at this day.

The inhabitants, whose house-lots extended to the Merrimack, were permitted to "use the bank for a fence." It appears that, in 1643, when the "accommodation grant" was surveyed and laid out, a strip of land adjoining the river, and another running from the river to the spot now occupied by the first Parish meeting-house, and from thence to the present location of Mr. Hale's Factory, was reserved for a road; though no mention was made of it in the grant. About this time, the road near Mr. William White's, was laid out; and, for more than a century, it was the principal, or "great road," as it was called, which led into the village.

1652.

7th June. The second division of plough-land was granted and ordered to be laid out, "after the proportion of four acres to an acre of houselot." This division begun at the head of pond-meadow, and extended north, east, and west, until each person received his due proportion. Forty-one persons received accommodations in this division. Five lot-layers were appointed to lay it out, who received two pence an acre for their services.

7th Sept. The town voted to Mr. Ward, their "Teacher," a salary of fifty pounds. This sum, which would be so inadequate for the support of a clergyman at this period, may be called a liberal salary, when we consider the resources and circumstances of the town. It shows their strong attachment to their pastor, and their desire to promote the christian religion.

Another curious substitute was provided for a bell. Instead of having the drum beaten, it was voted, "that Abraham Tylor shall blow his horn in the most convevient place every lord's day about half an hour before the meeting begins, and also on lecture days; for which he is to have one peck of corn * of every family for the year ensuing."

Stephen Kent was fined 10s. "for suffering five Indians to be drunk in his house of whom one was wounded. He is to pay for his cure." He afterwards petitioned the Court to diminish his fine, but without success.

This year a Mint was established at Boston, for coining silver; the pieces had the word Massachusetts, with a pine tree on one side, and the letters N. E. 1652, and III, VI, or XII, denoting the number of pence, on the other. It is said that the dies for coinage, were made by Joseph Jenks, at the Iron works in Lynn.†

---

* This passage, "one peck of corn," has often been read "one pound of pork," and is generally believed to be pork, instead of corn; but if any person will examine closely, he will find it to read *corn*, instead of *pork*.

† Lewis' Hist. of Lynn.

1653.

It was voted that "John Webster should enjoy that six acres of accommodation which was formerly granted unto Isaac Cousins, and is now returned into the Town's hands; provided, that the said John Webster live here five years from the last of March next, following the trade of a blacksmith in doing the town's work, when they have occasion." Mr. Webster was the first blacksmith in town; he followed the trade, however, but four years, when he returned to Newbury. His brother, Stephen, a tailor, came into town soon after, from Newbury; and is probably the ancestor of the Websters in this place. He was born in Ipswich, and moved with his mother, who married John Emery, sen., to Newbury. He had three brothers and four sisters. His brothers, John and Israel, remained in Newbury, and Nathan settled in Bradford. His mother, Mary, was a sister of Theophilus Shatswell; John, his father, died in Ipswich, about 1642.* The descendants of Stephen are numerous as the "leaves on the trees;" they are scattered in almost every city and village in the Union.

It seems that our ancestors liked the marshal sound of the drum better than the tooting of Abraham Tylor's dinner-horn; for it was this year laid aside, and Edward Clark was ordered to beat the drum again, on the "Lord's days and lecture days."

A second division of meadow was ordered to be laid out, "after the proportion of one acre to two acres of houselot." This division was situated in Spiggot-meadow, bordering on Spiggot-River, near the meeting-house in Salem, New-Hampshire.

The Island "over against the plain," was ordered to be divided. The Island referred to, is the one now owned by David How, Esq., situated three-fourths of a mile below Haverhill bridge. The number of persons who drew lots, was forty-five.

25th Feb. A third division of upland, or ploughland, was ordered to be laid out; it was situated west and north of west-meadow, in the West Parish.

---

* Coffin's MSS.

The wife of John Hutchins was presented for wearing a silk hood; but, "upon testimony of her being brought up above the ordinary way was discharged." The wife of Joseph Swett was presented at the same time and for the same offence, and was fined 10s.

It was a general custom of the inhabitants, at this early period, to turn their flocks together into one pasture; and we find that James George was appointed herdsman for the town. His salary was twelve shillings and six pence per week, to be paid "in Indian cor.. and butter. * * * * He is to keep ye heard faithfully as a heard ought to be kept; if any be left on the Sabbath when ye towne worship, they who keepe are to goe ye next day, doing their best indeavore to find them." He was not permitted to turn his flock into the pasture on the Sabbath, until the " second beating of y^e drum."

A lot of land, not exceeding four-score acres, was granted to the proprietors of the mill, so long as they kept it in use.

1654.

9th Feb. Liberty was granted to Stephen Kent to place a *wear* in Little River, to catch alewives, or any other fish, if he would sell to the inhabitants of the town " what alewives they stood in need of." This is the first notice we have of the fisheries, which were afterwards carried on to considerable extent.

A third division of staves was granted.

13th Dec. Some additions were made to the ox-common, and the whole was ordered to be enclosed with a suitable fence; " and all those that will join in the fencing of it, shall have a proportion in it according to the fence they make and maintain, provided that none shall keep more than four oxen in it." Thirty-four persons assisted to build the fence, and were entitled to keep ninety-two oxen within the enclosure. It was then voted that " the cattel that shall goe in the ox-common this day granted, shall be only oxen, steers and horses, and no other cattel." This is the first notice we have of an ox-common, though it appears that one was laid out some years previous. The present ox-common, so called, then constituted but a small portion of it. In a few years, the commoners, as they were designated, became quite numerous; and long disputes often existed between them and the non-commoners, which, not unfrequently, ended with bloody noses, swollen faces, and a dimness of the optical organs. The commoners held meetings, at which they transacted their business, and there are three large books, consisting of about 260 pages each, which contain their proceedings.

Commissioners were appointed by the General Court, to run the boundary line between Haverhill and Salisbury, as a *great mistake* was said to have been committed when it was run before. The Court approved of their return; but it appears that the bounds were not permanently settled, and that the parties soon became dissatisfied. We find the following on the Colony files, in May, 1667. "As a final issue of all differences between the two towns of Haverhill and Salisbury Newtown, in reference to their bounds, the Court having heard what all parties could say therein, judge meet to confirm the line which was run by the Committee and the agreement of both towns, beginning at a tree near Holt's Rocks, near Merrimack rivers' side, and running up on the N. W. line, as they apprehended, to Brandy Brow, and from thence to Darby Hill, and so to a white pine about a mile further, marked H. S. and this is to be the dividing line between them."

1655.

3d March. Some repairs were this year made upon the meeting-house, and it was voted that "Thomas Davis shall have three pounds allowed him by the town, for to ground-pin and dawb it; provided that Thomas Davis provide the stones and clay for the underpinnings; the town being at their own expence to bring ye clay into place for ye plaistering of the walls up to the beams."

In 1648, Thomas Hale was ferryman, probably for that year only; and afterward it does not appear that any was appointed; for, at the September term, "Y^e Courte being informed y^t there is no fery over Merrimack river, at Haverill, the courte orders Robert Haseltine to keepe a fery over the said river; and to have of strangers 4d a person, if they pay presently; and 6d if bookt; and to keepe entertaynement for horse and man, for one yeare, unless the General Court take further orders." Robert Haseltine lived on the Bradford shore.

The Constable, Thomas Davis, carried "Stephen Kent, Matthias Button, a Dutchman, and John Mac Clary, a Scotchman," to Court.

1656.

Considerable difficulty arose between Mr. Ward and a part of his people, concerning his salary, which was thought by the latter to be exorbitant, while he maintained to the contrary. It seems that the difficulty had become so great, it was deemed necessary to call a council of the neighboring clergymen; and we find that the Rev. Mr. [blank] Norton, was chosen by the first church in Boston, on the 14th of August, to attend an ecclesiastical council in Haverhill. On the same day the "Council of the Commonwealth took into consideration the sad contention and division of the Churches of Salisbury and Haverhill, and thereupon thought it necessary to send certain Elders and other messengers to compose that difference; which, through the blessing of God, upon their endeavours is in a good measure attained, and their officers * settled amongst them, which greatly concerns the welfare of those two towns. The Court do therefore order the Constable of Haverhill to levy, by way of Rate, on the inhabitants of Haverhill the sum of £12. 19s. for the satisfying of Mr. John Clements

---
* Ministers.

for the charges expended in Haverhill." The like course was pursued with Salisbury. The Town Records say that, on the 28th of August, it was voted in Council to pay Mr. Ward "fifty pounds;" twenty of which were to be paid in "wheat, Rye, and indian corn." We have not been able to ascertain any further account of the proceedings of this Council, nor of the members who composed it.

William White was exempted from doing military duty.

This year, Michael Emerson came into town, and settled, at first, near the house now owned by Mr. William White. The grantees told him that, if he would "go back into the woods," as they then called it, they would give him a tract of land. He accordingly moved, and settled between Little River and the house now occupied by his descendant, Capt. Nehemiah Emerson.

1657.

Goodman Simons was appointed to keep the ferry on the "Great River." If he had only a canoe he was to ferry a single person for two pence, and cattle for four pence a head; but, if he provided a suitable boat, his price should be established at six pence per head for cattle, two pence for sheep and hogs, and three pence for strangers.

6th March. Liberty was granted to Thomas Hutchins to set a *wear* in the Merrimack, near the falls, for the purpose of catching fish. He was to supply the town with "every kind of fish he might catch for what recompence it could afford." The works were to be finished by April, 1659, or the grant was to be considered void.

It was voted that, if any person moved into town and was not a freeholder, yet partook of the benefits of the "church and commonwealth," he should assist in paying the public taxes, according to his "visible estate, or by estimation."

1658.

17th Jan. A third division of meadow was granted, and ordered to be laid out before the fifteenth of May next, at the rate of half an acre to an acre of accommodation. Forty-one persons drew lots in this division.

At the same meeting it was voted that, if any person had no convenient road to his upland, or meadow, upon his complaint to the town, two men were to be chosen to lay one out, whose charges should be defrayed by the town.

It appears that the inhabitants suffered considerably for the want of a blacksmith. To obviate this difficulty, a contract was signed by Mr. Ward and nineteen others, in which each agree to pay Mr. Jewett his proportion of twenty pounds, to purchase his house and land, which the contractors gave to John Johnson, " provided he live here seven years, following the trade of a blacksmith in doing the town's work; also, the said John Johnson doth promise to refuse to work for any that refuse to pay towards this purchase, untill they bring under the Selectmen's hands that they will pay." This house stood on the ground now occupied by the mansion of the late Hon. Bailey Bartlett, who is a lineal descendant from John Johnson. He is likewise the ancestor of the Johnsons in this town.

Joseph Peasly was fined 40s. by the Court, for beating Peter Brown, and 20s. for abusing Timothy Swan—all to be paid in " corne." *

---

* A friend of ours thinks that the sentence of the Court would sound better in the following, which he wrote for us.

>Because you whipped old Timothy Swan,
>Please pay your fine in indian *corne*;
>Just twenty shillings must you pay,
>And that without the least delay.
>Also, for beating Peter Brown,
>Pay forty shillings quickly down.

1659.

14th Oct. A fourth division of upland was ordered to be laid out beyond Spiggot River, now in Salem, New-Hampshire, at the rate of twenty acres to an acre of accommodation. This division was ordered to be bounded, south by the Merrimack, north by Shatswell's pond, west by the town's bounds, and to run eastward until the lots were all drawn. It was divided into forty-nine lots, and forty-six were taken up; they were laid out a mile in length.

23d Nov. It was ordered that, if a town meeting was publickly warned on a *Lecture day*, it should be considered a sufficient notice. It was likewise voted that no man should be taken into the town as an inhabitant, or "town dweller, without the consent of the town."

The population had increased so rapidly, that the meeting-house was found too small and inconvenient to accommodate the worshippers. To lessen this evil, the town appointed a committee of four, and gave them power to enlarge and repair the house according to their best discretion; "and to finish it, and make seats in it, and also to sell land for to pay the workmen, not exceeding twenty acres in the cow-common."*

27th Nov. Daniel Ladd and Theophilus Shatswell, had liberty to erect a saw-mill, on Spiggot River. They accordingly built one, soon after, near that which is now owned by Mr. Clement, in Salem, N. H. This was the first mill erected on that stream; and the proprietors of it were obliged to pay five pounds per annum to the town.

Sometime this year, John Clement shipped for England, and on his outward voyage was cast away and drowned. At the September term, Robert, his brother, applied to the Court to be appointed administrator of his estate. This is the first notice we have of an adminis-

---

*This is the first notice we have of a cow-common: it appears that one was laid out, but no record was made of it. The present "common," as it is called, then constituted a part of it.

tratorship, and, for this reason, we have copied the following from the Court files.

"John Clements late of Haverhill, being by God's providence cast away and dying intestate, the worshipful Mr. Samuel Symonds, and Major General Denizen the Clarke, being present, granted administration unto Robert Clements of the estate of John Clements deceased, he to bring an inventory to Ipswich Court next, and then the Court to take further orders."

In the following year, 10th May, Robert Clement "brought in an accompt to this court of his charges expended in his voiage to England and Ireland, his brother John, his wife and children; and upon the request of his brother Job and Sisters, the court confirmed the administration unto Robert Clements of the estate of his brother John Clements."

1660.

30th August. James Davis and Theophilus Shatswell were chosen "to answer the warrant of the General Court, concerning the bounds." The town granted them each ten groats a day.

The town seems to have been rather negligent in providing a regular burial place, though we may presume that the dead were buried on the spot which was afterwards appointed for that purpose. On the 30th November, it was ordered that the land "behind the Meeting house should be reserved for a burial ground."

Ten acres of meadow, and two hundred acres of upland, were granted for a parsonage, to Mr. Ward and his successors.

A second ox-common was granted to the petition of six persons. It was situated between Merrie's Creek and a small brook which issues from West-meadow. Eighteen oxen were kept upon it.

The first public school was established about this time; the instructer was Thomas Wasse, whose salary was ten pounds per year. He also taught school in

Chebacco parish, [Ipswich] and at Newbury. He died at the latter place, Aug. 18, 1691.

Up to this time, a period of twenty years, there had been recorded nineteen marriages, one hundred and thirty-five births, and thirty deaths.

1661.

The road near "huckleberry-hill" was laid out.

The ox-common was divided into two parts; the division line run north and south. Those who lived east of Mill Brook, enjoyed their privileges in the eastern part; and those who lived west of the brook, enjoyed the opposite part.

A fourth division of meadow was granted, and fifty-one lots were drawn.

1662.

This year the first militia company was organized. William White was chosen Captain, and Daniel Ladd, Lieutenant. So early as 1648, the inhabitants were ordered by the Court to choose a Sergeant to "exercise them." We are very doubtful whether this order was promptly obeyed; but, allowing that it was, no company was collected and organized until this year.

The town, at this period, was intolerably infested with wolves, that nightly prowled around the farms and destroyed large numbers of sheep. The County and Colony had offered large premiums for every wolf's head; and this year, the town, to induce the Indians to assist in destroying so powerful an enemy, voted, "that if any Indian shall kill a wolf in Haverhill bounds, he, or they, shall have for every wolf so killed, forty shillings."

Michael Emerson was appointed to assist the men from Newbury, to lay out the high-way between that town and this.

Hugh Sherrit was permitted to keep an ordinary, and to sell "strong water and wine by retail."*

1663.

It was voted that there should be a general Town-meeting holden on the first Tuesday of March, annually. Previous to this they had no annual meeting; but each one was generally adjourned to some specified time, and the inhabitants were notified by the selectmen.

The selectmen were authorised to sell a quantity of land, to pay the expense of building a pound. This was the first building of the kind erected; it was built of wood, and stood nearly in the lot of land now occupied for a grave-yard.

William Simons was appointed to keep the ferry.

1664.

It was voted that, "if any man in this town should kill a wolf, or wolves, he shall be paid, by the town, forty shillings."

Mr. John Carlton was chosen Town Recorder and Clerk of the Writs; he continued in office till 1668.

An old manuscript states that there were sixty-four freemen in town this year; the list begins with "Mr. Ward our preacher."

Another cow-common was ordered to be laid out; it extended from Little River to a place then called North-meadow, and from thence to East-meadow.

---

*It is a fact that our earliest ancestors, when they spoke of ardent spirits, invariably called them "strong water;" and we do not remember of seeing the words, rum, gin, or brandy, at any period before 1700. The only terms they used, were "strong water and wine."

1665.

A road was ordered to be laid out from "Holts Rocks,"* just below the present Rock's Bridge, to the Country bridge, in the East-meadow.

It was voted that Mr. Ward, with three others, "should plan and seat the inhabitants of Haverhill in the seats built in the meeting house."

"In answer to the petition of the inhabitants of Haverhill, the Court Judgeth meet to allow and confirm their choice of Mr. Nathaniel Saltonstall to be their Capt. and George Brown to be their Ensign."†

1666.

Elizabeth Sherrit was licensed to keep an ordinary.

6th March. A Committee was chosen to lay out a parcel of land on which Mr. Ward might build a barn. It was built on the upper side of Hawke's meadow-brook. Mr. Ward owned a part of that meadow.

"It was this day voted and granted, y^t John Hutchins shall have lybertie to beuld a gallerey at y$_e$ westend of y^e meeting house, and to take any of y^e inhabitants of y^e towne to joyne with him, provided y^t he give nottise to y^e towne wheher he will or noe y^e next training day, soe y^t any of y^e inhabitants of y^e towne y^t hath a minde to joyne with him, may give in their naimes; and y^t there is none but ye inhabitants of ye towne is to have any interest in ye said gallerry."

John Barnard and his wife were fined for incontinency; the man was fined £3, and the woman 4s.

The Court fined John Carlton £3, for striking Robert Swan " several blows, and Robert Swan 30s., for striking John Carlton several blows." ‡

---

* Holt's Rocks were so called from one Nicholas Holt, one of the first settlers of Newbury, and who afterwards settled in Andover.

† Court Files.

‡ The Court determined to make sure work, by fining both parties. Perhaps it would be as well if the Courts of the present day, in such cases, would follow the example.

1667.

A highway was ordered to be laid out "down the valley to Holt's Rocks," and those who made use of it were ordered to keep it in repair.

1668.

The town continued to be exceedingly jealous for the timber; almost every year a vote was passed for its preservation, and this year, a fine of ten shillings was imposed upon any person, who should fall a white, red, or black oak-tree, within the town's limits, "for staves, heading, logs for boards, or any thing else for transportation, without leave from the Select men from year to year."

The first General Fast was holden this year.

John Griffin was permitted to keep the ferry; he lived in Bradford.

3d March. Nathaniel Saltonstall was chosen Town Recorder and Clerk of the Writs; he continued in office until 1700.

In answer to a petition, the Court authorised "Capt. Nathaniel Saltonstall to joyne persons in marriage."

1669.

2d March. It was ordered that a list of the voters should be read at every town-meeting, and if any one did not appear and answer to his name, who was lawfully warned, should pay a fine of eighteen pence, which was to be appropriated to the use of the town—"any former order to the contrary notwithstanding."

Upon a complaint made by Mr. Ward for want of wood, it was voted to add ten pounds to his salary, (which was fifty pounds,) and that the selectmen should annually expend it in procuring him cord-wood, at six shillings per cord.

3d March. At an adjourned meeting, the town passed the following singular vote:—"The town, by a major vote, did make choice of Andrew Greely, sen., to keep the ferry at Haverhill; provided that he agree and will carry over the Inhabitants of the town, and the inhabitants of the town of Merrimack, [Bradford] over against us, for three pence an horse, and a penny a man; and that he will carry all Ministers over free that come upon visitation to us, and in particular Mr. Symes; and that, if the inhabitants of the town over against us do come over to meet with us on the sabbath days, they shall have the free use of the ferry boat, or boats, for the occasion, without paying any thing, * * * * * * * and that he shall give the widow Simons forty shillings." *

A highway was laid out from Topsfield to Haverhill.

29th July. A Committee was chosen to build a bridge over Little River, where Hale's Factory now stands. It was voted that, "when any of the Inhabitants being warned, by one of the Committee, to appear at the works of said Bridge, and cometh not, nor brings with him such implements as he hath fitting for the work, shall be fined as followeth:—for the absence of a man one day, five shillings; for a yoke of oxen, two shillings and sixpence, and so proportionably." This was the first convenient bridge built over the stream; and it appears that all the inhabitants were obliged to contribute a certain portion of labor towards constructing it.

1670.

1st March. It was resolved that no vote should be valid that was passed after sunset. An excellent regulation, and we wish that it had been adopted, and continued in force, in every town.

---

* Widow Simons' husband was the former keeper of the ferry.

1671.

A thatched house, belonging to Matthias Button, was burnt.* He was a Dutchman, and quite a migrating animal. He lived in the village, in the western part of the town, in the eastern, and finally settled near the house now owned by Thomas West, Esq., where his house was burnt. He died in the following year. The Rev. Mr. Cobbett, of Ipswich, called him " old Button."

7th March. Robert Emerson and his wife, brought an orphan child of Richard and Hannah Mercier's, into the Meeting, and desired the town "to provide for it;" which it voted to do.

Liberty was granted to John Haseltine, or to any other man, to build a corn-mill upon "Sawmill River," or upon the East-meadow River.

1672.

7th March. The town, prior to this, had been destitute of a school-house; but, at this meeting, it ordered one to be built near the meeting-house, which was also used for "a watchhouse, and the entertainment of such persons on the sabbath days as should desire to repair thither."

The Selectmen were ordered to prepare a store-room in the Meeting-house, to secure the town's powder, and " all other amunition."

Simon and Samuel, two Indians, were fined five pounds by the Court, "for stealing Englishmen's horse." Simon made his principal residence in this town, but frequently migrated to Amesbury and Newbury.

Many of the laws enacted by our ancestors were of a most ludicrous character. Among them, was one, prohibiting a man from living alone, or, in other words, forbidding him to live a bachelor;—but John Littlehale, it seems, was not affected by the glowing descrip-

---

* Court Records.

tions which the advocates of matrimony would fain impose upon the honest bachelor; for we are told that he stoutly resisted this law, and "lived in an house by himself." When, however, he arrived at the age of twenty-two, his neighbors, feeling a friendly concern for his welfare, and a patriotic regard for legal enactments, began to think it high time for him to enter into a condition "for better for worse;" and not perceiving that he gave any indications of the matrimonial mania, sued him at the law for living a "solitary life," as appears by the following order of Court :—

"At a Courte holden at Hampton, 8th of 8th mo. This Court being informed that John Littlehale of Haverhill, liveth in an house by himself contrary to the law of the Country whereby hee is subject to much sin; and having had information of some of his accounts which are in no way to be allow'd of but disproved and discountenanced, doe therefore order that the said John doe forthwith, at farthest, within the time of six weeks next after the date hereof remove himself from the said place and solitary life and settle himself in some orderly family in the said towne and bee subject to the orderly rules of family government in said family (unless hee remove out of the said towne within the time) and if he doe not perform this order as abovesaid then this Courte doth order that the Selectmen doe forthwith order and place the said John to bee in some orderly family as abovesaid, which if he shall refuse to submit unto, then these are in his majesties name to require the Constable of said town upon his knowledge of it, or information, to apprehend the person of said John and carry him to the house of correction in Hampton, there to bee kept and sett to work untill hee shall be freed by order of authority; and this order shall bee a discharge and security."*

---

* In the remarks which precede this order of Court, it is stated that there was a law *prohibiting a man from living alone, or, in other words, forbidding him to live a bachelor.* That there was a law which prohibited a man from living alone, is evident from the order itself, which says:—*liveth in an house by himself contrary to the law of the Country.* We have no knowledge of one which expressly forbade a man to live in a state of celibacy,

He probably removed to some "orderly family," but lived a life of celibacy until he arrived at the advanced age of sixty-six, when he married, and became the father of two children.

1673.

The town seems to have been rather parsimonious in paying the Selectmen for their services,—for we find that it granted them an annual stipend of only fifty shillings, which was to be distributed among them, "to each man according to his services."

Nathaniel Emerson was admonished by the Court for "being in company with Peter Cross, and others, at Jonas Gregory's and drinking of stolen wine."

1674.

4th March. A viewer of staves and boards was appointed,—the first of which we have any account.—At the same meeting a person was hired to sweep the Meeting-house.

4th July. The bounds of Haverhill were again run.

Robert Swan was fined 20s. for "being drunk and cursing."

Michael Emerson was fined 5s. "for his cruel and excessive beating of his daughter with a flayle swingel, and kicking of her."

---

though the law, which prohibited him from living a "solitary life,"' in this case, was made to bear upon that point. John Littlehale, for aught that can be found, was a man of good morals; and this is the only time that he was prosecuted—at least, we can find no other order against *John Littlehale* upon the Court Files. Why then was he prosecuted?—because he was guilty of living a "solitary life;" or, in other words, (the remark may be safely applied in this case) of living without the pale of matrimony. These statements are made, because the remarks which precede the order have been objected to by one or two persons whose opinions we highly value.

The town still continued to be very jealous for its timber. At a meeting holden on the 4th of February, a long act was passed, forbidding any person to cut timber of any description on the common, for the purpose of transportation, under the penalty of 20s.

1675.

It was voted that the annual town-meetings should be holden on the last Tuesday in February, instead of the first Tuesday in March.

19th Feb. The inhabitants began to think seriously of taking measures to defend themselves from the Indians. It appears that a fortification was built around the Meeting-house some years previous; but, owing to the open and peaceable conduct of the savages, it was suffered to fall into decay. They had heretofore lived in security, and it seems that an unrestrained intercourse had existed between many of them and the natives. They did not hesitate to mingle with them, and even to admit them into their dwellings; but the Indians now began to show symptoms of hostility, and the whole town became considerably alarmed. At a meeting warned expressly for the purpose of concerting measures to prevent the threatened danger, it was voted that "the Selectmen shall forthwith cause the fortifications (around the Meeting-house) to be finished, to make port holes in the walls, to right up those places that are defective and likely to fall, and to make a flanker at the east corner, that the work, in case of need, may be made use of against the common enemy." At the same time, Daniel Ladd, Peter Ayer, and Thomas Whittier, were appointed to designate what houses should be garrisoned; and the "old brush and top wood" on the common, was ordered to be burnt.

Two daughters of Hanniel Bosworth were fined 10s. each, for wearing silk. The fine was remitted in 1677.

Hannah Button was sentenced by the Court to be whipped, or pay a fine of 40s. for misdemeanors. Daniel Ela was fined 10s. for "swearing," and 2s. for his "reviling speeches."

1676.

The Selectmen were ordered to remove the pound from the grave-yard, to a "more suitable and convenient place."

Sometime before this, the General Court passed a law prohibiting the Indians from going a mile from their wigwams. This year they were permitted to gather "chestnuts and other nuts in the wilderness," if two white men went with each company, whose charges were to be borne by the Indians.

2d May. Ephraim Kingsbury was killed by the Indians. He, it is believed, was the first person slain in this town by the savages; but the incidents connected with his death are buried in oblivion.

On the 3d of May, Mr. Thomas Kimball, of Bradford, was killed by the Indians; and his wife, Mary, and five children, Joanna, Thomas, Joseph, Priscilla and John, were captivated.* The Indians were led on by Simon, an Indian, who made his principal residence in this town.†

---

*Rev. Gardner Perry's Discourse.

† It seems that Mrs. Kimball soon after returned from her captivity; but by what means, we have not ascertained. Probably her children also returned, as Mr. Perry says nothing to the contrary. Soon after Mrs. Kimball's return, she addressed the following petition to the Governor and Council, which is correctly copied from the original.

"*To the Hon. Governor and Councell.*

The humble petition of Mary Kimball sheweth that Simon, the Indian who killed my husband, Thomas Kimball, hath threatened to kill me and my children if ever I goe to my own house, so that I dare not goe to looke after what little I have there left, for fear of my life being taken away by him; and therefore, doe humbly entreate the Hon. Governor and Councell that some course may be taken, as God shall direct, and your wisdoms shall think best, to secure him; for I am in continual fear of my life by him; and if any course may be taken for the recovery of what is yet left in their hands of my

1677.

The property of Hugh Sherrit, an old man whose name is attached to the deed, was illegally taken from him; and he was obliged to apply to the town for support. The town agreed with Peter Brown to keep him for five shillings per week, one moiety of which was to be paid in breadstuff, and the other in meat. We should suppose that money was a scarce article in those days, for the principal currency of the town was grain, butter, meat, or land. We copy the following, believing it will be interesting to many of our readers.

"Upon Peter Brown's conclusion to keep Hugh Sherrat, a motion was made to the inhabitants to know who would lend corn, or meat, to the town, for the supply of Hugh Sherrat; and they to be paid by the next town rates; and several engaged as followeth:—Robert Emerson, Bacon; Joseph Emerson, Beef, 6lb.; Daniel Ela, Beef, 12lb.; Samuel Gile, Beef, 6lb.; Henry Kingsbury, Indian, 1*; John Page, jun. 1 Ind. and meat, 2lb.; Thomas Eaton, 18lb. meat or corn; Robert Ford, jun. 1-2 Indian; Bartholomew Heath, Pork, 4lb.; Thomas Davis, Pork, 4lb. Butter, 1lb.; Michael Emerson, Pork, 4lb.; Thomas Whittier, Turnips, 1; Robert Ayer, Pork, 6lb.; Daniel Hendrick, meat, 2lb.; Peter Ayer, 3lb. meat, or corn; Thomas Ayer, jun. 1lb. meat."

Daniel Ela was licensed to keep an ordinary for one year; but the small pox breaking out in his family, he was unable to sell his liquors, and he petitioned the Court, at the fall term, to extend his license. The Court gave him liberty to sell "wine, liquore, Beere, Cyder, and provisions to horse and man, or travilers in Haverhill."

Bartholomew Heath was presented for "two acts of drunkenness."

---

goods that they have not destroyed (as there was two kittells and two or three baggs of linnen when I came from them) that I might have it restored, leaving myself and my concernes under God, to your wisdoms. Remaine your humble suppliant. Mary Kimball."

* Meaning one bushel of Indian Corn.

At this time there was but one Post Office in Massachusetts Colony, which was at Boston. John Hayward was appointed Post Master for the Colony, on the 3d December.

1678.

23d Dec. Benjamin Page, a child 4 years of age, was so scalded with hot water, that he died in a few hours.

1679.

24th Feb. The town passed the following vote:— "Upon the request of Benjamin Webster and Samuel Parker, two young men and shooemakers, that the towne would give them libertie to live in this towne to follow the trade, having hired a house to that end; the towne by their vote doe grant their motion, and accept of them so as to live in towne and follow the trade of shooemaking."

We have taken considerable pains to ascertain the name of the first shoemaker, and the time he came into town; but we have not been able to learn that any worked at the trade before this, and we are inclined to think that Benjamin Webster and Samuel Parker, were the first who had served a regular apprenticeship at the trade, and established themselves in this town. No doubt shoes were made many years before this, but probably every farmer could cobble a little, and almost every man was a cobbler.

1680.

Peter Pette was presented for being "absent from his wife several years." We cannot blame him much, for it is believed, that she was a termagant creature, and a common scold. In the following year, he was again presented for having another wife in Virginia. We have no remarks to make upon the last presentment.

Daniel Ela was fined 10s. for selling "drink" without a license.

Mr. Ward, the hardy and fearless pioneer of civilization, into the untrodden wilderness of Pentucket,—whose voice first sounded the praises and judgments of the unseen but terrible Jehovah, on the *then* shaded banks of the beautiful Merrimack,—had now become seared and decrepid with age. Time had passed over him like a blight, and left the traces of his invisible fingers upon his features. The form that stood erect in the pride of manhood, was bent to the earth, and trembled with weakness, like the ancient oak that has breasted the blasts of an hundred winters, and whose trunk is silently but rapidly crumbling to the dust. It was deemed expedient by the town to procure an assistant for him, and a committee was chosen for that purpose. The vote reads thus:—"And taking the advice of our present minister, to look out for, to agree with, and procure upon the best terms, some meet and able person to be a present help to Mr. Ward, our Minister, now in his old age, in the work of the ministry in preaching."

1681.

24th June. A gallery was ordered to be immediately erected in the east end of the Meeting-house, for the accommodation of the women.* The house had now become old and decayed, and was too small to accommodate the inhabitants. They began to talk considerably of building a new one, and a question was agitated, at this meeting, whether such a thing would be expedient? But it was voted down, to use the words of the

---

* It will be recollected that John Hutchins was permitted to build a gallery in the west end.

Recorder,—" by the additional and wilful votes of many prohibited by law from voting."

The town officers had generally been chosen by nomination, but it was this year voted that the selectmen should be chosen in future, " by the putting in of papers."

1682.

The inhabitants extended an invitation to Rev. Jeremiah Cushing, of Hingham, to settle among them as an assistant to Mr. Ward. Not hearing any thing from him, a messenger was ordered to be despatched immediately to procure his answer, or, "to get him to bring it himself." On the 13th of November, "at a general town-meeting called by the Selectmen to treat further in order about the settlement of Mr. Jeremiah Cushing, Thomas Whittier was chosen Moderator, who, declaring his inability to serve through sickness, was discharged, and Mr. William White was legally chosen Moderator for this present meeting;—nomine contradicente vel alium proponente.

Thus the French King, with twenty thousand men,
Went up a hill, and then came down again.

The meeting for the time is at an end."

This was all that was effected at the meeting; no vote was passed, but we conclude that there was considerable discussion, and probably it was rather violent. The excitement appears to have been great, and Mr. Cushing very wisely refused to accept of their invitation.

A committee was chosen to re-build the bridge over Little River, it " being by the great flood of waters much damnified."

Daniel Ela was prosecuted by his wife, and the Court ordered him to pay her 40s.

John Page was licensed to keep an ordinary; and at the next Court he was fined 40s. for selling " drink to Indians."

William White was licensed to sell cider for three years.

1683.

The people began to talk considerably of building a new Meeting-house, but there was great dissention concerning the spot on which it should stand. One party strenuously contended that the site of the old one was the most convenient, while the other, which was much the strongest, as strenuously opposed it. At a meeting holden on the 13th of June, a question was put to vote, "whether the order of the town made March 3, 1648, for the settlement of the meeting house place, should be adhered unto, and the house to be continued there?" A paper was presented to the Moderator, signed by fifteen persons, who were in favor of having the new house erected where the old one stood; and another was presented, signed by twenty-seven persons, who were opposed to it. On the margin of the last paper, was the following note:—"We, the above written, are not for, but against the setling of a meeting house where the meeting house now stands, forever—but, that the meeting house that now is may stand as long as convenient." It was something like settling a minister for life.

A complaint was made against John Keezar, for keeping his tan-vats open, by which means, some cattle and swine belonging to his neighbors, had been destroyed. "The Moderator, in ye name of ye towne, did publiquely give s^d Keezar a caution—warning and admonishing him upon his perill to secure his tan-yard and tan fatts that no damage be done by him, to other mens or his owne creatures; and in speciall that mischeif may not come unto children, w^c may occasion his owne life to come upon triall."

Daniel Ela, who was a coarse, unprincipled, hard hearted man, was prosecuted by William White, for turning his wife out of doors in a snow-storm, and shamefully abusing her. The following deposition of one of his neighbors, will exhibit his character.— "Goodman Ela said that Goodman White was an old knave, and that he would make it cost him souse for coming to him about his wife, and meddling about that which was none of his business. He said that she was his servant and his slave; and that she was no woman, but a devil in woman's apparel; and that she should never come into his house again; and that he would have her severely whipped, but that it would be a disgrace to him."

Another deposition said that Ela called his wife a "b——h," and she returned the compliment by calling him a "rogue."

1684.

27th Oct. A third committee was chosen, consisting of "Corporal Peter Ayer, Corporal Josiah Gage, and Robert Swan," to procure a minister.

More respect was shown to the office of a corporal, by our unsophisticated fathers, than is now shown to that of a General.

Abraham Whittaker and his wife were presented, for "absenting themselves from the public service of God on the Lord's day."

Simon Wainwright was permitted to sell "liquors out of doors."

1685.

24th Jan. This was an exceeding cold day; in Boston it was "so cold ye sacramental bread was frozen pretty hard and rattled sadly in ye plates."*

23d Feb. The act allowing 40s. for every wolf's head, and which was continued till now, was repealed; for, having heard that Amesbury people had repealed theirs a short time previous, it was supposed that it might be a temptation, if continued, for many to assert that the wolf was killed in Haverhill, rather than in Amesbury; or to decoy and kill it, within the bounds, to obtain the reward. We hardly think these men deemed it good policy to place temptations before a per-

---
* Sewall's Diary.

son, to see how long and how well he would resist them —at least, they were unwilling to try it in this case.

James Chadwick was hired to keep the school; he was the second master.

The Colony laws were promulgated by beat of drum.*

The town petitioned the Court for liberty to put "the yonge ones to sarvice, such as are not able to maintaine themselves." The petition was granted, if they could obtain the approbation of the "Worshipful Nath'l Saltonstall Esq."

The road from Amesbury to this place, was laid out by order of the town. The following is a synopsis of the return of the Committee appointed for that purpose. "We have laid out, and sufficiently marked, the Country highway between Haverhill and Amesbury, four rods wide, lying from Amesbury meeting-house to the widow Bette's; from thence to country Bridge in the east-meadow, and from thence to the meeting-house." A part of this route was travelled long before this, and was frequently called a "bridleway."

1686.

We find the following among the records of deaths, births and marriages:—"Elizabeth Emerson, single-woman, had Dorothy, born April 10—86; and a second time, though never married, Twins, born May 8—91, who were both made away with privately, and found dead May 10—91." The Recorder then says:—"The Mother lay long in prison, but at the long run, in the year 1691, as I take it, was executed at Boston for the murthering of the two babes, or one of them."†

---

* Sewall's Diary.

† The Recorder is correct. The author has seen a record of her trial, and looked over the evidences *pro* and *con*, and no one can imagine any thing more obscene than many of them. The deed for which she suffered, was truly horrid; but the man, who was married, and named Samuel Ladd, by what could be collected from the evidences, was equally guilty; at least he was no better at heart, and he should either have been executed at her side, or severely punished. Neither of which, however, was done, as the author can learn.

1687.

It was ordered that no "dams or wards" should be built across Sawmill, or any other river, so as to stop the free passage of the fish.

A bounty of 15s. was voted to any person, who should kill a full grown wolf within the town's bounds.

The town deeming it expedient, "for the sake of back, belly and purse"—so says the Recorder—to keep a stock of sheep, empowered the Selectmen to provide a place in the outskirts of the town, where they might be conveniently pastured. They were to warn the inhabitants to appear at the designated spot, with suitable tools, to clear it of the wood and brush, and prepare it for the above purpose. Any person who was warned, and did not appear accordingly, was to pay a fine of two shillings per day.

25th Oct. Richard Singletary died, aged 102 years.

1688.

It is evident, from the language of the Recorder, that some epidemic prevailed about this time, though we have no other account of it. He says:—"it being apparent that, by the *death of many persons* in this town, some of the seats are thined in the meeting house." The Selectmen were ordered to place other persons in their seats.

The Selectmen, or some other persons, were generally appointed to seat the people in the meeting-house. A few only, enjoyed pews, or seats, exclusively for themselves; and this privilege was generally confined to the most wealthy and respectable. The two sexes were not permitted to seat themselves promiscuously in the house of worship; but the males occupied one part, and the females the other. Our ancestors were sedate, orderly, and sober-spoken men, who loved to follow the rules of decorum in all things, deeming it almost an unpardonable sin for men to ogle the women, and be seated elbow to elbow with them, in the house of God. Could they have had the power of looking into futurity, and of seeing their degenerate posterity assembled to worship, as is now the custom—the well-dressed and sober husband beside his meek and comely wife, and the beardless youth beside the blushing and innocent maiden—how would their hearts have been pained, to see them wandering so carelessly from the paths which they had devoutly and perseveringly trod.

1689.

About this time there was a revolution in the government of the Colony, and the Council, "for the safety of the people and the preservation of peace," which was convened at Boston, on the 2d of May, deemed it expedient to hold a consultation with the people generally. A circular was sent to each town, advising it to choose "some discreet person, or persons, not exceeding two," to assemble at Boston on the 9th inst., at two o'clock, P. M. The town met on the sixth, and made choice of Mr. Peter Ayer to represent it in the Council.

A question was agitated at a meeting holden on the 24th of March, about the state of the town, and its ability to defend itself against the enemy. But little, however, was said, and the meeting was adjourned *sine die*.

The Indians, for some time past, had been hovering over the town in such a manner as kept the inhabitants in continual alarm. Small parties were almost daily seen traversing the adjacent woods, and slyly approaching the farm-houses in search of plunder. The friendly intercourse that had existed so many years between them was broken, and open hostility succeeded. So early as 1675, the fortifications around the meeting-house were repaired, and in the following year we find that Ephraim Kingsbury was slain; but it was in the summer of this year that they commenced the work of murder and desolation in good earnest. The tawny savage sharpened his knife and tomahawk for the work of blood, and glutted his imagination with the atrocities he should commit. The war began—the fierce and inhuman contest on the part of the savages. It proceeded, and what deeds of valor were performed—what acts of chivalry graced the lives of our Fathers! The plaided Highlander, armed with his claymore and battle-axe, was not more heroic; the stern and determined patriot, who rallied beneath the banner of Wallace, was no braver; the enthusiastic Crusader, who fought and bled on the plains of the Holy Land, never exhibited a more fearless and undaunted spirit. Some of their deeds have been emblazoned on the page of history; but many of them, until now, have been permitted to rust in obscurity.

There was but little genuine bravery among the savages; and in fact, we do not recollect one instance of the kind, on their part, where pure, high-souled and chivalrous courage was displayed, during the whole war, a period of nearly thirty years. But they were generally cruel, vindictive and treacherous. Such aged and infirm persons as were unable to perform a journey through the wilderness, were generally despatched. Infants, soon as they became troublesome, had their mouths filled with burning embers, or their brains dashed out against the nearest stone, or tree. But we have one thing to record which speaks highly in their favor; that is, the modesty with which they generally treated their captive women. We do not recollect of but one instance * where they attempted to abuse their chastity in word, or action. †

---

* This was in the case of Mrs. Hannah Dustin, when her captors told her that she, and her companions, must be stripped naked, and run the gauntlet.

† Testimonies in favor of the savages, in this particular, are very frequent. Mary Rowlandson, who was taken prisoner at Lancaster in 1675, says in her narrative, (page 55,)—"I have been in the midst of these roaring lions and savage bears, that feared neither God nor man, nor the devil, by day and night, alone and in company, sleeping all sorts together, and yet not one of them ever offered me the least abuse of unchastity in word or action." Elizabeth Hanson, who was captured in Dover, in 1724, says in her narrative, that "the Indians are very civil towards their captive women, not offering any incivility by any indecent carriage." Charlevoix, speak-

Haverhill was a frontier town for nearly seventy years, and but few towns suffered so severely from the Indians. At this period, we can have but a faint conception of the sufferings of the inhabitants. Surrounded with an immense and mostly unexplored forest—thinly scattered over a large tract of land—and constantly exposed to the attacks of savage hordes, are circumstances which have made us wonder, why they should continue to march onward and onward into the wilderness, terrific for its extent, and unfurl the banner of civilization under the very shadow of the enemy's wigwam. The contests between them and the savages, were not like those between civilized nations; but it was a war for extermination on one side, characterized with acts of the basest cruelty and revenge, and for defence on the other. The foemen frequently fought hand to hand; the bloody frays were frequent and sometimes long.

The Indians made their attacks slyly, and cautiously approached their enemy by skulking behind the intervening objects, until they came so near that they felt perfectly sure of their victim. At other times, they would fall upon the inhabitants before the break of day, and barbarously slaughter them while they were unprepared to defend themselves. The people always went armed to their daily labor, and on the sabbath they were seen on their way to the Church, with a psalm-book in one hand, and a gun, loaded and primed, in the other. But even then, while kneeling beneath the roof of the sanctuary, they were not safe; if they went into the fields at noontide, with their spades and mattocks, their foes were behind them; if they slept within their dwellings when the sun had gone down, the darkness would not protect them; but ere the light had stole upon the east, their blood, and the blood of their beloved, might pool together upon their hearths. In summer and winter, at the budding and searing of the leaf, they were alike exposed to hardships and to death.

Some of the most heroic deeds accomplished by the inhabitants of this town, were performed by women,—

---

ing of the Indians of Canada, says, (letter 7.) "there is no example that any have taken the least liberty with the French women, even when they were their prisoners."

by those whose limbs were not made to wield the weapons of war—whose hearts could never exult in a profusion of blood—and whose sphere of usefulness, of honor and of glory, was in the precincts of the domestic circle. Giddy, thoughtless and fearful as she often appears, there are times when these characteristics are laid aside, and she clothes herself with a steadiness, a thoughtfulness, and courage, which equals, and oftentimes surpasses, the same qualities in man.

8th July. Henry Barnsby, a young man living with Benjamin Singletary, was drowned.

A small party of Indians, on the 13th of August, made their appearance in the northerly part of the town, and killed Daniel Bradley.* They then went to the field of Nathaniel Singletary, where he, and his oldest son were at work. They approached in their slow and serpent-like manner, until they came within a few rods of them, when they shot Mr. Singletary, who fell and died on the spot; his son then attempted to escape, but was quickly overtaken and made prisoner. The Indians than scalped Mr. Singletary, and commenced a hasty retreat; but their prisoner soon eluded their vigilance, and returned to his home, on the same day, to make glad the hearts of his afflicted relatives. They again made their appearance on the 17th of October, when they wounded and made prisoner, Ezra Rolfe, who died on the 20th.

Two sons of Robert Swan, sen., Samuel and Joshua, went into the orchard of Simon Wainwright and cut down some of his best appletrees. The boys were arrested and brought before Major Nathaniel Saltonstall for examination. But the father wished that they might be examined before some other person, for he bit-

---

* On the 30th of September, 1690, the following petition of his son, Daniel, was addressed to the Court, which we have copied from the original manuscript.

"To the honord cortt now siting att ipswige this may signify to your honors that whereas by the prouvidence of God my father Daniel Bradly was slaine by the hand of the heathen and left no will as to the deposing of his outward estatte I request his brother Joseph may be apointed administrator.   DANIEL BRADLY."

This request was granted.

terly hated the Major, and wrote him the following letter on the occasion, which we copy from the original.

"Dec 16 1689 the hon Major saltonstall is quire i understand there is a contrivance in towne to bring my boys y^t bee onder my government samuel and joshua before youre honer for exsamminasion for mischief don by somebody upon Simon wainwrits estate which i doe forbid and forwarn youre honers having any thing to doe with the exsamminasion of theas my boys but i am willing mr simon wainwrigt should have them to any other magistraticall athority for exsamminasion if he pleas and then i shall bee in hops ye exsamminasion will not be altord when it comes to corte as witnesse my hand
                    ROBERT SWAN sen."

There is but one mark of punctuation in the whole letter, and that is after *sen.*; still it is a biting thing as ever was written, and indirectly charged the Major with altering the tenor of the examination before it was presented to Court. It was too foul an insult to be given to a magistrate, unless it could be supported by positive proof; and the Major considered it too important to be overlooked. Accordingly on the 17th of February following, he entered a complaint to the Court, against Robert Swan, sen., "for a high contempt of authority, and endeavoring to hinder him in the execution of his office as Magistrate, and casting abominable wicked reflections upon him to y^e high defamation of his name."

1690.

Near the close of the last year, Rev. Benjamin Rolfe, a native of Newbury, began to preach, and assist Mr. Ward in other parochial duties. The town voted him a salary of forty pounds, during Mr. Ward's life, in wheat, rye, and indian. There was a strong opposition to this measure, and three lines recorded at the bottom of the vote, were blotted out by order of the town. Having again met in the afternoon, this vote was revised, and another passed, in the absence of "Mr. Ward and his son Saltonstall." The marginal reference to it says:—" £20 taken from Mr. Ward for Mr. Rolfe's diet in —90 without consent."

The inhabitants grew more and more alarmed on account of the Indians, and, on the 7th of April, a meeting was called to provide means for their safety, when a petition was ordered to be drawn up and presented to the General Court, requesting a company of forty men at " the Country's charges, as this was a frontier town, —to be on constant service, and stationed without the outmost garrisons, so as to watch the enemy and prevent any surprise, or give notice to others within, that they may be encouraged to do somewhat in order to future livelihood, and, in case of need, to stand for their lives."

Six garrisons were appointed, and ordered to be kept in a state of defence; and four houses were appointed for refuge, then called " houses for refuge." One of the garrisons was commanded by Sergeant John Haseltine. A part of the house is now standing, and is occupied by Mr. Samuel Pecker.* He had seven men under his command:—Onesiphorus Marsh, sen., Onesiphorus Marsh, jun., Nathaniel Haseltine, Eben Webster, Joseph Holt, Thomas Ayer, and Joseph Bond. Another was commanded by Sergeant John Webster; this is supposed to be the brick house which stands on the bank of the river, three fourths of a mile east of the bridge, and is now occupied by Widow Nathaniel Whittier. He had eight men under his command:—Stephen Webster, Samuel Watts, Nicholas Brown, Jacob Whittaker, John Marsh, Robert Ford, Samuel Ford, and Thomas Kingsbury. The third was owned and commanded by Jonathan Emerson; a part of it is now standing, a few rods west of the house now occupied by Capt. Nehemiah Emerson, and is owned by Mr. Jonathan K. Smith. The fourth was commanded by James

---

* This garrison was owned by Onesiphorus Marsh, sen., who is the ancestor of those of that name in this town. The first notice we have of him, is in 1684, when he built a house a few rods north of that owned by Mr. Pecker. He owned the principal part of that hill, and for many years it was known by the name of Marsh's hill. The name was generally spelt Mash. Another account states that the garrison was commanded by Jonathan Marsh.

Ayer; it stood nearly opposite to the house now occupied by Capt. John Ayer, 2d. The fifth was commanded by Joseph Bradley, and was situated in the northerly part of the town, not far from the house of the late Zebulon Sargent; it was long since torn down, and no traces of it now remain. The sixth was owned and commanded by Capt. John White; and was situated near the house now owned by Mr. William White. He had six men under his command:—Stephen Dow, sen., Stephen Dow, jun., John Dow, Edward Brumidgo, Israel Hendrick, Israel [MS. defaced] jun. Two brick houses, belonging to Joseph and Nathaniel Peaslee, in the easterly part of the town, the houses of Major Nathaniel Saltonstall and Capt. Simon Wainwright, were appointed for houses of refuge.* A few soldiers were stationed in them, who were under the command of the owners. Two watch-houses were erected, one of which stood near the house now occupied by Mr. John Dow, and the other was on the bank of the river, a few rods east of Wid. Samuel W. Duncan's house. The school-house, which stood near the grave-yard, was likewise made use of for that purpose. A guard of soldiers was stationed in each of them, who were on the look-out for the enemy, night and day. Beside these, many private houses were barricaded, and the inhabitants generally were prepared for any emergency.

Most of the garrisons, and two of the refuge houses, those belonging to Joseph and Nathaniel Peaslee, were built of brick, and were two stories high; those that

---

* The houses of Joseph and Nathaniel Peaslee are now standing; the former was owned by the late Nathan Sawyer, and the latter is owned and occupied by Capt. Jesse Newcomb. The house of Mr. Saltonstall stood near that of Wid. Samuel W. Duncan's. The house of Capt. Simon Wainwright stood on the spot now covered by that of Capt. Nehemiah Emerson.

The garrisons here spoken of, it is presumed, were not all appointed in the year 1690; nor can the precise time be ascertained, when they were; though we find them all before 1696. Sergeant John Haseltine took the command of a garrison in the spring of 1690, and it is most probable that the others were appointed at such times as the town authorities deemed proper. But it was thought best to put them all in one year, as the time of their appointment could not be exactly designated.

were not built of this material, had a single laying of it between the outer and inner walls. They had but one outside door, which was often so small that but one person could enter at a time; their windows were about two feet and a half in length, eighteen inches in breadth, and were secured on the inside with iron bars. Their glass was very small, cut in the shape of a diamond, was extremely thick, and fastened in with lead instead of putty. There were generally but two rooms in the basement story, and tradition says that they entered the chamber with the help of a ladder, instead of stairs, so that the inmates could retreat into them, and take it up if the basement-story should be taken by the enemy. Their fire-places were of such enormous sizes, that they could burn their wood sled-length, very conveniently; and the ovens opened on the outside of the building, generally at one end, behind the fire-place; and were of such dimensions that we should suppose a sufficient quantity of bread might have been baked in them, without much difficulty, to supply a regiment of hungry mouths.

It was truly an age of terror with these hardy and courageous men; and their descendants can have but a faint idea of the difficulties they encountered, and of the dangers that continually hung over their heads, threatening every moment to overwhelm them like a torrent, and sweep them, with those whom they dearly loved, to the silent tomb. Almost every man was a soldier; and many, who lived in remote parts of the town, moved, with their families, into the vicinity of a garrison, or a house of refuge.*

On the 31st of August, Samuel Parker, and a small boy, were employed in the east-meadow, in curing hay.

---

* This was the case with Stephen Dow and his son, who lived in the East part of the town, and moved near to the garrrison of Capt. John White. The Indians had a peculiar whistle, which was made by placing both hands to the mouth, and was known to be their call, or watch-word. It was frequently heard in the adjacent woods, and tradition says, that Stephen Dow, jun. was the only person in the garrison who could exactly imitate it; and that he frequently concealed himself, and endeavored to decoy them within the range of the soldiers' bullets. But it does not say that he ever succeeded.

A party of Indians approached them while they were at work, and shot Mr. Parker dead on the spot; the boy ran in an opposite direction from the smoke of the assailants, and, by concealing himself in the tall grass, escaped uninjured, and was the first to bear the melancholy tidings to Mr. Parker's family.*

To add to the horrors of savage warfare, the small pox broke out among the inhabitants. This loathsome and deadly disease was then but little understood, and was much more terrific than at the present day. The town seems to have been somewhat alarmed, and about this time, ordered a pest-house to be erected, which was situated on the hill, east of the house now occupied by Mr. Joseph Bradley. We can learn of but six persons who died with this disease. They were Abraham Hendrick, Mary Ford, and her daughter Mary, Josiah Starling, Ruth Hartshorne, and Thomas Marsh. The records say that John Stockbridge "went to sea and died of the small pox."

Samuel Swan, son of Robert Swan, sen., wantonly stabbed a valuable horse belonging to Capt. Simon Wainwright, with "a half pike." At the Court holden on the 25th of September, Samuel Ingalls swore to the following testimony, which we insert merely for the oddity of its expressions. It is copied correctly from the Court Records. He says—"I and samuel swan was at work to gether in the field of Robert Swan jun and goodman Swan sen came to us and asked us to goe into the hous with him and then he asked Sam¹ why he stabed mr Wainwright horse—Samuel said nothing—then said his father to him what is the reason yo doe wickedly in sinning against God in abusing the dum creature and his father was so grievd at it y^t he weped and then he said I am resolved I will give you coreksion and then he pulled of his close to his shurt and took a stick as big as a good ordinary nailing rod and then he took Sam¹ by one hand and streek him as hard I thought as he was eable to strike and streek him many blows. His father was a considerable while beating him and Samuel

* Tradition.

cryed out and beged of his father vari much y^t he would beat him no more." The boy was convicted and sent to jail.

1691.

On the 16th of June, John Robie* was killed by the Indians; and his son, Ichabod, was taken prisoner, but soon after returned. At the same time they shot Nathaniel Ladd, who soon after died of his wounds. In October, says Mr. Hutchinson, " a family was killed at Rowley and one at Haverhill."† Perhaps he had reference to the above persons; if not, the name of that family must remain in obscurity, for there is no account of the death of any other person, this year, by the Indians. The family killed at Rowley was named Goodridge. ‡

1692.

The witchcraft delusion, so celebrated in the annals of New-England History, commenced in February, in Danvers. Within six months, thirteen women and six men were hung, and one man was pressed to death. More than one hundred other persons were imprisoned within the same time. This fatal delusion, which hung like a tempest-cloud over the whole Colony, showering death and infamy upon those who should be convicted of the diabolical charge, and carrying terror to the hearts of men, did not make its appearance, either in this town, or Newbury. There was not a solitary instance of the kind to stain the characters of our fathers.

2d March. Nathaniel Smith and his wife were presented for drunkenness, " and especially upon the 27th of

---

* After his death, an inventory was taken of his property, which amounted to £120. 5s. 1d.
† Vol. 1, page 359.
‡ Coffin's MSS.

January last." The Court Files say:—" at 9 1-2 P. M., the said Smith's wife came to the house of Samuel Child, in said Haverhill, being very drunk, hardly able to speak for drink, and was very abusive to the great disturbance of the said Samuel's family."

Stephen Dow, 3d., and Daniel Ladd, jun., were chosen jurymen.

The following letter was written by Nathaniel Saltonstall, Esq., to the Court holden at Salem.

"HAVERHILL, March 29, 1692.

Gentlemen:—I do not remember since I belonged to any Court, that a greater or so strong a desire to give my personal appearance at any time than now. Business, transient business, hinders me not. The affaires of ye court (all y^t I have yet heard of,) divert me not. My heart is with you and my prayer shall be for you. Were I with you I could not set in court to hear any case; and besides that, this very day I have met with such a fall that puts me by any possibilitie of moving this day. If I may be capable of serving the country tomorrow, I purpose to come, and do w^t I can. I'll try in the morning.

Gentlemen, proceed, I beseech you, and if in any case there wants a cypher to be added to the number (as soon as I can) you shall have me. I cannot compliment—I have not time for any thing now but to tell you, gentlemen, I am your servant.

NATHANIEL SALTONSTALL."

18th July. Hannah Whittaker was killed by the Indians.

Sometime in August, John Keezar took his scythe and his gun, and went into the Pond Meadow to cut the grass. He laid his gun down beside a tree, and while mowing, a short distance from it, an Indian, who had secretly observed his motions, crept silently along, concealing himself in the grass, and secured the gun before Keezar was aware of it. The Indian then brought the britch of it to his shoulder, and exultingly exclaimed— "me kill you now." Keezar saw that an attempt to fly, would be attended with certain death, and his only recourse was to stratagem. Soon as he saw that the Indian had secured his gun, he faced about and ran towards him, shouting at the top of his voice, swinging his glittering scythe, and threatening to cut him in pieces. This daring conduct, in one whom the Indian expected would fly, or beg for his life, his terrible threatenings, and the formidable appearance of his weapon, completely affrighted him; and he threw down his stolen gun and fled for his life. Keezar followed close upon his heels, striking at him all the time with his scythe. At length he reached him, and at one stroke, buried it in his bowels.* Thus, by a courageous action, which, if it had not succeeded, would have been stigmatized as rash, he saved his life and took that of his opponent.

1693.

19th March. Jonathan Franklin was killed by the Indians.

Joseph Greely and Joseph Peasley, agreed with the town to build a corn-mill on the East-meadow-brook. Mr. Greely, some years before, had partly finished a dam on the same stream; but being unable to bear the expense, he was obliged to leave it. This was the first mill erected on that stream.

8th May. A Committee of four was appointed, to ask Mr. Ward how much he would abate of his annual salary after the settlement of Mr. Rolfe. The record reads thus:—"the messenger, by word of mouth, returned Mr. Ward's answer, that from and after Mr. Rolfe's settlement, he would abate all except twenty pounds in wheat and indian, annually, and sixty cords of sound wood corded at his house; and that a Committee be appointed to attend to his house upon a sett day, to receive and take account of what shall be brought in, and sett the price thereof, if it be not merchantable, that so it come not in by pitiful driblets as formerly."

The venerable Mr. Ward died on the 27th of December, in the eighty-eighth year of his age, and was buried on the following day. He was the projector of

---
* Tradition.

the settlement, and in fact, the father of the town. He had heard the first sound of the woodman's axe—he had seen the first tree fallen, and the first house reared in the wild forest. These hills had never heard the glad sounds of the gospel, until his voice was echoed among them; these green and beautiful vallies had long laid in moral darkness and desolation, trodden only by the feet of the savage, until he came among them as a messenger from God. The waters of the broad Merrimack became glad at the sound of his voice, and rolled onward to their ocean-home,—to the assemblage of the mighty waters.

If we may be permitted to judge from the records, and from what the early writers have said of him, we should say that no preacher ever had a stronger hold on the affections of his people, than Mr. Ward. As a minister, he was honored; as a man, he was respected; as a neighbor, he was beloved. His father was the celebrated Rev. Nathaniel Ward, the author of "the Simple Cobler of Agawam in America." Dr. Cotton Mather calls him one of the worthies of New-England. In his peculiar style, he says:—"Mr. John Ward was born, I think, in Haverhill, [England] on Nov. 5, 1606. His grandfather was that worthy minister of Haverhill, and his father was that N. Ward, whose wit made him known to more Englands than one. He was a person of a quick apprehension, a clear understanding, a strong memory, a facetious conversation; he was an exact grammarian, and expert physician, and which is the top of all, a thorough divine; but which rarely happens, these endowments of his mind were accompanied with a most healthy, hardy and agile constitution of body, which enabled him to make nothing of walking, on foot, a journey as long as thirty miles together.

"Though he had great offers of rich matches in England, yet he chose to marry a meaner person, whom exemplary piety had recommended. He lived with her more than forty years in such an happy harmony, that when she died, he confessed that in all this time he never received one displeasing word or look from her. Although she would so faithfully tell him of every thing that might seem amendable in him, that he would pleasantly compare her to an accusing conscience; yet she pleased him wonderfully. When he lost his mate he caused those words to be fairly written on his tableboard—*In Lugenda Compare, Vitœ Spacium Compleat Orbus.*

"This diligent servant of the Lord Jesus Christ continued under and against many temptations, watching over his flock at Haverhill more than thrice as long as Jacob continued with his unkle, yea, for as many years as there are sabbaths in the year. On Nov. 19 1693, he preached an excellent sermon, entering the eighty-eighth year of his age, the only one that ever was, and perhaps ever will be, preached in this country at such an age.* On Dec. 27th he went off bringing up the rear of our first generation."†

Mr. Rolfe, on the day of his ordination, speaking of him, says, that "these four years past have been the happiest and most profitable to me of my whole life. I have had the counsels of wisdom and experience, the admonitions of a father and friend, and an example constantly before me, of undissembled virtue, ardent piety and burning zeal."

The following is an extract from his will, which was dated on the 27th of May, 1680.

"O Lord, into thy hands commit I my spirit.—Credo languida fide sed tamen fide.

Concerning that portion of worldly goods which God of his rich bounty hath bestowed upon me, I make this my last will and testament. I give to my beloved son, Benja. Woodbridge, and to my beloved daughter, Mary, his wife, one parcell of land containing thirty acres, more or less, lying att the norwest end of the towne of Haverhill, in N. England. * * * * * I give to my beloved son, Nathl. Saltonstall, and to my beloved daughter, Elizabeth, his wife, my house, and land adjoyning thereto, commonly called the houselott, lying in the town of Haverhill. * * * * * Lastly, I constitute and appoynt my beloved son, Saltonstall, the ex-

---

*The Dr. was incorrect in his prediction.
†Magnalia.

ecutor of this my last will and testament, and do hereby make void all former Wills made by me.

Witness my hand and seal.

JOHN WARD. [SEAL.]

Signed and sealed in the presence of us;
WILLIAM WHITE, THOMAS EATON, BENJA. ROLFE.
Jan. 23, 92-3, owned before JOHN WHITE."

1694.

A large portion of the town was opposed to the settlement of Mr. Rolfe, and considerable violence was used. The town voted to make provision for his ordination, if it did not exceed ten pounds; but the opposition was so strong, that—to use the words of the Recorder—the vote was " withdrawn and nullified." His answer to the call of the Church and town was then read, in which he expressed his willingness to settle among them, if they would subscribe to three articles—to which they agreed; and he was accordingly settled the 7th of January.

26th Feb. The annual Town-meeting had been holden on the last Tuesday in February, but, the day on which the assembly met was changed, and it became necessary to alter the day on which the town met, or it would be obliged to hold two annual meetings. To prevent this, the first Tuesday in March was appointed for that purpose.

The garrison commanded by Sergeant Nathaniel Haseltine,* it is believed, was never attacked; but a laughable circumstance happened in it, about this period, which we will narrate. In the dead of night, when the moon shone fitfully through the ragged clouds, and the winds moaned solemnly on the wooded hills, the watch, the only person awake in the garrison, perceived something standing within the paling that surrounded it, which he supposed to be an Indian; and who was, as he

---

* Then owned by Jonathan Marsh, and now owned by Mr. Samuel Pecker.

thought, endeavoring to gain an entrance. Being considerably affrighted, he did not wait to consider the object coolly, but raised his musket and fired. The report alarmed the whole garrison. The women and children were awakened from their slumbers, and ran hither and thither like maniacs, expecting that they should fall beneath the tomahawk. The men, equally affrighted, jumped into their breeches as though their lives depended on their speed, seized their guns, and hastened to the port-holes. Every man now displayed his heroism. Volley after volley was fired at the suspicious looking object—but it fell not. There it remained, just as it did when the watch first observed it. This was truly a mystery, that had no whys nor wherefores. It is presumed a consultation was held at this important crisis; but we have never been informed of the result. Let that be as it may,—they ceased firing, but continued under arms till morning, all prepared for immediate action, and keeping a good look-out for the supposed enemy. At length, the morning began to dawn, and all eyes were turned toward the daring intruder. They soon discovered the cause of their alarm—and what do you suppose it was, reader?—Why, it was nothing but an old maid's old black quilted petticoat, which she had washed the day previous, hung it on the clothes-line to dry, and neglected to take it in at night. When it was taken down, every part of it was pierced with bullet-holes, and, for aught we know, the poor old maid had no other to wear. It is thought that those excellent marksmen ought to have provided her with another—and doubtless they did.*

4th Sept. Joseph Pike and Richard Long, were slain by the Indians, as they were travelling near the north end of the Pond Plain. "The enemy lay in a deserted house by the way, or in a clump of bushes, or both."† They were both of Newbury, and Joseph Pike was a cousin of Rev. John Pike, of Amesbury.

---

* Tradition.
† Rev. John Pike's Journal. Mr. Pike was a minister of Dover, and kept a journal of Indian depredations, from 1682 to 1710.

1695.

2d April. There had been many but ineffectual attempts to settle the boundary line between this town and Amesbury. At this meeting the Selectmen were ordered to have it done immediately. It was then ordered, that the "necessary repairs should be made on the meeting house;" and then they voted that a new one should be erected "with what speed it may be." A question was started, whether the contemplated house should stand on the site of the old one, or on the common land, "near Mr. Keezar's dwelling;"* and the latter place was chosen by a large majority.

"Two persons were wounded by the Indians in Haverhill, in 1695." †

4th Sept. Two persons were killed at Pond Plain.†

Early in the fall, a party of the Indians appeared in the northerly part of the town, where they surprised and made prisoners of Isaac Bradley, aged fifteen, and Joseph Whittaker, aged eleven, who were at work in the open fields near Mr. Joseph Bradley's house. The Indians instantly retreated with their prisoners, without committing any further violence, and pursued their journey through the wilderness until they arrived at their homes, on the shores of Lake Winnipiseoge. Isaac, says tradition, was rather small in stature, but full of vigor and very active; and he certainly possessed more shrewdness than most of the boys of that age. But Joseph was a large, overgrown boy, and exceedingly clumsy in his movements.

Immediately after their arrival at the Lake, the two boys were placed in an Indian family, consisting of the man, his squaw, and two or three children. While they were in this situation, they soon became so well acquainted with the language, that they learned from the occasional conversations carried on in their presence, between their master and the neighboring Indians of the

---

* The present training-field was meant by the common land, and Mr. Keezar then lived near the house now occupied by Mr. John Appleton.

† Farmer's edition of Belknap's Hist. of N. H.

same tribe, that they intended to carry them to Canada,* the following spring. This discovery was very afflicting to them. If their designs were carried into execution, they knew that there would be but little chance for them to escape; and from that time the active mind of Isaac was continually planning a mode to effect it. A deep and unbroken wilderness, pathless mountains, and swollen and almost impassable rivers, lay between them and their beloved homes; and the boys feared, if they were carried still further northward, that they should never again hear the kind voice of a father, or feel the fervent kiss of an affectionate mother, or the fond embrace of a beloved sister. They feared, should they die in a strange land, that there would be none to close their eyes—none to shed for them the tear of affection —none to place the green turf on their graves—and none who would fondly treasure up their memories.

Such were the melancholy thoughts of the young boys, and they determined to escape before their masters started with them for Canada. The winter came with its snow and wind—the spring succeeded, with its early buds and flowers, and its pleasant south wind— and still they were prisoners. Within that period, Isaac was brought nigh to the grave—a burning fever had raged in his veins, and for many days he languished on a bed of sickness; but by the care of the squaw, his mistress, who treated them both with considerable kind-

---

* The derivation of the word Canada is so singular, it was thought that its insertion in this work would be acceptable to the curious, and that the digression would be pardoned by the general reader. "Mr. Bozman, in his excellent 'Introduction to a History of Maryland,' 34, says that it is a traditional report, that previous to the visiting of Newfoundland by Cartier, in 1534, some Spaniards visited that coast in search of gold, but its appearance discouraged them, and they quitted it in haste, crying out as they went on board their vessel, '*Aca nada, Aca nada;*' that is in English, '*there's nothing here.*' The Indians retained these words in their memories, and afterward, when the French came to the country, they were saluted with the same words, and mistook them for the name of the country. And in time the first letter was lost, hence the name, *Canada.*" Samuel G. Drake's "History of Philip's war and the French and Indian wars at the Eastward," page 177. There is something in Mather's Magnalia amounting to nearly the same—II. 522.

ness, he recovered. Again he felt a strong desire to escape, which increased with his strength; and in April he matured a plan for that purpose. He appointed a night to put it in execution, without informing his companion, till the day previous, when he told him of his intentions. Joseph wished to accompany him; to this Isaac demurred, and said to him, " I'm afraid you wont wake." Joseph promised that he would, and at night they laid down in their master's wigwam, in the midst of his family. Joseph soon fell asleep, and began to snore lustily; but there was no sleep for Isaac—his strong desire to escape—the fear that he should not succeed in his attempt, and of the punishment that would doubtless be inflicted if he did not—and the danger, hunger and fatigue that awaited him, all were vividly painted in his imagination, and kept sleep or even drowsiness far from him. His daring attempt was environed with darkness and danger—he often revolved it in his mind, yet his resolution remained unshaken. At length the midnight came, and its holy stillness rested on the surrounding forest;—it passed—and slowly and cautiously he arose. All was silent save the deep drawn breath of the savage sleepers. The voice of the wind was scarcely audible on the hills, and the moon, at times, would shine brightly through the scattered clouds, and silver the broad lake, as though the robe of an angel had fallen on its sleeping waters.

Isaac stepped softly and tremblingly over the tawny bodies, lest they should awake and discover his design, and secured his master's fire-works, and a portion of his moose-meat and bread; these he carried to a little distance from the wigwam, and concealed them in a clump of bushes. He then returned, and bending over Joseph, who had, all this time, been snoring in his sleep, carefully shook him. Joseph, more asleep than awake, turned partly over, and asked aloud, "what do you want?"—This egregious blunder alarmed Isaac, and he instantly laid down in his proper place, and began to snore as loudly as any of them. Soon as his alarm had somewhat subsided, he again arose, and listened long for the heavy breath of the sleepers. He determined to fly from his master, before the morning dawned. Perceiving that they all slept, he resolved to make his escape, without again attempting to awake Joseph, lest, by his thoughtlessness, he should again put him in jeopardy. He then arose and stepped softly out of the wigwam, and walked slowly and cautiously from it, until he had nearly reached the place where his provisions were concealed, when he heard footsteps approaching hastily behind him. With a beating heart he looked backward, and saw Joseph, who had aroused himself, and finding that his companion had gone, concluded to follow. They then secured the fire-works and provisions, and without chart or compass, struck into the woods in a southerly direction, aiming for the distant settlement of Haverhill. They ran at the top of their speed until day-light appeared, when they concealed themselves in a hollow log, deeming it too dangerous to continue their journey in the day time.

Their master, when he awoke in the morning, was astonished to find his prisoners had escaped, and immediately collected a small party with their dogs, and pursued them. The dogs struck upon the tracks, and in a short time came up to the log where the boys were concealed, when they made a stand, and began a loud barking. The boys trembled with fear lest they should be re-captured, and perhaps fall beneath the tomahawk of their enraged master. In this situation, they hardly knew what was best to do—but they spoke kindly to the dogs, who knew their voices, ceased barking, and wagged their tails with delight. They then threw before them all the moose-meat they had taken from the wigwam, which the dogs instantly siezed, and began to devour it as though they highly relished so choice a breakfast. While they were thus employed, the Indians made their appearance, and passed close to the log in which they were concealed, without noticing the employment of their dogs. The boys saw them as they passed, and were nearly breathless with anxiety. They followed them with their eyes till they were out of sight, and hope again took possession of their bosoms. The dogs soon devoured their meat, and trotted after their masters.

They lay in the log during the day, and at night pursued their journey, taking a different route from the one travelled by the Indians. They made only one or two meals on their bread, and after that was gone they were obliged to subsist on roots and buds. On the second day they concealed themselves, but travelled the third night and day without resting; and on that day, towards night, they luckily killed a pigeon and a turtle, a part of which they ate raw, not daring to build a fire, lest they should be discovered. The fragments of their unsavory meal they carried with them, and ate of them as their hunger required, making their dessert on such roots as they happened to find. They continued their journey night and day as fast as their wearied and mangled limbs would carry them. On the sixth day, they struck into an Indian path and followed it till night, when they suddenly came within sight of an Indian encampment, saw their savage enemy seated around the fire, and distinctly heard their voices. This alarmed them exceedingly; and wearied and exhausted as they were, they had rather seek an asylum in the wide forest, and die within the shadow of its trees, than trust to the kindness of foes whose bosoms had never been moved by its silent workings. They precipitately fled, fearing lest they should be discovered and pursued, and all night retraced their steps. The morning came and found them seated side by side on the bank of a small stream, their feet torn and covered with blood, and each of them weeping bitterly over his misfortunes. Thus far their hearts had been filled with courage, and their hopes grew, and were invigorated with the pleasant thoughts of home, as they flitted vividly across their minds. But now their courage had fled, and their hopes had given way to despair. They thought of the green fields in which they had so often played—of the tall trees whose branches had so often overshadowed them—and of the hearth around which they had delighted to gather with their brothers and sisters, on a winter's evening, and listen to a story told by their parents. They thought of these, yea, of more—but as things from which they were forever parted—as things that had once given 'forever passed away.

They were, however, unwilling to give up all further exertions. The philosophy of Isaac taught him that the stream must eventually lead to a large body of water, and after refreshing themselves with a few roots, they again commenced their journey, and followed its windings. They continued to follow it during that day and a part of the night. On the eighth morning, Joseph found himself completely exhausted; his limbs were weak and mangled, his body was emaciated, and despair was the mistress of his bosom. Isaac endeavored to encourage him to proceed; he dug roots for him to eat, and brought water to quench his thirst—but all was in vain. He laid himself down on the bank of the stream, in the shade of the budding trees, to die, far from his friends, with none for companions but the howling beasts of the forest. Isaac left him to his fate, and with a bleeding heart, slowly and wearily pursued his journey. He had travelled but a short distance when he came to a newly raised building. Rejoiced at his good fortune, and believing that inhabitants were nigh, he immediately retraced his steps, and soon found Joseph in the same place and position in which he left him. He told him what he had seen, talked very encouragingly, and after rubbing his limbs a long while, he succeeded in making him stand on his feet. They then started together, Isaac part of the time leading him by the hand, and part of the time carrying him on his back; and in this manner, with their naked limbs mangled and wearied with travelling, their strength exhausted by sickness, and their bodies emaciated almost to skeletons, they arrived at Saco fort, sometime in the following night.

Thus, on the ninth night, they arrived among their countrymen, after travelling over an immense forest, subsisting on a little bread, on buds and berries, and on one raw turtle and a pigeon, and without seeing the face of a friend, or warming themselves over a fire. Isaac, soon as he regained his strength, started for Haverhill, and arrived safely at his father's dwelling, who had heard nothing from him since he was taken, and expected never to see him again. But Joseph had more to suffer

—he was seized with a raging fever soon as he reached the fort, and was for a long time confined to his bed. His father, when Isaac returned, went to Saco, and brought home his long lost son, soon as his health permitted.*

1696.

On the 11th May, a Committee was chosen to hire a man who would build the Meeting-house by the "lump" —to examine the houses for public worship in the neighboring towns, and draw up such a plan as they thought would best accommodate the inhabitants. On the 28th of July next the doings of the Committee were read before a full meeting, when much contention again arose about the place on which it should stand; and only that part of the Committee's report was accepted which related to its dimensions, which was "fifty feet in length, forty feet in breadth, and eighteen feet studd." † The meeting was then dissolved, and nothing more was done until the next year.

13th Aug. Old John Hoyt, so called, and Mr. Peters, a young man, both of Amesbury, were slain by the Indians on the road between Andover and Haverhill. ‡

15th Aug. Jonathan Haines, who lived in the westerly part of the town, and his four children, ‡ Mary,

---

* We do not recollect of ever seeing an account of this truly heroic escape in print. The "Sketch of Haverhill" merely gives it a passing notice, without going into particulars. It is deemed a daring attempt on the part of the boys, considering their ages and the great distance they were from their homes; and as such was well worthy of being faithfully recorded. It has been taken wholly from tradition—but, from so many lips, and the narrators agreed so perfectly in all the essential points, we have no hesitation in declaring that every word of it is truth. It has been preserved in the families and handed down from father to son with singular accuracy; and is even now, often told by their descendants, to help fill up a winter evening's amusement. The Rev. Abiel Abbot, while he was pastor of the first parish, collected the facts, and left them in manuscript.

† Committee's Report.
‡ John Pike's Journal.

Joseph, Ruth, and Elizabeth, were captivated by the Indians. The children were in a field near Bradley's Mills, picking beans, and the father was reaping near by. The Indians, with their captives, immediately started for Penacook, [Concord.] When they arrived, they separated, and divided their prisoners—one party taking the father and Joseph, and the other the three girls. The party which took the men started for their homes, in Maine, where they soon arrived. The prisoners had remained with them but a short time, before they escaped; and after travelling two or three days with little or nothing to satisfy their craving appetites, the old man became wholly exhausted, and laid down beneath the branching trees to die. The son, who was young and vigorous, finding his efforts vain to encourage his father, started onward. He soon found himself upon a hill, where he climbed a tall tree to discover signs of civilization; and heard indistinctly the sound of a saw-mill. With a glad heart he hastily descended, and following the sound, soon arrived at the settlement of Saco. Here he told the story of his escape, the forlorn situation of his father, and getting assistance and a bottle of milk, hastened back to him, and found him still lying on the ground without the expectation of ever seeing the face of a friend. He drank some of the milk, which revived him considerably, and with some assistance, reached Saco. Here they remained until their strength was somewhat recruited, when they started for Haverhill, where they arrived without any further difficulty.

The party which took the three girls, went to Canada, where, it is presumed, they were sold to the French;—for Joseph Haynes, a relative, visited them some years after, and found one of them married to a Frenchman. They had all forgotten their mother tongue, and were obliged to converse with Mr. Haynes through an interpreter. Though they had forgotten the language of their childhood, they had not forgotten its incidents—for one of them, a short time before she was captivated, had one of her fingers accidentally cut off by a young lad, a son of a neighbor; and she asked Mr. Haynes if the lad was then living. They had become so fascinated with the manners and customs of the French, that

Mr. Haynes could not persuade them to return to their relatives. But there they lived and died, and their descendants are now in that quarter.

Timothy Eaton petitioned the town to grant him a bounty, more than the country allowed, for killing a full grown she-wolf on the ox-common. The town granted him ten shillings "for killing said wolf since he declares it was a bitch wolf and that she will not bring any more whelps."

Peter Pettee, says the Recorder, "entered a strange motion for keeping a tavern at his house, and offered his conditions, which, if done or endeavored, would have been prejudicial to the town. Being moved and fully agitated the town declared against his having any allowance for it."

The winter of this year was the coldest since the settlement of New-England.*

1697.

On the 15th† of March, a body‡ of Indians made a descent on the westerly part of the town, and approached the house of Mr. Thomas Dustin.§ They came as they were wont, arrayed with all the terrors of a savage war-dress, with their muskets charged for the contest, their tomahawks drawn for the slaughter, and their

---

* Sewall's Journal.

† The day on which the attack took place, is variously stated. The Magnalia says it happened on the fifth, and Mr. Drake, in his Appendix to "the History of King Philip's War, &c." falls into the same error. I have my information from the Town Records, where the deaths are dated on the 15th of March, 1696–7.

‡ The Appendix to the History of King Phillip's War, says about twenty. Page 316.

§ This name was variously spelt;—in the Town Records, it is spelt Dustin, Duston and Dustan. In a Petition to the General Court, he signs his name Dunstan. Perhaps he was a descendant of St. Dunstan in the monkish legends, who fought and vanquished the devil, by pinching his nose with a pair of red-hot tongs. The name is now spelt Dustin.

scalping knives unsheathed and glittering in the sunbeams. Mr. Dustin, at this time, was engaged abroad in his daily labor. When the terrific shouts of the blood-hounds first fell on his ear, he seized his gun, mounted his horse, and hastened to his house with the hope of escorting to a place of safety his family, which consisted of his wife, whom he tenderly and passionately loved, and who had been confined only seven days in childbed, her nurse, Mrs. Mary Neff,* and eight young children. Immediately upon his arrival, he rushed into his house, and found it a scene of confusion—the women trembling for their safety, and the children weeping and calling on their mother for protection. He instantly ordered seven of his children to fly in an opposite direction from that in which the danger was approaching, and went himself to assist his wife. But he was too late—before she could arise from her bed, the enemy were upon them.

Mr. Dustin seeing there was no hope of saving his wife from the clutches of the foe, flew from the house, mounted his horse, and rode full speed after his flying children. The agonized father supposed it impossible to save them all, and he determined to snatch from death, the child which shared the most of his affections. He soon came up with the infant brood—he heard their glad voices and saw the cheerful looks that overspread their countenances, for they felt themselves safe, while under his protection. He looked for the child of his love—where was it?—He scanned the little group from the oldest to the youngest, but he could not find it. They all fondly loved him—they called him by the endearing title of father, were flesh of his flesh, and stretched out their little arms toward him for protection. He gazed upon them, and faltered in his resolution, for there was none whom he could leave behind, and indeed, what parent could, in such a situation, select the child which shared the most of his affections?—He could not do it, and therefore resolved to defend them from the murderers, or die at their side.

---

* She was the daughter of George Corliss, and married William Neff,—her husband went after the army, and died at Pemaquid, in February, 1688.

A small party of the Indians pursued Mr. Dustin, as he fled from the house, and soon overtook him and his flying children. They did not, however, approach very near, for they saw his determination, and feared the vengeance of a father,—but skulked behind the trees and fences, and fired upon him and his little company. Mr. Dustin dismounted from his horse, placed himself in the rear of his children, and returned the fire of the enemy often and with good success. In this manner he retreated for more than a mile, alternately encouraging his terrified charge, and loading and firing his gun, until he lodged them safely in a forsaken house. The Indians, finding that they could not conquer him, returned to their companions, expecting, no doubt, that they should there find victims, on which they might exercise their savage cruelty.

It is truly astonishing that no one of that little company was killed or wounded. When we reflect upon the skill of the Indians as marksmen, upon their great superiority of strength, and the advantage they possessed in skulking behind every fence and tree, it cannot but be confessed that the arm of the Almighty was outstretched for their preservation. Not a ball from the enemy took effect; but, so surely, says tradition, as Mr. Dustin raised his gun to his eye, so surely some one of the enemy would welter in his blood.

The party which entered the house when Mr. Dustin left it, found Mrs. Dustin in bed, and the nurse attempting to fly with the infant in her arms. They ordered Mrs. Dustin to rise instantly, while one of them took the infant from the arms of the nurse, carried it out, and dashed out its brains against an apple-tree.* After plundering the house they set it on fire, and commenced their retreat, though Mrs. Dustin had but partly dressed herself, and was without a shoe on one of her feet. Mercy was a stranger to the breasts of the conquerors, and the unhappy women expected to receive

---

*We have been informed by a gentleman, that he has heard his grandmother, who lived to an advanced age, often relate this fact, and that she had frequently ate apples that grew on the same tree. We have also been informed by an aged female, that she had often heard her mother tell of eating of the fruit of the same tree.

no kindnesses from their hands. The weather at the time was exceedingly cold—the March-wind blew keen and piercing, and the earth was alternately covered with snow and deep mud.

They travelled twelve miles the first day,* and continued their retreat, day by day, following a circuitous route, until they reached the home of the Indian, who claimed them as his property, which was on a small Island, now called Dustin's Island, at the mouth of Contoocook River, about six miles above the State House in Concord, New-Hampshire. Notwithstanding their intense suffering for the death of the child—their anxiety for those whom they had left behind, and who they expected had been cruelly butchered—their sufferings from cold and hunger, and from sleeping on the damp earth, with nothing but an inclement sky for a covering—and their terror for themselves, lest the arm that, as they supposed, had slaughtered those whom they dearly loved, would soon be made red with their blood,—notwithstanding all this, they performed the journey without yielding, and arrived at their destination in comparative health.

The family of their Indian master consisted of two men, three women and seven children; besides an English boy,† named Samuel Lennardson, who was taken prisoner about a year previous, at Worcester. Their master, some years before, had lived in the family of Rev. Mr. Rowlandson, of Lancaster, and he told Mrs. Dustin that, "when he prayed the English way he thought it was good, but now he found the French way better." ‡

These unfortunate women had been but a few days with the Indians, when they were informed that they must soon start for a distant Indian settlement, and that, upon their arrival, they would be obliged to conform to the regulations always required of prisoners, whenever they entered the village, which was, to be stripped, scourged, and run the gauntlet in a state of nudity. The gauntlet consisted of two files of Indians of both

---

* Appendix to History of King Philip's War—page 317.
† Hutchinson, vol. II. page 101.
‡ Sewall's Diary.

sexes and of all ages, containing all that could be mustered in the village; and the unhappy prisoners were obliged to run between them, when they were scoffed at and beaten by each one as they passed, and were sometimes marks at which the younger Indians threw their hatchets. This cruel custom was often practised by many of the tribes, and not unfrequently the poor prisoner sunk beneath it. Soon as the two women were informed of this, they determined to escape as speedily as possible. They could not bear to be exposed to the scoffs and unrestrained gaze of their savage conquerors —death would be preferable. Mrs. Dustin soon planned a mode of escape, appointed the 31st inst. for its accomplishment, and prevailed upon her nurse and the boy to join her. The Indians kept no watch—for the boy had lived with them so long they considered him as one of their children, and they did not expect that the women, unadvised, and unaided, would attempt to escape, when success, at the best, appeared so desperate.

On the day previous to the 31st, Mrs. Dustin wished to learn on what part of the body the Indians struck their victims when they would despatch them suddenly, and how they took off a scalp. With this view she instructed the boy to make inquiries of one of the men. Accordingly, at a convenient opportunity, he asked one of them where he would strike a man, if he would kill him instantly, and how to take off a scalp. The man laid his finger on his temple—" strike 'em there," said he; and then instructed him how to scalp.* The boy then communicated his information to Mrs. Dustin.

The night at length arrived, and the whole family retired to rest, little suspecting that the most of them would never behold another sun. Long before the break of day, Mrs. Dustin arose, and having ascertained that they were all in a deep sleep, awoke her nurse and the boy, when they armed themselves with tomahawks, and despatched ten of the twelve. A favorite boy they designedly left; and one of the squaws, whom they left for dead, jumped up, and ran with him into the woods. Mrs. Dustin killed her master, and Samuel

---

* Sewall's Diary, and tradition.

Lennardson despatched the very Indian who told him where to strike, and how to take off a scalp.* The deed was accomplished before the day began to break, and after securing what little provision the wigwam of their dead master afforded, they scuttled all the boats but one, to prevent pursuit, and with that, started for their homes. Mrs. Dustin took with her a gun that belonged to her master, and the tomahawk † with which she committed the tragical deed. They had not proceeded far, however, when Mrs. Dustin perceived that they had neglected to take their scalps, and feared that her neighbors, if they ever arrived at their homes, would not credit their story, and would ask them for some token, or proof. She told her fears to her companions, and they immediately returned to the silent wigwam, took off the scalps of the fallen, and put them into a bag. They then started on their journey anew, with the gun, tomahawk, and the bleeding trophies,—palpable witnesses of their heroic and unparalleled deed.

A long and weary journey was before them, but they commenced it with cheerful hearts, each alternately rowing and steering their little bark. Though they had escaped from the clutches of their unfeeling master, still they were surrounded with dangers. They were thinly clad—the sky was still inclement—and they were liable to be re-captured by strolling bands of Indians, or by those who would undoubtedly pursue them so soon as the squaw and the boy had reported their departure, and the terrible vengeance they had taken; and were they again made prisoners, they well knew that a speedy death would follow. This array of danger, however, did not appal them, for home was their beacon-light, and the thoughts of their fire-sides, nerved their hearts. They continued to drop silently down the river, keeping a good look-out for strolling Indians; and in the night two of them only slept, while the third managed the boat. In this manner they pursued their journey, until they arrived safely, with their trophies, to their homes,

---

* M. D. Fairfield's Diary, and Sewall's.

† It has not been ascertained whether Mrs. Neff or the boy took their tomahawks or any thing else, with them; it is presumed, however, that they did not.

totally unexpected by their mourning friends, who supposed that they had been butchered by their ruthless conquerors. It must truly have been an affecting meeting for Mrs. Dustin, who likewise supposed that all she loved—all she held dear on earth—was laid in the silent tomb.

After recovering from the fatigue of the journey, they started for Boston, where they arrived on the 21st of April. They carried with them the gun and tomahawk, and their ten scalps—those witnesses that would not lie; and while there, the General Court gave them fifty pounds,* as a reward for their heroism. The report of their daring deed soon spread into every part of the country, and when Colonel Nicholson, Governor of Maryland, heard of it, he sent them a very valuable present,† and many presents were also made to them by their neighbors. ‡

Various opinions are afloat concerning the justness of this certainly heroic deed. Perhaps the strict moralizer would say that, the fear of the gauntlet, which, perhaps, appeared worse to them than torture or death, or of suffering their danger anew, would not justify the act. And it surely seems that she had lost a great portion of that sensibility, that fear of blood, that sympathy for another's wo, which is at once the delight and ornament of her sex; and which we have been taught to believe is an inmate and constant virtue of her bosom. But a prisoner among the savages—a wife who has seen her dwelling in flames, her infant cruelly slaughtered, and who expects that her husband and the rest of

---

* Hutchinson.

† Magnalia.

‡ M. D. Fairfield thus speaks of this exploit in his Diary. "April 21, 1696-7. At the latter end of this month, two women and a young lad that had been taken captive from Haverhill the March before, watching their opportunity when the Indians were asleep, killed ten of them, scalped them all, and came home to Boston, brought a gun with some other things. The Chief of these Indians took one of the women captive when she had been in childbed but a few days, and knocked her child in head before her eyes, while the women killed and scalped that very Indian. This was done just about the time the Council of this Province had concluded on a day of fasting and prayer throughout the province."

her children have been butchered, who is herself threatened with immediate torture, and with disgrace worse than death—a wife in such a situation would not be apt to critically analyze the morality of the deed.

But let what will be said of her conduct, there is something in the actions of the father and husband, disinterested perhaps, beyond comparison, and noble beyond example. But few acts, if any, are recorded on the page of history, more exalted, more generous, more free from every gross and selfish passion of the heart. In most of the daring and noble actions that are spoken of with enthusiasm by historians, we find that the actors were prompted by some powerful stimulus—glory, ambition, or a lust for gain—which acted as a spur to their flagging spirits. But in this he was not urged on by ambition; he thought not of glory; he cared not for his property;—but it was only a deep, chaste and uncontaminated love for his wife and children, that prompted him to the action.

Mrs. Dustin was the daughter of Michael and Hannah Emerson, and the eldest of fifteen children. She was born 23d December, 1657, and was married to Thomas Dustin, 3d December, 1677. She had thirteen children, Hannah, Elizabeth, Mary, Thomas, Nathaniel, John, Sarah, Abigail, Jonathan, Timothy and Mehitable, twins, Martha, whose brains were dashed out against an apple-tree, and Lydia. Mrs. Dustin was in the fortieth year of her age when she was captured by the Indians. The time when she, or her husband died, cannot be positively ascertained. The Town Records are defective in this particular. Their descendants are quite numerous, both in this State and in New-Hampshire.

The following beautiful lines are from the pen of Mrs. Sarah J. Hale, Editor of the Ladies' Magazine, and copied from the Boston Lyceum.

THE FATHER'S CHOICE.

Now fly, as flies the rushing wind—
Urge, urge, thy lagging steed!
The savage yell is fierce behind,
And life is on thy speed.

And from those dear ones make thy choice;
　　The group he wildly eyed,
When "father!" burst from every voice,
　　And "child!" his heart replied.

There's one that now can share his toil,
　　And one he meant for fame,
And one that wears her mother's smile,
　　And one that bears her name.

And one will prattle on his knee,
　　Or slumber on his breast;
And one whose joys of infancy,
　　Are still by smiles expressed.

They feel no fear while he is near;
　　He'll shield them from the foe;
But oh! his ear must thrill to hear
　　Their shriekings, should he go.

In vain his quivering lips would speak,
　　No words his thoughts allow;
There's burning tears upon his cheek—
　　Death's marble on his brow.

And twice he smote his clenched hand—
　　Then bade his children fly!
And turned, and e'en that savage band
　　Cowered at his wrathful eye.

Swift as the lightning winged with death,
　　Flashed forth the quivering flame!
Their fiercest warrior bows beneath
　　The father's deadly aim.

Not the wild cries, that rend the skies,
　　His heart of purpose move;
He saves his children, or he dies
　　The sacrifice of love.

Ambition goads the conqueror on,
　　Hate points the murderer's brand—
But love and duty, these alone
　　Can nerve the good man's hand.

The hero may resign the field,
　　The coward murd'rer flee;
He cannot fear, he will not yield,
　　That strikes, sweet love, for thee.

They come, they come—he heeds no cry,
　　Save the soft child-like wail,
"O father save!" "My children, fly!"
　　Were mingled on the gale.

And firmer still he drew his breath,
And sterner flash'd his eye,
As fast he hurls the leaden death,
Still shouting, " children fly !"

No shadow on his brow appeared,
Nor tremor shook his frame,
Save when at intervals he heard
Some trembler lisp his name.

In vain the foe, those fiends unchained,
Like famished tigers chafe,
The sheltering roof is near'd, is gain'd,
All, all the dear ones safe !

We have not yet finished narrating the tragedy of that eventful day. The Indians dispersed themselves in small parties, and attacked the houses in the vicinity. Eight,* besides the house of Mr. Dustin, were conquered, plundered, and reduced to ashes.† Their owners in every case were slain while defending them—their blood stained their door-sills, and the blood of their beloved pooled upon their hearths. The houses that were burnt belonged to John Keezar, John Kimball, Thomas Eaton, Thomas Emerson, Daniel Bradley, Thomas Wood, John Woodman and —— Kingsbury; making nine in all. The persons slain, were John Keezar, his father, and son, George; John Kimball and his mother, Hannah; Sarah Eastman; Thomas Eaton; Thomas Emerson, his wife, Elizabeth, and two children, Timothy and Sarah; Daniel Bradley, his wife Hannah, and two children, Mary and Hannah; Martha Dow, daughter of Stephen Dow; Joseph, Martha and Sarah Bradley, children of Joseph Bradley; Thomas and Mehitable Kingsbury; Thomas Wood and his daughter Susannah; John Woodman and his daughter Susannah; Zechariah White, and Martha, the infant daughter of Mr. Dustin; —making the round number of twenty-seven, who were

---

* Mr. Drake, in his Appendix to Philip's War, &c., page 315, says, they "took and killed thirty-nine persons and burnt about a half a dozen houses."

† Fairfield thus notices it in his Diary· "March 15. The Indians did much damage at Haverhill; burnt nine houses—killed and took captive near forty prisoners."

slaughtered, fifteen of whom were children, besides thirteen who were captured.

The savages were now glutted with murder and desolation, and breaking up into small parties, as was their general practice, they commenced a hasty retreat. One of their number stole the old or first town-book, and with a few others retreated up the river. In the westerly part of the town, now Methuen, they came upon a yoke of oxen, and with that hellish barbarity which is their principal characteristic in war, cut out their tongues, struck up a fire and broiled them. Had they despatched the oxen, after their tongues were out, it would have been a deed of mercy; but instead of doing that, they left them in that dreadful situation. After their repast was over, they continued their retreat, but, either designedly or intentionally, left the town-book. It was soon found, but so damaged with water that many of the records were perfectly illegible. The rumor of this attack soon reached the village, when an armed party was collected and immediately pursued them. But the Indians eluded their vigilance, and they returned without seeing any of them.

This was truly a terrible day for the infant settlement; some of its most useful citizens were slain, and many of its promising youth. Terror seized the hearts of the inhabitants, and well it might, for they were liable, every day, to be swept from the stage of existence without even a moment's warning. They were now on the alert to prevent, if possible, another attack; guards were stationed in many of the houses, and the brick house of Thomas Dustin, that had been partly finished the year before, but had not been occupied, was ordered to be garrisoned.* The following is a copy of the order to Mr. Dustin when he was appointed to command it.

"To Thomas Dustin, upon the settlement of garrisons. April 5 1696–7. You being appointed master of the garrison at your house, you are hereby, in his Maj's [Majesty's] name, required to see that a good

---

* A part of this building is now standing, and is occupied by Mr. Joshua Dustin, his descendant, for an out-house.

watch be kept at your garrison both by night and by day, by those persons hereafter named who are to be under your command and inspection in building or repairing your garrison; and if any person refuse or neglect their duty, you are accordingly required to make return of the same, under your hand, to the Committee of militia in Haverhill. The persons appointed are as followeth:—Josiah Heath, sen., Josiah Heath, jun., Joseph Bradley, John Heath, Joseph Kingsbury, and Thomas Kingsbury.

By order of the Committee of militia.

SAMUEL AYER, Capt."

Thomas Dustin was a man of considerable ingenuity, and tradition says that he had a "vast deal of mother wit;" that he possessed unshaken courage and the purest and loftiest feelings of affection, cannot be doubted. It is said that he made his own almanacks, and furthermore, that he always made them on *rainy days*. How true this is, we will not attempt to say. He had a grandson, Joshua, who was said to have been his counterpart. He once took it into his head to weave a bed-quilt, and succeeded in making an excellent one, consisting of as many colors as Joseph's coat. This curious relic is now preserved by his descendants.

The business of brick-making was carried on extensively, for that period, by Mr. Dustin, and the spot where the kilns were burnt, is still visible. It was, however, attended with considerable danger, for the Indians were continually lurking in the vicinity, watching an opportunity to shoot them from their hiding places, or to successfully attack them. The pits, where the clay was dug, were situated only a few rods south of the garrison, but the enemy were so bold that those who brought the clay from the pits to the yard, near the house, where it was made into bricks, were constantly attended by a file of soldiers.

We will here narrate a laughable incident that happened at this garrison, while it was commanded by Mr. Dustin. One Joseph Whittaker was quartered there, to serve on the watch, assist in defending it against the enemy, and perform such other duties as were from time to time required of him. He was a young unmarried man, and full of "marcury," as the story goes; but whether or no, he was tall in person, had a high brow, a beautiful countenance, and an elegant and courtly mien, we have never been informed. But that he was unmarried, is positively true, and this unlucky circumstance seemed to trouble his mind;—for it was considered, by our worthy fathers, something of a sin to live long without the pale of matrimony; yes, they positively deemed it better for young men and young women to be linked together by the holy and inseparable banns of wedlock, "soon as convenient,"— blessed be their memories for that! Our young gentleman mourned bitterly over his sinful situation, as he considered it, and came to a solemn resolution to change it immediately "for better for worse." It must have been a trying time with him, and doubtless he weighed the matter carefully before he came to a final determination. But he came to it at last, and accordingly he began to cast many inquisitive glances upon the buxom lasses of his acquaintance, and to resolve, in his own mind, which of them should have the *honor* of accepting his heart and hand.

It so happened that a young lady, jogging on in the joyless state of celibacy, yeclped Mary Whittaker, but of no kith nor kin to Joseph, says tradition, was then living in the garrison, who evidently was not averse to a state of double blessedness. Mary was undoubtedly a fascinating creature, sensitive as the gossamer, beautiful as an Houri, and combined in her actions the three grand secrets of loveliness,—gentleness, gracefulness, and delicacy. It is impossible to state the exact color of her hair—perhaps it was black ;—perhaps her neck was shaded with "flaxen ringlets," such as Burns has immortalized. The color of her eyes is also a mystery; but Joseph, no doubt, clearly saw heaven in their every wink. But, whether black, blue, or grey, she stole his heart, and would not return it to the rightful owner.

The days and nights passed rapidly on, as they always do to persons who begin to feel the silent workings of young love, and Joseph found himself sinking deeper and deeper each day, in the miry pit, with only one remedy within his grasp—and this was matrimony.

Accordingly he thought it best to make a declaration, as it is called, and learn if the object of his devoted affection returned "love for love." Agreeably to this manful resolution, he sedulously watched an opportunity, and assisted a little by the young lady, who, no doubt, suspected his design, luckily found one.

> 'Twas when the shades of evening fell
> O'er forest deep, and hill and dell.

But whether the sky was cloudless, the stars came out like beautiful spirits, and the western breezes warbled among the aged oaks;—or whether the clouds rolled upward in black and frightful masses, and the lightnings flashed vividly along their torn and sable edges, and the deep and heavy thunder vaulted from pole to pole—we have yet to learn. But the evening was probably calm and beautiful, for love is positively afraid of thunder, and will never show its delicate proportions when it is heard. It was in the night-time, however, and they began "to court a little," to use the phrase of our narrator. At length, Joseph nerved his shrinking courage, and with a palpitating heart, and in broken accents, made a declaration of his love, and ended the interesting harangue by offering his heart and hand.

Mary heard his story very attentively, and then flatly refused to have any thing to do with him. What a hard hearted creature! Joseph was somewhat staggered at so prompt a denial, but determined not to suffer her to escape so easily; he had probably heard of the old adage, "faint heart never won fair lady," and resolved to persevere in the good work until he triumphed. He pleaded his cause most manfully—but it was all in vain; she remained stubborn and hard-hearted as at first. As a last resource, he told her that, if she would not accept of his offer, he would go and "jump into the well." This was truly a desperate resolution; but it had no effect on the cruel heart of the maiden—she still persisted in her refusal. Joseph then arose—probably from a kneeling posture—and casting a long, lingering look on the unfeeling girl, left the garrison. He went to the well, and looking into "the deep and dark abyss," anxiously weighed the matter before he took the final leap. It was a stern resolve—he thought of it earnestly—he wavered—and at last determined not to throw away his life for such a hard-hearted creature. While "casting himself about" to see how he could escape from this sad dilemma, and still preserve some appearance of having done the deed, a new idea happily flashed across his cranium. A large log was lying near, which he resolved should be the Joseph to jump into the well, instead of himself. Soon as this commendable determination was formed, he seized the log, plunged it into the "watery deep," and immediately concealed himself behind the curb.

But where was Mary all the while?—She had been listening attentively at the door, half sorry that she had denied him so long, and hardly believing that he would commit so rash an act. But when she heard the heavy plunge of the wooden Joseph, her heart completely relented, and oh! how fervently she then wished that she had not refused his offer! She hastily ran to the well, and bending over the curb, with a bleeding and agonized heart, exclaimed—"Oh! Joseph, Joseph! if you are in the land of the living, I will have you." Joseph saw and heard the whole, and his heart leaped for gladness at this intelligence, and instantly leaving his place of concealment, he rushed into her arms and exclaimed—"Oh! Mary, Mary! I will take you at your word!" How Mary looked and acted on this occasion, we have not been informed; but no doubt,

"Her pure and eloquent blood
Spoke in her cheeks, and so distinctly wrought,
That one would almost say her body thought."

The long embrace—the mutual reconciliation—and the many tears of unfeigned joy that probably followed, we will not attempt to describe.

On the 19th of April, a Committee was chosen "to agree with Mr. John Haseltine about the peculiar work of the meeting house, the workmen providing all to the turning of the key, the other work without and within being done; and a turret also for a bell, provided the whole do not exceed four hundred pounds in money."

At a meeting, on the fifth of July, it was again voted, "that it should stand on the common land near Mr. Keezar's dwelling house." The second house was accordingly built, about fifty feet in front of the present Congregational church. It was built without a cupola, or tower, as it was then more frequently called, and with two doors, one for the women and one for the men. The Committee that was appointed to examine it after it was finished, reported that it was "50 1-2 feet in length, 40 1-2 feet in breadth and 19 feet studd."

A severe cold, attended with a cough and high fever, prevailed in the whole Province. In Braintree, 120 persons died.*

1698.

9th Jan. A meeting was warned by the Selectmen to appoint Assessors for a tax of £40, demanded of the town by the Assembly. Four of the Selectmen and three others only were present. The meeting was therefore dissolved without appointing them, but it was *understood*—says the Recorder—that the four Selectmen should perform that duty.

On the 22d February, Jonathan Haynes and Samuel Ladd, who lived in the western part of the town, started with their eldest sons, Joseph and Daniel, and a team of oxen and horses, to procure a load of hay which was stacked some distance from their dwellings. While they were slowly driving their teams, without suspecting any danger, they suddenly found themselves between two files of Indians, who had concealed themselves in the bushes on each side of their path. There were seven of them on a side, who were on their return from an attack on Andover. Their guns were presented and cocked, and the fathers seeing that it was impossible to escape, called for quarter;—"*boon quarter! boon quarter!*"—(meaning good quarter,) they twice exclaimed in answer to their call. But Daniel, the son of Ladd, did

---
* Fairfield's Diary.

not wish to be taken prisoner without making an effort to escape; and he told his father that he would mount the fleetest horse and endeavor to flee. But the old gentleman forbid him to make the attempt, telling him that he had better remain a prisoner. He cut the horses loose, however, gave them the lash, when they started off full speed, and soon arrived uninjured to their stables; though they were repeatedly fired at by the Indians. Two of them then stepped behind the fathers, and struck them violently on their heads, without the least provocation. Mr. Haynes, who was quite aged, instantly fell, but Mr. Ladd did not. Another then stepped before him and raised his hatchet with the intention of striking him in the face. Mr. Ladd closed his eyes, expecting that the blow would fall—but it came not—and when he opened them, he saw the tawny fellow laughing at, and mocking his fears. Another Indian then stepped behind him and struck him down.

The Indians, on being asked why they killed the old men, said that they killed Haynes because he was "*so old he no go with us;*"—meaning that he was too aged and infirm to travel; and that they killed Ladd, who was a fierce, stern looking man, because "*he so sour.*" They then started for Penacook, where they arrived, with the two boys. Young Ladd soon grew weary of his situation, and one night after his Indian master and family had fell asleep, he attempted to escape. He had proceeded but a short distance, when he thought that he should want a hatchet to fell trees to assist him in crossing the streams. He accordingly returned, entered a wigwam near his master's, where an old squaw lay sick, and took a hatchet. The squaw watched his movements, and probably thinking that he intended to kill her, vociferated with all her strength. This awakened the Indians in the wigwam, who instantly arose, re-captured him, and delivered him again to his master, who bound his hands, laid him upon his back, fastened one of his feet to a tree, and in that manner kept him fourteen nights. They then gashed his face with their knives, filled the wounds with powder, and kept him on his back until it was so indented in the flesh, that it was impossible to extract it. He carried the scars to his grave, and is now frequently spoken of by his descendants as the "marked man." Some years after he found means to return, and his scarred and powdered countenance produced many witticisms at his expense. He was one day walking the streets of Boston, and a parrot observing his "marked" features, vociferated, "a rogue! a rogue!" Haynes remained a prisoner with the Indians some years, and was at last redeemed by his relatives.

5th March. A party of about forty Indians again attacked Andover, killed five persons, burnt two houses, and two barns with the cattle in them. On their return, "they made spoil on Haverhill."*

A general contribution was taken in the Province, for the relief of those who were prisoners with the French and Indians.

1699.

Joseph Peasly moved that the town should allow him and others "to meet at the new house for and in their way of worship, which is according to the quakers. It was read and refused to be voted upon."

This is the first notice we have of the Friends; and probably their number was small. Though the bitter persecutions carried on against them, in this Province, by the prevailing sect were considerably abated, they were still looked upon with contempt, and as a designing and wicked people. The detestable bigotry that spread its mantle of darkness over the minds of men at that period, prevented them from thinking charitably of those persons, whose religious tenets were opposed to theirs. The arm of the strong was raised to crush the weak, or those who could not conscientiously worship with them.

20th Nov. A meeting was warned to choose a Committee to seat the people in the new meeting house, "that they may know where to sit, and not disorderly

---

* Hutchinson, vol. II. page 101.

crowd upon one another in the time of God's worship." The Selectmen were then ordered to designate seats for the above Committee, "that there may be no grumbling for picking and placing themselves."

Capt. Samuel Ayer and Nathaniel Saltonstall, Esq., were chosen to dispose of the old meeting-house to the best advantage.

It is supposed that the well-known disease, ycelped mumps, made its appearance in the Colonies this year. A journalist* says, "many persons died of an *unusual* distemper, called the mumps." Doubtless it was much more mortal than at the present day.

1700.

15th Jan. A meeting was warned to raise money to pay the town debts, and there seems to have been considerable confusion, for the Recorder says that "the meeting was opened and mouths too."

5th March. A building was ordered to be erected for a watch-house, school-house, and for any other use to which it might be appropriated. It was built on Main-street, north of the present parsonage house, and faced the Merrimack.

On the 3d of June, a grammar-school was ordered to be established immediately, and Mr. Richard Saltonstall was appointed to procure a suitable instructer. In July, thirty pounds were raised to be appropriated for that purpose; and the Selectmen were ordered to "write a letter to the scholar that Richard Saltonstall had treated with, or to some other meet person, to invite him to come and be the school-master for this town of Haverhill." It is presumed that the school was not established; for in the following year, we find that there was none; and it cannot be ascertained that there was any from 1690, till the Indian war was terminated. We are not much surprised at their negligence on this point, for the inhabitants had enough to do to defend themselves.

A son of John Merrill was scalded to death.

---

* Sewall.

1701.

3d March. A Clerk of the market was chosen; and it was also voted that ten pounds should be added to Mr. Rolfe's salary.

4th March. A Committee was chosen purposely to seat strangers in the meeting-house. A very good plan; and it would be well if some of the churches would learn a little politeness, and practice it at the present day. It was further ordered that, "if any of the inhabitants did sit in any seat where he or she was not seated, should pay a fine of one shilling in money."

It appears that Joseph Peasly suffered considerably by fire, for the town "voted to give him his rates" on that account.

Early in the spring the Indians made their appearance in small parties, traversing the woods in every direction. They soon became very bold, and attacked the garrison of Jonathan Emerson; but were repulsed with the loss of two killed, while the whites sustained no injury. One of the soldiers, after the war was over, meeting one of the Indians, spoke of the attack, when the following dialogue ensued:

"You had two of your number slain," said the garrison man.

"How do you know that?" asked the Indian.

"We saw your biers," was the reply.

"Hah, hah!" grunted the tawny fellow of the woods, and was the only answer he condescended to make.—"And you put them in the great hole," continued the garrison man.

"Hah, hah! no, we did not," muttered the surly fellow, feeling that he was questioned too closely.

"What did you do with them?" asked the garrison man, laughing in his sleeves, as the saying is, confident that he had the best end of the dispute.

"We carried them to the deep hole above," he replied, sharply; and immediately wheeled about and marched for his native woods."*

---

* Tradition.

The "deep holes" referred to, were situated in the low lands, south-west of the tavern now occupied by Mr. Pingree. One of them, many years since, was near fifteen feet in depth, and was called the great hole; and the other was called the deep hole. Soon after the attack on the garrison, two Indian biers were found near them, which led them to suppose that two of the enemy were slain.

The Colony, at this time, was computed to contain 70,000 inhabitants.*

1702.

A garrison was ordered to be kept in the northerly part of the town, in the house of one Saunders, which stood on land now owned by Capt. Richard Stuart. It was the custom for the nearest neighbors to sleep in the garrison at night; but Thomas Whittier, a member of the Society of Friends, who lived nearly opposite, refused to shelter himself and family beneath it. His own house was unguarded—no palisades surrounded it—and he carried with him no weapon of war. When urged by his friends to fly to the garrison for safety, or prepare himself with the means of defence, he refused to comply with their desires, for he depended more upon the weapons of his faith than on those of steel. The Indians frequently visited him, and the family often heard them whispering beneath the windows, and saw them put their copper faces to the glass to take a view of the apartments. Friend Whittier, however, treated them civilly, and they ever retired without otherwise molesting him.

The government, on account of the extreme scarcity of silver, began to emit bills, since called "Old Tenor." They were then called bills of credit, and read thus:—
"This indented bill of [amount] due from the Province of the Massachusetts Bay to the Possessor thereof, shall be in value equal to money, and shall be accord-

---

* Sewall's Diary.

ingly accepted by the Treasurer, and Receivers subordinates to him, in all public payments, and for any stock at any time in the Treasury.

Boston [date.] By order of the Great and General Court of Assembly."

Silver was this year valued at 8s. per ounce.

1703.

18th Aug. At a meeting holden this day, "after some discourse about getting a school-master, the town, on consideration of their troubles with the Indians, resolved that nothing should be done about it, and the meeting was dissolved."

The Selectmen were ordered to petition the Assembly for an abatement of their country taxes, " by reason of their uncomfortable circumstances by reason of the Indians."

1704.

The Indians had been quite peaceable for the last two years, and the inhabitants pleased themselves with the hope that they should see no more of them. They had shaken off a portion of their watchfulness, and neglected to guard their dwellings so securely as in former years. On the 8th of February, about 3 or 4 o'clock in the afternoon,* a party of six Indians attacked the garrison of Joseph Bradley, which was unhappily in an unguarded state—even the sentrics had left their stations, and the gates were open. The Indians approached cautiously, and were rushing into the open gates, before they were discovered. Jonathan Johnson, a sentinel, who was standing in the house, shot at and wounded the foremost, and Mrs. Bradley, who had a kettle of

---

* Pike's Journal.

boiling soap over the fire, seized her ladle, and filling it with the steaming liquid, discharged it on his tawny pate—a *soap*-orific that almost instantly brought on a *sleep*, from which he has never since awoke.* The rest of the party immediately rushed forward, killed Johnson,† made prisoner of the intrepid woman, and of some others. Pike, in his Journal, says four.‡ Three persons escaped from the garrison. The Indians, then fearing lest they should soon be attacked by a stronger party, commenced a hasty retreat, aiming for Canada, which was their place of resort when they had been so successful as to take a number of prisoners.

Mrs. Bradley was in delicate circumstances, and in slender health; still she received no kindness from her savage conquerors. No situation of woman would ever protect her from their demon-like cruelties. The weather was cold, the wind blew keenly over the hills, and the ground was covered with a deep snow,—yet they obliged her to travel on foot, and carry

---

* Penhallow.
† Town Records.
‡ We copy the following from Mr. Pike's Journal—it is all that he says of the affair. "Feb. 8. About 3 or 4 o'clock, afternoon, Joseph Bradley's house, at Haverhill, was taken by six Indians; 13 persons killed and 5 carried away, whereof one returned. 3 more persons escaped out of the house, and 1 Indian was slain in it by Jonathan Johnson." Mr. Pike is the only one, that we can find, who says that thirteen persons were killed in this attack. Penhallow, in his history of the "Indian Wars," speaks of no other slain than Jonathan Johnson and the Indian; and if there were thirteen killed, it appears rather singular that he did not mention it. Mr. Pike says there were only six Indians, and thirteen slain—the disparity of the two parties seem to invalidate his statement, for, unless they were all children, which is not probable, they must have been positive cowards, or been taken extremely unawares. Or, if they were women, it hardly seems probable to us, for women at that period, seem to possess, at times, as much courage and fortitude as the men. Another reason we have for doubting the statement of Mr. Pike, is the silence of the Town-Records on the subject. The death of Mr. Johnson is there faithfully recorded, thus:—" Jonathan Johnson [birth] killed by the Indians, Feb. 8, 1703-4." Why did they neglect to record the deaths of the others?—It appears to us that, if other persons were slain, their deaths would have been recorded as well as that of Mr. Johnson.

a heavy burthen, too large even for the strength of man. In this manner they proceeded through the wild wilderness; and Mrs. Bradley informed her family, after she returned, that for many days in succession, she subsisted on nothing but bits of skin, ground-nuts, the bark of trees, wild onions, and lily roots.

While in this situation, with none but savages for her assistants and protectors, and in the midst of a thick forest, she gave birth to a child. The Indians then, as if they were not satisfied with persecuting the mother, extended their cruelties to the innocent and almost friendless babe. For the want of proper attention, it was sickly, and probably troublesome; and when it cried, these remorseless fiends showed their pity, by throwing embers into its mouth.* They told the mother that, if she would permit them to baptize it in their manner, they would suffer it to live. Unwilling to deny their request, lest it should enrage their fierce and diabolical passions, and hoping that the little innocent would receive kindness at their hands, she complied with their request. They took it from her, and baptized it by gashing its forehead with their knives.† The feelings of the mother, when the child was returned to her with its smooth and white forehead gashed with the knife, and its warm blood coursing down its cheeks, can be better imagined than described.

Soon as Mrs. Bradley had regained sufficient strength to travel, the Indians again took up their march for Canada. But before they arrived at their place of rendezvous, she had occasion to go a little distance from the party, and when she returned, she beheld a sight shocking to a mother, and to every feeling of humanity. Her child, which was born in sorrow, and nursed in the lap of affliction, and on which she doted with maternal fondness, was piked upon a pole.‡ Its excruciating agonies were over—it could no more feel the tortures of the merciless savages—and its mother could only weep over its memory. Soon after, they proceeded to

---
* Penhallow.
† Tradition.
‡ Rev. Abiel Abbot's MSS.

Canada, where Mrs. Bradley was sold to the French for eighty livres. She informed her friends, after her return, that she was treated kindly by the family in which she lived. It was her custom, morning and evening, when she milked her master's cow, to take with her a crust of bread, soak it with milk, and eat it; with this, and with the rations allowed her by her master, she eked out a comfortable subsistance.*

In March, 1705, her husband, hearing that she was in the possession of the French, started for Canada with the intention of redeeming her. He travelled on foot, accompanied only by a dog that drew a small sled, in which he carried a bag of snuff, as a present from the Governor of this Province to the Governor of Canada.† When he arrived, he immediately redeemed her,‡ and set sail from Montreal for Boston, which they reached in safety; and from thence travelled to Haverhill.

Penhallow§ mentions this as her second captivity, and Hutchinson says the same; but Penhallow is, without doubt, his authority. Diligent search has been made to learn the history of her first; but, thus far, it has been unsuccessful. Very accurate traditions of the captivities of the other members of the family, have been transmitted to their descendants, but they have never heard their fathers tell that this person was taken at any other time; at least, they can give no account of such a fact. We extract the following, from Rev. Abiel Abbot's MS., taken by him from Judith Whiting:—"Destitute of nurses and necessaries, the child was sickly, and apt to cry, and they would put hot embers in its mouth. Being obliged to leave it a short time, on her return, she found it piked on a pole. * * * * Having been brought home by her husband, she was taken a second time, but not before she had finished and wounded an Indian by pouring boiling soap into his mouth." From this, it appears that she was twice

---
* Tradition.

† The only authority we have of the dog, the sled, and bag of snuff, is tradition, which we heard related very minutely by his descendants.

‡ Penhallow, page 10.

§ Hist. of the Indian Wars, page 10.

captivated; but of the truth of the statement, in this particular, we will not undertake to judge. It certainly does not agree with Penhallow's, and if we rely on one we must throw up the other, at least, in part.*

21st March. Major Richard Saltonstall was chosen by the town to appear at Court, "to answer in the town's behalf their presentment for not being provided with a school master as the law requires."

4th Aug. Joseph Page and Bartholomew Heath, were killed by the Indians; a lad who was with them, narrowly escaped.†

1705.

6th March. Mr. Rolfe petitioned the town for another addition to his salary; and ten pounds more were granted him.

A reward of twenty shillings was offered to any person who should kill a full-grown wolf within the limits of the town.

4th April. A general fast was held throughout the New-England Colonies, on account of the war with France and Spain.

1706.

In the month of February, there was a great fresh in the Merrimack. The ice stopped in the river and caused the water to overflow its banks in many places.‡

Samuel Swan had his house broken open and robbed of about fifty pounds. He petitioned the town, on the 4th of March, to make up a part of his loss, but the people did not see fit to comply.

---

* See Penhallow, page 10.
† Pike's Journal.
‡ Coffin's MSS.

The town was again presented for being destitute of a school-master, and Major Richard Saltonstall was chosen to answer it.

Sometime in the summer of this year, the Indians again visited the garrison of Joseph Bradley; and it is said that he, his wife and children, and a hired man, were the only persons in it at the time. It was in the night, the moon shone brightly, and they could be easily seen, silently and cautiously approaching. Mr. Bradley armed himself, his wife and man, each with a gun, and such of his children as could shoulder one. Mrs. Bradley supposing that they had come purposely for her, told her husband that she had rather be killed than be again taken. The Indians rushed upon the garrison, and endeavored to beat down the door. They succeeded in pushing it partly open, and when one of the Indians began to crowd himself through the opening, Mrs. Bradley fired her gun and shot him dead. The rest of the party, seeing their companion fall, desisted from their purpose and hastily retreated.*

3d July. Sergeant Kingsbury was killed or taken prisoner.†

1707.

Colonel Nathaniel Saltonstall, one of the firmest pillars of the town, and a prominent man in the Colony, died on the 21st of May, after being ill with a consumption nearly half a year.† He was the grandson of Sir Richard Saltonstall, who was one of the patentees of the Colonies of Massachusetts and Connecticut,‡ was styled one of the fathers of the former, and projected and settled a plantation, and "called it Watertown." Col. Saltonstall possessed a vigorous and well-cultivated intellect, was beloved by his neighbors and friends, and appeared comparatively free from the bigotry and gross

---

* Tradition.
† Pike's Journal.
‡ Trumbull's Hist. Connecticut.

superstition of the age in which he lived. He was born in 1639, and graduated at Harvard College in 1659, and soon after settled on that beautiful situation, now owned by Wid. Samuel W. Duncan. He married Elizabeth Ward, daughter of Rev. John Ward, and the estate on which he lived, was conveyed to him in consideration of this marriage.* It was known for many years by the name of the "Saltonstall seat." He had five children; Guerdon, born 27th March, 1666, was a minister at New-London, and afterwards Governor of Connecticut, and died 1724; Elizabeth, born 17th Sept., 1668, and married, 1st, Mr. Denizen, 2d, Rev. Rowland Cotton; Richard, born 25th April, 1672, graduated at Harvard College, 1695; Nathaniel, born 5th Sept., 1674, and graduated at Harvard College, 1695; John, born 14th Aug., 1678, and died 2d Oct., 1681. His wife died 29th April, 1714.

He took the oath of freeman, 1665, was chosen Representative, 1666, 1669 to 1671, Captain, 1690, elected assistant, 1679 to 1682, and again, 1689 to 1692.† He was Colonel of the Essex Regiment. A bitter and violent enemy of New-England, Edward Randolph, who was the chief instrument in depriving this Colony of its charter, "included him among those whom he called a faction of the General Court in 1681, and against whom he exhibited articles of high misdemeanor to the lords of the Council."‡ When the old charter was taken away, in 1686, he was named as one of the "Council for the government of Massachusetts Bay;" but it seems that he had taken the oath of Assistant under the old charter a few days before, and refused to accept of the appointment.

Soon after Sir Edmund Andross was seized and removed, he accepted of an invitation to join the Council which took the government into their hands, and continued in this office until the charter of William and Mary, when he was appointed one of his Majesty's Council.

---
* Sketch of Haverhill.
† Farmer's Genealogical Register.
‡ We are indebted for this fact, and for many others concerning this family, to the "Sketch of Haverhill."

Randolph, whose name has been once mentioned, in his "answer to heads of inquiry concerning New-England," speaks of him as one among the "most popular and well principled military men." In August, 1680, he accompanied the deputy-Governor and others, "with sixty soldiers in a ship and sloop from Boston, to still the people at Casco Bay and prevent Governor Andross' usurpation." In 1683, he was appointed one of the commissioners by Charles II, "to examine and inquire into the claims and titles as well of his Majesty as others to the Narragansett country."

It has been said that he was comparatively free from the bigotry and gross superstition which then prevailed. His conduct is our proof. He was opposed to the proceedings of the Court against the witchcraft mania that commenced in 1692. He was then one of the Judges; but he vacated his seat, and openly expressed his dissatisfaction at the violence of the Court. We are astonished at his independence—his moral energy—and his fearlessness, in declaring his sentiments, though in opposition to the united opinion of his cotemporaries of the bench, and against that of nearly the whole Colony. A torrent of madness and delusion had overwhelmed it, and swept onward, carrying terror to every heart, and leaving death and desolation in its pathway. The Judges of the land, the ministers, whose voices were heard in the sacred desks—the high and gifted in mind—were victims to this terrible fanaticism; and it is deemed an honor to Mr. Saltonstall, which will ever be attached to his memory, that he went forth from among them, and stood aloof from their councils.

Mr. Brattle, speaking of this in his account of the witchcraft, says, "Maj. N. Saltonstall Esq. who was one of the Judges, has left the court, and is very much dissatisfied with the proceedings of it." Upon this, Mr. Bentley, in his history of Salem, remarks, "Saltonstall left the bench; but ought he not, as the friend to justice, to have been upon it?"—What effect, we ask, would his single voice have had against the united voices of the other Assistants? Had he remained on the bench and opposed the delusion while there, his life would have been in jeopardy, and he would have exhibited a paucity of judgment—a fanaticism, nearly or quite equal to that displayed by his opponents. There was no other way for him to act, and even then he was not free from danger.

It was thought that a short biography of Guerdon, eldest son of Nathaniel Saltonstall, deserved a place in this history; for perhaps it is not known to all of our readers, that one of the most accomplished Governors of Connecticut, and one of the most distinguished men in New-England, was a native of this town. He graduated at Cambridge, in 1684, where he was a profound scholar, and gave promise of his future greatness. In 1691, he was ordained pastor of the church at New-London. He soon became a celebrated preacher, and so rapid was the growth of his reputation, that in 1707, upon the death of Fitz-John Winthrop, he was chosen Governor by the Legislature. So great was the respect for his character, that "the Assembly repealed the law which required that the Governor should always be chosen from among the magistrates in nomination, and gave liberty for the freemen to elect him from among themselves at large." Mr. Saltonstall accepted of the appointment, and entered upon the duties of his office, 1st January, 1708. He was continued in office until his death, which was very sudden, on the 20th September, 1724.

He is said to have been a powerful reasoner, and an eloquent orator. "In 1722, when Timothy Cutler, rector of Yale College, and five other ministers, exhibited to the trustees of the College a written declaration against the validity of Presbyterian ordination, a public disputation and conference on the subject, between them and the trustees, was held soon after in the College library, at which conference, Gov. Saltonstall presided; and three of the ministers retracted, 'being satisfied of the validity of ordination by presbyters, chiefly by his earned reasonings.'"

The Boston News Letter,* speaking of his death, says: "On the 19th he dined well and so continued till about 4 P. M. when he seemed something indisposed

---

* "No. 1074, Oct. 1, 1724."

and quickly complained of a pain in his head; about 6 he betook himself to his bed, his pain and illness increasing he then said, *See what need we have to be always ready, &c.* At twelve the next day he expired, to the almost unexampled sorrow of all that saw or since heard of it, not only through all that government, but the whole land."

The Rev. Eliphalet Adams of New-London, in a sermon upon his death, says:—"How doth the whole land shake at his fall! How much of our glory, how much of our peace and safety is buried in this one grave! Every heart aches at the hearing of it, and every eye plentifully pours out tears unto God! The heavy tidings passeth swiftly from place to place, astonishing all as it goes, and every man amazed at the news tells it to his trembling neighbor, and all with one consent begin to cry, *The crown is fallen from our head, wo unto us that we have sinned.*

"Often have I trembled to think how much of our glory and safety was bound up in him, and what a mighty blow we should be made to feel in the day when it should please God to remove him from us. The melancholy hour is at length come, this wise, great, and good man is fallen, with all his glories yet fresh about him, as if the sun should go down at noon. Every mouth is filled with his praises, and can scarce speak of any thing else but our heavy loss. And indeed, here is a most copious subject for panegyric—it is hard to say what should be passed in silence, when every thing may be said, and too much *plenty* makes us *poor*.

"Who did not admire his consummate wisdom, profound learning, his dexterity in business and indefatigable application, his intimate acquaintance with men and things, and his superior genius? and what was more than all this, his unaffected piety and love to God's house, his exact life and exemplary conversation? In what part of learning did he not excel?"

This is truly an exalted eulogy—but Mr. Saltonstall was an extraordinary man, and was an honor to the Colony of which he was Governor, and to the town from which he originated.

24th June. Joseph and Ebenezer Page, sons of Joseph Page, were killed by the Indians.

1708.

In the latter part of the year 1707, and the commencement of this, but few Indians were seen lurking in the adjoining woods. The frontier settlements began to feel somewhat secure, and consequently remitted their vigilance; but it was ascertained, early in the spring, that the enemy were collecting forces in Canada for some important attack. Intelligence was carried to Governor Dudley, at Boston, that an army, consisting of eight hundred men, was about marching for some one of the frontier settlements. Upon the receipt of this, he " ordered guards in the most exposed places of both his provinces." A body of troops, under Capt. Robert Coffin, patrolled from Kingston to Cochecho, and scouts were ordered to be kept out continually. Four hundred Massachusetts Militia were posted in N. H. Province. The guard sent to this town, consisted of about forty men, accompanied with three choice officers, from Salem, Major Turner, afterwards Colonel, a principal merchant of that place, and for many years a member of the council; Capt. Price, and Capt. Gardner, and soon after their arrival, they were posted in the frontier houses and garrisons.

Early in the year a grand council was held at Montreal, when an extensive engagement was agreed upon; which was to be joined by the principal Indians of every tribe in Canada, the Abenakis tribe, one hundred select French Canadians, and a number of volunteers, several of whom were officers in the French army, composing a formidable body of about four hundred men. The French were commanded by DeChaillons, and the infamous Hertel de Rouville, the sacker of Deerfield,* and

---

* Deerfield was desolated in the winter of 1704. The French and Indians were commanded by this same Hertel de Rouville, whose name will ever be coupled with infamy, " assisted by four of his brothers; all of which had been trained up to the business by their father, who had been a famous partizan in their former wars." They slaughtered forty-seven of the inhabitants, plundered the village, and set it on fire. They then retreated, carrying with them one hundred and twelve, as prisoners of war. Dr. Samuel Williams, the imme-

the Indians by La Perriere. The Indians were merciless, insolent and revengeful; but the French at that period equalled, and we had almost said, exceeded them in acts of wantonness and barbarity. When the former were weary of murdering "poor, helpless women and children"—when they were glutted with blood, it is said that M. Vaudreuil, then Governor of Canada, employed the latter to do it.*

To excite less surprise among the English, they divided their army into two bodies; the French with the Algonquin, the St. Francois and Huron Indians, were to take the route by the river St. Francois, and La Perriere and the French Mohawks, were to pass by Lake Champlain. Lake Nickisipigue was appointed the place of rendezvous, and there they were to meet the Norridgewock, the Penobscot, and other eastern tribes.* These arrangements being completed, they commenced their march on the 16th of July; but before the first named party had arrived to the St. Francois, a Huron was accidentally killed by a companion, which was considered by the tribe as an ill-omen, and that the expedition, though commenced under such favorable auspices, would certainly prove unfortunate. Strongly impressed with this idea, and not wishing to be connected with it if it should so prove, they deserted. The Mohawks then pretended that an infectious distemper had broken out among them, and that it would soon spread among the rest of the tribes, if they remained—and they also returned. M. Vaudreuil, when he heard of this, immediately sent word to the French officers to proceed, and fall upon some of the English settlements, even if they should be deserted by the Algonquin and St. Francois tribes. These, however, remained firm to their allegiance, and they continued their march; but when they arrived at Nickisipigue, their rendezvous, what was their astonishment at finding that the eastern Indians had broken faith with them.

---

diate descendant of one of the principal sufferers, and the accomplished historian of Vermont, has given an interesting account of the whole affair.

* Hutchinson.

It is said that their first design was to attack Portsmouth, and then, marching rapidly onward to other settlements, spread terror and desolation along the whole frontier. But being unable to accomplish this on account of the unexpected desertions, they were obliged to compress their views. Their whole force was now about 250, a small number when compared with that which started from Canada. Probably the French officers felt ashamed to return without effecting something, after they had been at so much trouble and expense; accordingly, Haverhill, a compact village, consisting of about thirty houses,* was selected for the slaughter.

At the break of day, on the 29th of August, they passed the frontier garrisons undiscovered, and were first seen near the pound, marching two and two, by John Keezar,† who was returning from Amesbury. He immediately ran into the village and alarmed the inhabitants, who seem to have slept totally unguarded, by fir-

---

* Hutchinson.

† This Keezar, the son of John Keezar, who was killed when Mrs. Dustin was captivated, was a very eccentric man, and a jack at all trades. He was said to be exceedingly proud of his proficiency in walking, leaping, and other manual exercises; and, if tradition may be relied upon, he was certainly a great walker and leaper; for it is said that he walked to Boston and back again in one night, and jumped over a cart with two large pails full of milk in his hands. It was his custom to go from this town to Amesbury and pitch his tent on the side of a hill, where he worked at the trade of shoemaking, and lived in all respects, while there, like an austere hermit. Some say, that when he discovered the enemy, he was out to take in his horse, which, according to his custom, he had turned into his neighbor's field to feed. Others say they were discovered by one Hutchins, who was out to steal milk from his neighbors' cows.

Another account says that the slaughter might have been prevented had it not been for the agitation of a young man, who, intending to start very early that morning for a distant town, went up on the Common to catch his horse, and while there, discovered the enemy advancing toward the village. He immediately hastened to the town, but in his extreme agitation, he thought only of the safety of the young lady to whom he had paid very particular attention some time previous. It is said that he passed through a part of the village, went directly to the abode of his mistress, and concealed her in a pile of boards. He then, after seeing his own property safe, and which, perhaps, was all he possessed in the wide world, gave the alarm; but the attack had already commenced.

ing his gun near the meeting-house. The enemy soon appeared, making the air ring with terrific yells, with a sort of whistle, which, says tradition, could be heard as far as a horn, and clothed in all the terrors of a savage war-dress. They scattered in every direction over the village, so that they might accomplish their bloody work with more despatch. The first person they saw, was Mrs. Smith, whom they shot as she was flying from her house to a garrison. The foremost party attacked the house* of Rev. Benjamin Rolfe, which was then garrisoned with three soldiers, and he, and a part of his beloved and accomplished family, were suddenly awakened from their slumbers, only to hear the horrid knell for their departure. Mr. Rolfe instantly leaped from his bed, placed himself against the door, which they were endeavoring to beat in, and called on the soldiers for assistance; but these craven-hearted men refused to give it, for they were palsied with fear, and walked to and fro through the chambers, crying and swinging their arms. Had they displayed but half the ordinary courage of men, no doubt they would have successfully defended the house. But, instead of that, they did not fire a gun, or even lift a finger towards its defence. The enemy finding their entrance strenuously opposed, fired two balls through the door, one of which took effect, and wounded Mr. Rolfe in the elbow. They then pressed against it with their united strength, and Mr. Rolfe finding it impossible to resist them any longer, fled precipitately through the house, and out at the back door. The Indians followed, overtook him at the well, and despatched him with their tomahawks.† They then

---

* Where the parsonage house now stands.

† Another account says that he was killed by one of the bullets shot through the door, and this we believe is the prevailing opinion; but we feel confident that it is untrue. We know that it is hard for others, as well as ourselves, to give up a tradition which we have often heard repeated by our neighbors, and by our fathers; but in this case we think it must be done, if the truth is desired. When we first began to develope the affair, we felt confident, almost to a certainty, that he was killed through the door, because every body said so; and indeed, we had once so wrote it, and read it to a friend of ours, who agreed with us on that point, at least he made no objections to it. But while examining other affairs, we were shown

searched every part of the house for plunder, and also for other victims, on whom they might inflict their savage cruelties. They soon found Mrs. Rolfe and her youngest child, Mehitable, and while one of them sunk his hatchet deep in her head, another took the infant from her dying grasp, and dashed its head against a stone near the door.

Two of Mr. Rolfe's children, about six and eight years of age,* were providentially saved by the sagacity and courage of Hagar, a negro slave, who was an inmate of the family. Upon the first alarm, she leaped from her bed, carried them into the cellar, covered them with two tubs, and then concealed herself. The enemy entered the cellar and plundered it of every thing valuable. They repeatedly passed the tubs that covered the two children, and even trod on the foot of one, without discovering them. They drank milk from the pans, then dashed them on the cellar bottom, and took meat from the barrel, behind which Hagar was concealed.

Anna Whittaker, who was then living in the family of Mr. Rolfe, concealed herself in an apple-chest, under the stairs, and escaped unharmed. But it fared differently with the cowardly soldiers. They earnestly begged for mercy, of their inhuman conquerors, but their cries were unheeded; and when the massacre was over, their bodies were numbered with the slain. We can have no pity for the fate of such contemptible cowards. A man who will shrink from danger at such a time, and in such a situation, while he holds the weapons of defence in his hands, should be ranked with the reptile, and ever be looked upon with scorn by the world.

---

some extracts from the manuscript account of Rev. Abiel Abbot, taken by him from the lips of Judith Whiting, and which has been before mentioned in this work. Mrs. Whiting was eight years old when the attack happened, and when she gave the account to Mr. Abbot, though very aged, her faculties were unimpaired; and she stated that he was shot through the elbow, fled through the house, and was tomahawked at the well. We place much reliance on her statement, and no doubt, the story of Mr. Rolfe's being killed through the door, arose from the wound which he received in his elbow. It appears to us very probable that it should.

* One was afterwards married to Col. Hatch, of Dorchester, the other to the Rev. Samuel Checkley, sen., of Boston.

The names of such, should sink in oblivion, or survive as memorials of surpassing infamy.

The family of Thomas Hartshorne suffered as severely as that of Mr. Rolfe. He saw a party approaching to assault his house, which stood a few rods west of the meeting-house, and escaped out of it, followed by two of his sons, to call assistance; but all three were shot dead immediately after leaving it. A third son was tomahawked as he was coming out at the door. Mrs. Hartshorne, with that presence of mind which is a characteristic of her sex, when surrounded with danger, instantly took the rest of her children—except an infant which she left on a bed in the garret, and which she was afraid would, by its cries, betray their place of concealment, if she took it with her—through a trap-door into the cellar. The enemy entered the house, and began to plunder it, but happily did not discover them. They went into the garret, took the infant from its bed, and threw it out at the window. It fell on a pile of clapboards, and when the action was over, it was found completely stunned. It lived, however, and became a man of uncommon stature, and of remarkable strength. His neighbors would frequently joke him, and say that the Indians *stunted* him when they threw him from the garret-window.*

One of the parties proceeded towards the river, and attacked the house† of Lieut. John Johnson. Mr. Johnson and his wife, with an infant a year old in her arms, were standing at the door, when the enemy made their appearance. Mr. Johnson was shot, and his wife fled through the house into the garden,‡ carrying her babe, where she was overtaken by the foe, and immediately despatched. But when she fell, she was careful not to injure her child, and it seemed as if her last thoughts were for its safety. The enemy, it appears, did not murder it, and it is somewhat remarkable that they did not; for they always took great delight in torturing and

---

* Abbot's MSS.
† It stood on the spot now covered by the mansion of the late Hon. Bailey Bartlett.
‡ The garden was where the Post-office now stands.

dashing out the brains of innocent babes. Perhaps it was because the mother was not alive to witness its agonies. After the massacre was over, it was found at the breast of its dead mother.*

Another party rifled and burnt the house of Mr. Silver, which stood within ten rods of the meeting-house, and others attacked the watch-house, which was, however, successfully defended. Another party went to the house of Capt. Simon Wainwright,† whom they killed at the first fire. The soldiers stationed in the chambers, were preparing to defend the house till the last, when Mrs. Wainwright fearlessly unbarred the door, and let them in. She spoke to them kindly, waited upon them with seeming alacrity, and promised to procure them whatever they desired. The enemy knew not what to make of this;—the apparent cheerfulness with which they were received, and the kindness with which they were treated, was so different from what they expected to meet with, that it seemed to paralyze their energies. They, however, demanded money of Mrs. Wainwright, and upon her retiring "to bring it," as she said, she fled with all of her children, except one daughter who was taken captive, and were not afterwards discovered. The enemy, so soon as they found out how completely they had been deceived, were greatly enraged, and attacked the chambers with great violence; but the soldiers courageously defended them, and after attempting to fire the house, they retreated, taking with them three prisoners. In the mean-time, two Indians skulked behind a large stone, which stood in the field a few rods east of the house, where they could fire upon its inmates at their leisure. The soldiers in the chambers fired upon them, and killed them both. They were afterwards buried in the same field, a few rods south, and but a few years since, the water washed their skeletons from their places of repose.

Two Indians attacked the house of Mr. Swan, which stood in the field now called White's lot, nearly opposite to the house of Capt. Emerson. Swan and his

---

* Tradition.

† Capt. Wainwright lived in a house which stood on the ground now covered by Capt. Nehemiah Emerson's.

wife saw them approaching, and determined, if possible, to save their own lives, and the lives of their children, from the knives of the ruthless butchers. They immediately placed themselves against the door, which was so narrow that two could scarcely enter abreast. The Indians rushed against it, but finding that it could not be easily opened, they commenced their operations more systematically. One of them placed his back to the door, so that he could make his whole strength bear upon it, while the other pushed against him. The strength of the besiegers was greater than that of the besieged, and Mr. Swan, being rather a timid man, said our venerable narrator, almost despaired of saving himself and family, and told his wife that he thought it would be better to let them in. But this resolute and courageous woman had no such idea. The Indians had now succeeded in partly opening the door, and one of them was crowding himself in, while the other was pushing lustily after. The heroic wife saw that there was no time for parleying—she seized her spit, which was nearly three feet in length, and a deadly weapon in the hands of woman, as it proved, and collecting all the strength she possessed, drove it through the body of the foremost. This was too warm a reception for the besiegers—it was resistance from a source, and with a weapon they little expected; and surely, who else would ever think of spitting a man?—The two Indians, thus repulsed, immediately retreated, and did not molest them again. Thus, by the fortitude and heroic courage of a wife and mother, this family was probably saved from a bloody grave.*

One of the parties set fire to the back side of the meeting-house, a new, and for that period, an elegant building. These transactions were all performed about the same time; but they were not permitted to continue their work of murder and conflagration long, before they became panic-struck. Mr. Davis, an intrepid man, went behind Mr. Rolfe's barn, which stood near the

---

* The account of this deed is received wholly from tradition. We heard it related by an aged and venerable gentleman, Capt. Nehemiah Emerson, who has often heard it told by his grand-father, who then lived in the garrison of his father, Jonathan Emerson.

house, struck it violently with a large club, called on men by name, gave the word of command, as though he were ordering an attack, and shouted with a loud voice, "Come on! come on! we will have them!" The party in Mr. Rolfe's house, supposing that a large body of the English had come upon them, began the cry of "The English are come!"* and after attempting to fire the house, precipitately left it. About this time, Major Turner arrived with a company of soldiers, and the whole body of the enemy then commenced a rapid retreat, taking with them a number of prisoners. The retreat commenced about the rising of the sun. Meantime, Mr. Davis ran to the meeting-house, and with the aid of a few others, succeeded in extinguishing the devouring element; but it was mostly owing to his exertions, that the house was saved.

The town, by this time, was generally alarmed. Joseph Bradley collected a small party, in the northerly part of it, and secured the medicine-box and packs of the enemy, which they had left about three miles from the village. Capt. Samuel Ayer, a fearless man, and of great strength, collected a body of about twenty men, and pursued the retreating foe. He came up with them just as they were entering the woods, when they faced about, and though they numbered thirteen or more to one, still Capt. Ayer did not hesitate to give them battle. These gallant men were soon reinforced by another party, under the command of his son; and after a severe skirmish, which lasted about an hour, they re-took some of the prisoners, and the enemy precipitately retreated, leaving nine of their number dead.

The French and Indians continued their retreat, and so great were their sufferings, arising from the loss of their packs, and their consequent exposure to famine, that many of the Frenchmen returned and surrendered themselves prisoners of war; and some of the captives were dismissed, with a message that, if they were pursued, the others should be put to death. Perhaps, if they had been pursued, nearly the whole of their force might have been conquered; for the Governor, in his

---

* Sketch of Haverhill.

address to the Assembly, says, "we might have done more against them if we had followed their tracks." As it was, they left thirty of their number dead, in both engagements, and many were wounded, whom they carried with them. The French, when they returned, reported very differently from this; they said that they "faced about, and that our people, being astonished, were all killed or taken, except ten or twelve, who escaped."*

The inhabitants were now left to perform the sorrowful office of burying their dead—and it was a sorrowful one indeed. The day was somewhat advanced when the battle was over, and it being extremely warm, the interment was necessarily hurried. Coffins could not be made for all, and a large pit was dug in the burying-ground, in which several of them were laid. Some of those who fell in the last engagement, it is presumed, were buried on the spot.

The following is a list of the slain who belonged to this town; perhaps it is not full, though we have taken great pains to make it so.—Rev. Benjamin Rolfe, his wife and one child; Mrs. Smith, Thomas Hartshorne and three sons; Lieut. John Johnson and his wife, Catharine; Capt. Simon Wainwright, Capt. Samuel Ayer, John Dalton, Ruth Ayer, wife of Thomas Ayer, and one daughter, and Ruth Johnson, wife of Thomas Johnson. The whole number is sixteen. We have not been able to collect the names of those who were taken prisoners, and the exact number. Mr. Pike, in his journal, says that the enemy "killed and carried away 33 persons, and burnt several houses." Mr. Hutchinson says, "about forty" were killed and taken prisoners; perhaps the truth would fall between. A daughter of Capt. Simon Wainwright, who was not so fortunate as to escape with her mother, when she fled with the rest of her children, was made prisoner; and in 1710, her mother, Mary, petitioned the General Court to redeem her. The following is her petition.

"HAVERHILL, 29th April, 1710.

To his Excellency, Joseph Dudley, Captain-General and Governor in chief, &c. &c., to the Honorable council

---
* Hutchinson.

and General Assembly now mett; the petition of Mary Wainwright sheweth that, whereas my daughter hath been for a long time in captivity with the French of Canada, and I have late reason to fear that her soul is in great danger if not already captivated and she brought to their way; therefore I humbly intreate your Excellency, that some care may be taken for her redemption before Canada be so endeared to her that I shall never have my daughter more. Some are ready to say that there are so few captives in Canada that it is not worthe while to put the country to the charges for them; but I hope your Excellency, nor any other good, judicious man, will think so; for St. James has instructed us, as you may see, chapter 5, v 20—Let him know that he which converteth the sinner from the error of his way shall save a soul from death, and shall hide a multitude of sins. This is all I can do at present, but I desire humbly to begg of God that he would direct the hearts of our rulers to do that which may be most for his glory and for the good of his poor distressed creatures, and so I take leave to subscribe myself your most humble petitioner.   WIDOW MARY WAINWRIGHT.

In the house of Representatives read and recommended 12th June."

One of the soldiers, Joseph Bartlett, stationed at Capt. Wainwright's house, was also taken prisoner; he was a native of Newbury, was born 18th Nov. 1686, taken prisoner 29th Aug. 1708, returned 8th Nov. 1712, and died 1754, aged 68. After his return, he published a narrative* of his captivity, and perhaps the History of Haverhill will not be deemed an improper place to give a short account of him.

"In the year 1707—says the narrative—in Nov. I, Joseph Bartlett, was pressed and sent to Haverhill. My quarters were in the house of Capt. Waindret, [wright.] August 29, 1708, there came about 100 French and 30 Indians† and beset the town of Haverhill—set fire to several houses; among which was that of Capt. W."

---

* We have never seen but one copy of this narrative, and that was obtained for us by John Farmer, Esq., of Concord.

† Most of the accounts agree in stating that there was about 250 of the enemy.

After the enemy entered the house, they took him and another soldier, named Newmarsh, and the daughter of Mrs. Wainwright, prisoners. Soon after the different parties commenced their retreat, they knocked one of their prisoners in head, named Lindall, a soldier belonging to Salem. He then says: "They then marched on together, when Capt. Eaires [Ayer,] with a small company waylaid and shot upon them, which put them to flight, so that they did not get together again until three days after." Bartlett said that he was first taken by the French, but after the battle they gave him to the Indians. The three first days they travelled hard.

He was compelled to carry a heavy pack, and travel with his hands tied behind him. A part of the time he was led by an Indian, who carried a hatchet in his hand and a pistol in his girdle, with a cord tied about his neck. On arriving at Lake Winnipiseoge, the French and Indians parted. The latter crossed the Lake; but before they reached the opposite shore, they killed a bear which was swimming in the water, towed it to the shore, and cooked it. They then fared sumptuously, and remained in that place about a day and a half, when they proceeded on their journey, and travelled five days, with scarcely any other sustenance than pounded corn. Having arrived at a river, the Indians made some canoes in a day and a half, when they sailed down the stream three days, eating nothing for four, but a few sour grapes and thorn plums. They then killed a hawk and divided it among fifteen—the head fell to the share of Mr. Bartlett, which, he says, "was the largest meal I had these four days." From thence they proceeded to Chamble, and on their passage they met with some Indians who gave them a little corn and a few pumpkins. He there saw an Englishman, named Littlefield, taken from Wells. The Indians shaved the hair from one side of his head, greased the other, and painted his face. They then started for Montreal, and when they arrived, he was examined by the Governor, and from thence went to the house of a Roman Catholic Priest, where he lodged over night. The next morning they started for an Indian fort, nine miles distant. When about half way, they came to a fire, surrounded by "fifteen men and thirty boys," where they held a consultation about burning him; but before it was closed, the Indians, who owned him, and the boys, marched away. Soon as they arrived at the fort, they began to abuse their prisoner—a squaw cut off his little finger, and another beat him with a pole. The Indians danced and sung all night, and invited him to join them, but he refused; they pulled him into the ring, however, and he went once round it. An Indian then came to him, and, after making a long speech, gave him to an old squaw, who took him to her wigwam. In February next, he went to live with a Frenchman, named Delude, and remained with him until Sunday, October 5, 1712, when he started to return to his friends in Newbury, and arrived on the 8th November, after a captivity of four years, two months, and nine days.

After his return, the General Court ordered that "the sum of £20. 15s. be allowed and paid to Joseph Bartlett in full of his petition of charges and expenses to obtain his liberty from the Indians, being taken prisoner by the Indians at Haverhill when in her Majesties service in the year 1708, and for his support during four years captivity and for the loss of his arms."

Mr. Pike, in his journal, says that "many soldiers belonging to Salem were here slain." Among them was William Coffin, who distinguished himself for his bravery; and soon after, his widow petitioned the General Court for relief, when it passed the following resolve:

"Nov. 3, 1708.—Resolved that the sum of £5 be allowed and paid out of the publick Treasury to the Petitioner, Mrs. Sarah Coffin, on account of the remarkable forwardness and courage which her husband, William Coffin of Salem, distinguished himself by, in the action at Haverhill where he was slain."

Mr. Rolfe, his wife and child, were buried in one grave, near the south end of the burial-ground. A single monument was erected to their memory, on which was chiselled an inscription for each; but the hand of time has been rough with them—they are overgrown with moss, and the epitaphs are now almost illegible.

The following is the epitaph of Mr. Rolfe:

"*Clauditur hoc tumulo corpus Reverendi pii doctique viri. D. Benjamin Rolfe, ecclesiæ Christi quæ est in haverhill pastoris fidelissimi; qui domi suæ ad hostibus barbare trucidatus. A laboribus suis requievit mane diei sacræ quietis, Aug. XXIX anno domini, MDCCVIII. Ætatis suæ XLVI.*"

The sense of this epitaph is contained in the following: " Enclosed in this tomb is the body of the revered, pious and learned man, Benjamin Rolfe, who was a most faithful pastor of the Church of Christ in Haverhill. He was barbarously slain by the enemy at his own house, on the morning of the sabbath, the 29th of Aug., in the year of our Lord, 1708, and in the 46th year of his age."

This worthy man was born in Newbury, 1662, and graduated at Cambridge, 1684. He seems to have been a pious and upright man, ardently devoting his time and talents to forward the cause of his Saviour. He was respected and beloved by his people, and we cannot learn that any difficulty arose between them, after his settlement.

The grave-stones of Capt. Ayer, Capt. Wainwright, and Lieut. Johnson, are nigh to Mr. Rolfe's, but are considerably damaged, and their inscriptions have become nearly illegible.

Capt. Ayer was slain in the last engagement, before the reinforcement arrived. He was shot in the groin, and being a large, robust man, bled profusely. When his son arrived, he was told that his father was killed, and the informant pointed him out. He looked at the corpse a while, as it lay on the grass, all covered with blood, and told his informant that that person could not be his father, for he (meaning the person slain,) had on a pair of red breeches. Capt. Ayer was one of the Selectmen, a Deacon of the church, and one of the most worthy, active and intelligent citizens of the town. He lived near the house of Capt. John Ayer, 2d. Lieut. Johnson was also a Deacon of the church, and was an active and useful citizen. He is supposed to be descended from Capt. Edward Johnson, the author of the "*Wonder Working Providence of Zion's Saviour*" in New-England, and who, in company with Jonathan Ince, of Cambridge, and Sergeant John Sherman of

Watertown, surveyed the northern bounds of the Patent of Massachusetts, in 1652.

Capt. Wainwright came from Ipswich; he had two brothers, John and Francis. His father, whose name was Francis, came from Chelmsford, in England, when a boy, and died about 1690. He is particularly noticed in the Pequot war, where he was simultaneously attacked by two Indians, and while defending himself broke the stock of his gun; he then used the barrel and finally killed them both.

Capt. Wainwright was a high-minded and influential citizen. He was supposed to be very rich, and there is a tradition which states that he had a large chest filled with dollars—and that he offered a man the whole if he would extract one of them with his fingers. The man "pulled and tugged," as our informant said, with all his strength, but alas! the thing was impossible, and he was obliged to leave it, and be satisfied with only looking at the precious stuff. It was also said that he buried much of his money, and a part of the field, south of Capt. Nehemiah Emerson's house, has been dug over, for the purpose of finding it. The large oak-tree, near Little River, has been twice dug around for the same object, within the remembrance of many of our citizens; but the tantalizing dreams of the "money-diggers," it is believed, were never realized.

This 29th of August will ever be remembered by the inhabitants of Haverhill—its history is yet related by many of the descendants of the sufferers, and the door through which Mr. Rolfe was wounded, is now nailed up in the porch of the First Parish Meeting-house, for a memorial of that bloody tragedy. Some of the most influential and worthy citizens were slain. The tenderest ties of earth were broken and left to bleed. Nearly all of some families were swept from the stage of existence—in a moment they were separated from all they loved on earth, to appear before their Maker and Judge. They laid their heads on their pillows the night before, and little thought that the sword of death was suspended over them—that the yell of a savage horde would awake them from their slumbers, only to witness the hand which plunged the knife into their bosoms.

It has been a melancholy task to record the events of that day. Though more than a century has elapsed—though the names of many of the actors had nearly passed into oblivion—yet it has lost none of its interest.

The following lines were suggested after we had written the foregoing account.

    Down came the foemen, fierce and strong,
        Just at the break of day,
    Nor sound was heard, save curses deep,
        Along their dark array;
    For swift and cautiously they came,
        Like tigers seeking prey.

    With stealthy step they crept along,
        And spread themselves about,
    The cold, remorseless Frenchman here,
        And there the Indian stout;
    And they swung their knives and hatchets keen,
        Like demons on a rout.

    The white man on his bed was stretched,
        Nor a thought of foes had he;
    Close at his side his wife reposed,
        Nor a thought of blood had she;
    And neither dreamed their infant ones,
        All murdered soon would be.

    On—on, the ruthless foemen came,
        With loud and thrilling yell;
    As wolves upon a fold come down,
        On the sleeping men they fell,
    And would that none should then escape,
        Their bloody deeds to tell!

    How thickly were the dead men strewed
        On that eventful day!
    For a corse was here, and another there,
        And pale and chill were they;
    And blood was there, and blood was here,
        And all around it lay.

    Here lay the man with a bloodless face,
        The man so strong and bold;
    There lay the wife with wilted lip,
        And bosom stiff and cold;
    And further on, with mangled limbs,
        Her child of two years old.

Oh, God! they were a cursed band—
   A reckless company,
Far bloodier than the bucanier
   Who sails the briny sea,
And fiercer than the leopardess
   That roams the desert free.

The fray was o'er—the smoke blew o'er,
   And fast the foemen fled;
Then many a man and wife were seen
   Among the stiffened dead,
To seek the pale and lifeless one,
   Whose infant steps they led.

And forth they went with sorrow blent,
   Where lay a friend or foe;
And o'er the field where the strong did yield,
   They travelled to and fro;
With burning fears and scalding tears,
   The man and wife did go.

Over their heads the sun looked down,
   And he was fiercely hot;
Nor a cloud went o'er his scorching eye,
   And cooling winds blew not;
And they hastened on the funeral hour,
   Lest all the dead would rot.

In the grave-yard lone they dug a pit,
   They dug it wide and deep,
And in it laid the corses pale—
   They laid them there to sleep;
Then flung the cold, dank clay upon
   The stiff and ghastly heap.

On the 26th of October, "A petition of the Selectmen of Haverhill representing the distress'd condition of the said town, by reason of the havoc lately made on them by the enemy, praying for an abatement of their quota to yᵉ Province Tax with the vote passed thereon by the house of Representatives, viz: ordered that the sum of £30 be abated of the tax of Haverhill was read and passed in concurrence.*

8th Nov. Fifty pounds were raised to pay the town debts.

---

* Colony Files.

1709.

Feb. The town invited Mr. Nicholas Seaver to settle; but his propositions were such that the town would not agree to them.

The house of Col. Richard Saltonstall,* was blown up by a negro wench, on the night of the 29th of March. In Mr. Pike's journal, it is mentioned thus:—"Colo. Saltonstall's house blown up by negroes 29th March 1709. Though many lodged that night in the house, yet nobody hurt. A marvellous providence." Tradition has hoarded many stories concerning this affair, some of which are extremely ridiculous. The following, it is believed, is a true statement of the case. It appears that the Col. had severely corrected the wench, some time previous, for misbehaviour, and ever after, she cherished a feeling of hatred toward him, and determined to take signal revenge. In the dead of night, on the 29th, when the house was wrapped in profound stillness, she carried a quantity of powder into the room, directly under that which was then occupied by the Col. and his wife. Having fixed a long train and connected it with the powder, she dropped a match upon it, and fled precipitately to the farm-house, which stood but a few rods distant. She had scarcely secured herself, when the powder went off with a tremendous explosion, and nearly or quite demolished the house. The Col. and his wife, were thrown in their bed, some distance from the house, without receiving any injury. The soldiers stationed in the house, were scattered in every direction, but happily, no lives were lost. The Col., after recovering from his surprise, went directly to the farm-house and found his servants all up, excepting this wench, who feigned sleep. He suspected and charged her with the deed, but it could never be proved.

12th Sept. "The town and church being convened," it was voted, without a dissenting voice, that a committee should be chosen to express their thanks to

---

* It was the same which was occupied by his father, Nathaniel Saltonstall, Esq.

Mr. Richard Brown for the faithfulness with which he had preached the gospel and discharged the duties of a minister, the past season—and to invite him to settle. Mr. Brown declined the invitation.

5th Dec. Liberty was obtained from the town, by a number of individuals, to build two seats " in the hind seat in the west gallery" of the meeting-house, if they would build them so high " as not to damnify the light of the windows."

Samuel Hutchins petitioned the General Court for relief, stating that he broke his leg in her Majesty's service;—whereupon it was resolved, "that the sum of £3. 4s. be allowed and paid out of the Public Treasury to the Petitioner, Samuel Hutchins, to defray therein mentioned of his cure."

1710.

20th June. The parsonage house was ordered to be repaired and fortified.

On the 20th October, at a church-meeting, held at ten o'clock, A. M., it was unanimously voted to invite Mr. Joshua Gardner to become their settled minister. At two o'clock, P. M., a town meeting was holden, when the proceedings of the church were read, and approved of without a dissenting vote. They then granted an annual salary of seventy pounds to Mr. Gardner, if he accepted of their invitation. His answer to their proposals was read on the 11th of December, at a meeting called for that purpose, in which he consented to comply with their request, and it was agreed that he should be ordained on the 11th of January next. "Col. Richard Saltonstall then gave notice to John White, that by reason of his wife's illness, and the coldness of the season, he could not provide for the ordination, and therefore did wholly relinquish it, and the said White took care of it."

Mr. Gardner was accordingly ordained on the 11th of January, 1711.

1711.

John Swett, a native of Newbury, was appointed ferryman at the Rocks;—hence the name of "Swett's ferry." It is believed that there were then no more than two houses at that place; and, indeed, the whole town had increased but very little, if any, in population, during the last thirty years. Strangers would not move into it, on account of the danger arising from the Indian war, and it is probable that those who sickened and died, and those who were slain by the enemy, nearly equalled the births.

22d Oct. A motion was made in town-meeting, to raise five pounds to support a grammar-school, "provided those that sent their children should make up the rest," and was immediately voted down.

1712.

The town was again presented for being destitute of a school-master, and on the 12th of May, Nathaniel Haseltine was chosen to appear at the Court of General Sessions, held at Salem, to answer it.

The bounty of twenty shillings for every wolf's head was still continued.

1713.

2d March. The Selectmen and Constables were ordered "to regulate the conduct of disorderly boys on the Sabbath, in the meeting house."

1714.

In the month of September, a fire raged through the woods, and did considerable damage. Much standing timber was destroyed and some hay. At a town-meeting, warned on the 14th, so few attended on this account that a Moderator only was chosen, and it was adjourned to the 21st. On that day, Nathaniel Merrill presented an account of three shillings for warning the negroes to leave the town, and another of twelve shillings, for carrying them away.

1715.

Daniel Bradley was drowned on the 22d of January.

9th March. A weekly contribution was ordered to be collected for Mr. Gardner, "if he desired it."

Mr. Gardner died on the 21st March. At the early age of thirteen, he made a profession of religion, entered Cambridge College at sixteen, and graduated at twenty. In his twenty-first year, he began to preach, and was ordained when only twenty-three. He was a man of earnest and devoted piety, of brilliant talents, and his early death was deeply lamented. Mr. Barnard, his second successor, in a sermon, thus speaks of him:—" Mr. Gardner, who is warm in the hearts of a few of you to this day, was soon ripe for heaven, according to the account which was handed down of him. He was not suffered to remain long by reason of death. Neither prayers nor tears could detain him from his inheritance above. In a few years he finished his course with joy."

Mr. Gardner died just as he had entered upon the stage of usefulness; yet he left an unspotted name, and his memory was cherished as sacred by his people, as though he had lived till his head was silvered with age. He was respected and loved for his piety; and his talents, had he lived, would have placed him in the foremost rank of the New-England clergy. The following epitaph is taken from the simple monument raised to his memory:

"*Rev. Joshua Gardner died March 21, 1715, a man good betimes and full of the Holy Ghost and faith, of an excellent temper, of great integrity, prudence and courage*

—pastor of the church in Haverhill five years—who, having faithfully improved his talents, fell asleep in Jesus, and went triumphantly to recieve his reward in heaven."

After his death, the town voted to pay the expenses of his funeral, which amounted to £34. 9s. 6d.

A petition was presented, signed by thirty of the inhabitants, desiring that the obstruction in Merrie's creek, and the Fishing, or Little River, might be removed, " so that a free passage for the fish might be obtained." The petition was granted.

24th Oct. Two hundred pounds were ordered to be raised to pay the town-debts.

Silver was this year valued at 9s. per oz.

1716.

At a church meeting, called on the 27th July, to make choice of a minister to supply the place of the late Mr. Gardner, twenty votes were cast for Mr. Jonathan Cushing, and fifteen for Mr. Robert Stanton. At a town-meeting, holden for the same purpose, on the same day, one hundred and two votes were cast for the former, and thirty-four for the latter. An invitation was accordingly extended to Mr. Cushing, but he declined.

Considerable difficulty existed among the inhabitants about settling another minister. The church was nearly equally divided, and the shameful animosities which are so frequently created by religious controversies, then existed, and exercised an undue influence over the minds of the people. At length, their difficulties became so great, and the breach becoming wider between the two parties, it was resolved to choose a committee to wait upon the Rev. Mr. Leverett and Rev. Mr. Brattle, of Cambridge, to ask of them what method they should adopt to assuage their difficulties, and procure a settled minister. Accordingly a committee of six was chosen, three from each party. This, however, produced no good effect. A meeting was then warned on the 22d of January, and the sixth day of February next was appointed for a public fast, in which the neighboring ministers were requested to join, as was then the general custom. The advice of the Reverend gentlemen was then asked and given; and at a meeting holden on the 12th of February, it was voted to accept of it, and by a vote only. At the same time, a Mr. Fiske preached as a candidate, but was not accepted. It was then voted to give a call to Mr. Joseph Pearson, and at a meeting in August, all the votes passed on the subject were revoked.

1717.

The difficulties about settling a new minister, still continued, and the Rev. Thomas Symmes, Edward Payson, and Moses Hale,* were consulted, who replied, that they thought it "advisable that the town, laying aside further attempts for a settlement in the way they have been in, together with their awful animosities in respect thereof, now unite in looking out for some other person to come amongst them." This good advice, as it was called, was taken by a vote in the affirmative, and that was all; for they immediately negatived a recommendation from two of the same persons, that a new committee should be chosen from both of the contending parties, to consult the President of Cambridge College concerning their difficulties.

1718.

23d April. The town gave an invitation to Mr. Samuel Checkley, "to settle among them in the work of the ministry;" but he did not accept.

Ann Emerson, the widow of Robert Emerson, was drowned, July 28.

---

* Rev. Thomas Symmes was of Bradford, Rev. Edward Payson, of Rowley, and Rev. Moses Hale, of Newbury.

The ferry, established in 1711, at Holt's Rocks, and kept by John Swett, was granted by the General Court to Haverhill and Newbury for the term of forty years. In answer to Mr. Swett's petition, this town granted him all of its right in the ferry, if he would engage to carry the inhabitants over the river "for a penny a single person and four pence for a man and horse."

The bounty for wolves was continued; and the Selectmen were ordered "to seat both men and women that belong to our meeting-house, in this town, according to their best discretion."

The Colony received an unexpected accession of Irishmen, from the North of Ireland, who landed at Boston on the 14th of October. Soon after their arrival, they petitioned the Assembly for a grant of land, and obtained liberty to make a settlement of six miles square in any of the unappropriated lands at the eastward. After a tedious search along the sea-shore, and not being able to find a place that suited them, sixteen families hearing of a tract of land above Haverhill, called Nutfield, from the large quantity of chestnut and walnut trees growing there, and being informed that it was unappropriated, determined to take up their grant in that place. They immediately came to this town, and while crossing the river, just before they had reached the shore, the boat unluckily capsized, and men, women, and children, were thrown promiscuously into the river. This adventure afforded much amusement to the inhabitants of this town, at the expense of the poor Irishmen, whom they thoroughly hated and were not at all delicate in making it manifest. It soon awakened the muse of some delighted swain, who composed a song about the matter, which was frequently sung for the edification of his attentive auditors. Of this song, tradition has preserved only the following lines:—

"Then they began to scream and bawl,
And if the devil had spread his net,
He would have made a glorious haul."

In the following spring, 1719, on the 11th of April, the men went to Nutfield, leaving their families in this town, and erected a few huts near a brook, which they called West-running-brook. The next evening after their arrival, a sermon was preached to them under a large oak-tree.* In 1722, their settlement was incorporated by the name of Londonderry, from a city in the north of Ireland, in which many of them suffered the hardships of a memorable siege.† The use of potatoes was first introduced by the Irish, which were early planted in the garden of Nathaniel Walker, of Andover.* They were first planted in this town by William White, who raised four bushels; but he knew not how to make use of so large a quantity, and gave many of them to his neighbors.

The town unanimously voted to extend an invitation to Mr. John Brown, of Little Cambridge, now Brighton, to supply the vacant pulpit. He complied with their request, and was ordained on the 13th of May, 1719. He preached the funeral sermon of Rev. Thomas Symmes of Bradford, which was published.

Mr. Brown graduated at Cambridge, in 1714. He married Joanna Cotton, daughter of Rev. Rowland Cotton, of Sandwich, and she was famed as an "eminently pious and worthy Lady." He had seven children, four sons and three daughters. The sons were all educated at Cambridge. John graduated in 1741, and was ordained in Cohasset. He died 1792, aged 69.

Cotton graduated in 1743, was ordained at Brookline, on 26th of October, 1748, and died 13th of April, 1751. Dr. Cooper notices him as one who "had raised in his friends the fairest hopes, and given them just reason to expect in him one of the brightest ornaments of society, and a peculiar blessing to the church."

Ward graduated in 1748, and died the same year.

Thomas graduated in 1752, and was a minister at Stroudwater. He died in 1797.

His eldest daughter was married to John Chipman, Esq., of Marblehead; his second to ——— Dana, of Brookline, and his third to Rev. Edward Brooks, of Medford, formerly minister at North Yarmouth.‡

---

* Farmer's edition of Belknap's History of N. H.

† This city was besieged near six months, in 1689, by King James's army.

‡ Sketch of Haverhill.

1719.

1st March. The burial-ground was ordered to be suitably fenced with boards, and a convenient gate erected and swung on hinges.

1720.

7th March. The trees on the Cow-common were ordered to be marked with the letter **H** that they might be preserved for the "creatures in the summer time;" and a fine of twenty shillings was imposed on any person who should fall a tree that was thus marked.

Samuel White and William White, erected a cornmill and fulling-mill on Sawmill River.

This year, Capt. Ebenezer Eastman and several others from this town, explored the lands in the vicinity of Penacook, now Concord, New-Hampshire, and noticing the richness of the intervals, resolved to procure a grant of it, and commence a settlement. Accordingly, in the following year, they petitioned the General Court of this Province for a tract of land, about eight miles square, "situated on the river Merrymake at the lower end of Penacook." Their petition was twice allowed, in 1721, and 1722, but the Governor refused to sanction it. In 1724, a Committee was appointed to view the lands; and on the 17th January, 1725, "The Great and General Court," granted to the petition of Benjamin Stevens, of Andover, Ebenezer Eastman, of this town, and others, a tract of land, about seven miles square, which was appropriated for a township, by the name of "the Plantation of Penacook." The conditions of the grant were extremely rigid. It was required that the lands should be divided into one hundred and three lots; that one hundred families, "able to make a settlement" should be admitted. Each settler was to pay three pounds for his lot, and was obliged to build a good house for his family within three years—break up and fence in six acres of land, and completely finish a convenient house for the public worship of God within the time aforesaid. They were also required to pay 20s. each for the privilege of admittance, to defray the expense of laying out the lots, of cutting a road from Haverhill to the Plantation, and the charges of the Committee of the Great and General Court. Had they not been men of great resolution, such conditions would have deterred them from attempting the settlement.

On the same day that the petition was granted, the Court appointed a standing committee of nine, to "bring forward" the intended settlement, and "take special care" that the conditions were complied with. This committee met in this town, in February, 1725, for the purpose of admitting settlers; yet, they did not presume to rely solely on their own judgments, and voted that some of the principal inhabitants of the towns, to which the petitioners belonged, should be desired to wait upon the committee, and inform them of the circumstances of the petitioners. The first day they "admitted several of them," and on the next, they completed the number, 100 in all. The remaining three rights were reserved —one for the first settled minister, one for the parsonage, and one for the "use of the school forever."

These conditions met the views of the intended settlers. On the 7th of February, they held a meeting in this place, and resolved that they would "well and truly fulfil the conditions of the Great and General Court for bringing forward the settlement at Penacook—that such and so many of the intended settlers, as shall fail of ploughing, fencing or clearing of one acre of land, within twelve months from the first day of June next, shall each of them forfeit and pay to the community or settlers, the sum of five pounds;" and if any failed of complying with the above article within two years, and of having his timber for his house within six months "after receiving orders to do it from the committee"—to forfeit and pay the sum of ten pounds; and in case of failure to comply with the orders of the Court for bringing forward the settlement within two years and a half, "absolutely to forfeit the lot or lots, by him or them drawn, with all the improvements that shall be made thereon, to the other settlers." And finally, to exclude all persons from the plantation, but those of approved character.

In 1726, a Committee was appointed by the Court to lay out the lands at Penacook. They belonged principally to this town, and were headed by John Wainwright, who kept a journal of their proceedings, from which the following is extracted:—

12th May. The Committee left the town and proceeded as far as Amoskeag.

13th. "This morning we proceeded on our journey —very hilly and mountaneous land. About 8 o'clock, we passed a fall called *Annahookline*, [Hooksett] in Merrimack river which is taken from a hill of the same name. About 10 or 11 o'clock, we forded Suncook river which is a rapid stream and many loose stones of considerable bigness in it, making it difficult to pass. About 1 o'clock we passed Penacook river, [Soucook] pretty deep and very rocky. In a short time after, we came up as far as Penacook falls, [Garven's] and steered our course north over a large pitch pine plain, three miles at least in length, and about 5 o'clock afternoon, arrived at Penacook, and encamped on a piece of interval called Sugar Ball plain, from a very large hill called Sugar Ball hill, whereon was the first Indian fort, as we were informed, which the Indians in old times built to defend themselves against the Maquois, [Mohawks] and others their enemies. This Sugar Ball plain is a pretty large tract of land encompassed on all parts with very high and mountainous land, as steep as the roof of a house ordinarily—only where the river runs round it, which encompasses the other parts of it. It is altogether impractible for a team or even a horse-cart to get on the plain, the land is so mountainous round it; and there is no spring on it as we could find.

14th. About 12 o'clock this day, Messrs. Nathaniel Ware, Richard Waldron, jun., and Theodore Atkinson, a committee appointed by the governor and council of New-Hampshire, came up to our camp, (being attended with about half a score of Irishmen, who kept at some distance from the camp) and acquainted us that the Goverment of New-Hampshire, being informed of our business here, had sent them to desire us that we would not proceed in appropriating these lands to any private or particular persons, for that they lay in their goverment; and our goverment's making a grant which might be attended with very ill consequences to the settlers, when it appeared that the lands fell in the N. H. goverment. And they delivered a copy of an order passed by his honor the Lieutenant governor and council of New Hampshire, respecting the settling of the lands of Penacook, to which we refer. We made them answer, that the goverment of Massachusetts Bay had sent us to lay out the lands here into a township; and they had made a grant of it to some particular men, and that we should proceed to do the business we were come upon; and made no doubt but our goverment would be always ready to support and justifie their own grants; and that it was the business of the public, and not ours, to engage in, in order to determine any controversy about the lands. We sent our salutes to the Lieutenant governor of New Hampshire, and the gentlemen took their leaves of us, and set homewards this afternoon.

15th. Sunday.—Mr. Enoch Coffin,* our chaplain, performed divine service both parts of the day.

16th. At sunrise this morning, according to notification, we chose a representative, *nem. con.*, viz: Mr. John Sanders.

18th. It may be observed, that divers rattlesnakes were killed by several surveying companies; but, thanks be to God, nobody received any hurt from them."

This year, 1726, considerable progress was made in the settlement, and a road was cut through the wilderness from this town to that. In the fall of 1727, the first family, that of Capt. Ebenezer Eastman, moved into the place. His team was drove by Jacob Shute, who was, by birth, a Frenchman; and he is said to have been the first person who drove a team through the wilderness. Soon after, says tradition, ——— Ayer, a lad of 18, drove a team, consisting of ten yoke of oxen, to Penacook, swam the river, and ploughed a portion of

---

* Mr. Enoch Coffin was a native of Newbury, and grandson of Tristram Coffin, who signed the Indian Deed.

the interval. He is supposed to have been the first person who ploughed land in that place. After he had completed his work, he started on his return at sun-rise, drowned a yoke of oxen, while re-crossing the river, and arrived at Haverhill about midnight. The crank to the first grist-mill, was manufactured in this place, and carried to Penacook on a horse.

On the 18th November, 1730, their first church was organized, and Rev. Timothy Walker was ordained. Rev. John Brown, of this town, " gave to the Pastor and the Church the Right Hand of Fellowship."

The following is a list of those persons, belonging to this town, who were among the original proprietors of Penacook:—Ebenezer Eastman, Nathaniel Clement, Edward Clark, Joseph Davis, Samuel Davis, Ephraim Davis, Stephen Emerson, Nehemiah Heath, Moses Hazzen, Richard Hazzen, jun., Timothy Johnson, Robert Peaslee, Nathaniel Peaslee, Nathaniel Page, William White, Nicholas White, William Whittier, Christopher Carlton, Samuel Ayer, and John Ayer. They were mostly young men.

The life of Capt. Ebenezer Eastman was full of adventures, and perhaps a short biography of him will not be uninteresting to many of our readers, as he was a native of this town. He was born 1689, and at the early age of 18 joined the regiment under the command of Col. Wainwright, in the expedition against Port Royal. In 1711, he had the command of a company, and went with the fleet designed for the conquest of Canada, under the command of Admiral Walker. While sailing up the St. Lawrence, the weather being foggy and a strong wind rising, the Admiral asked the pilot what it was best to do? The pilot advised him that " as the fleet was on the north shore it would be best to bring to, with their heads to the southward." This the Admiral obstinately refused to do, and the consequence was the total failure of the expedition, the loss of nine ships, and many lives. Eastman, observing the imminent danger which surrounded them, beseeched the Captain of the vessel " to haul to windward, that they might escape the breakers." The Captain was a true loyalist, and exclaimed, that " he would follow his Commodore if he went to h—l." Eastman, finding that he could gain nothing by parleying with him, stated the circumstances to his men, and told them that, if they would support him, he would assume the control of the vessel, and attempt to shun the rocks. This was agreed to, and Eastman ordered the Captain to his cabin, and the helmsman to alter his course. They escaped shipwreck, and the next morning, the self-willed and wonderfully loyal Captain, was quite humbled, and on his knees acknowledged his deliverer, and desired his friendship. In the morning, Capt. Eastman appeared before the Admiral, who abruptly asked—" Capt. Eastman, where were you when the fleet was cast away?"—" I was following my Commodore," he replied. " Following your Commodore!"—exclaimed the Admiral in surprise—" you d——d Yankees are a pack of praying devils; you saved your own lives and prayed my men all to h—l." Soon after his return, he entered with zeal into the projected settlement of Penacook, and was one of its most influential, persevering and useful citizens. In 1744, he marched at the head of a company, with the provincial forces, against Louisburg.

Concord did not escape the depredations of the Indians; and it also appears to us that the deadly enmity frequently entertained by them toward particular families, did not cease at the death of the parties; but was transmitted, on the part of the Indians, without any diminution of strength and bitterness, from generation to generation.

In 1746, we find that Jonathan Bradley, and Samuel Bradley, descendants of Joseph Bradley of this town, were at Concord. On Monday morning, on the 11th of August of the same year, a party of seven, including the two Bradleys, set out from that place for Hopkinton, two on horses, and the others on foot, all armed. " They marched on leisurely, and Obadiah Peters, having proceeded some distance forward of the others into a hollow, about a mile and a half from the street, sat down his gun and waited the approach of his friends. The Indians"—who were concealed in the woods with the design to intercept a party of men whom they supposed would pass that way the same morning—"thinking themselves discovered, rose from their hiding places, fired and killed Peters on the spot. At this moment, Jonathan Bradley and the rest of his party had gained the summit of the hill. Bradley was deceived in the number of the enemy, supposing the few he saw near Peters to compose the whole party. He ordered his men to fire, and they rushed down among them. The whole body of the Indians instantly rose, being about 100 in number. Bradley now urged his men to fly for safety; but it was too late—the work of destruction had commenced. Samuel Bradley was shot through the body, stripped of his clothing and scalped. To Jonathan they offered 'good quarter,' having been acquainted with him; but he refused their protection, his heroic spirit thirsting to revenge the death of his comrades. He fought with his gun against the cloud of enemies, until they struck him on the face repeatedly with their knives and tomahawks, and literally hewed him down. They then pierced his body, and took off his scalp and clothes.

"Jonathan Bradley was an officer in Capt. Ladd's company, from Exeter, and stationed here [Concord] for the defence of the inhabitants. He was about thirty years of age when killed, and was the elder brother of Samuel Bradley. He was a man of much coolness and decision; and his vigorous defence against the overwhelming force which crushed him to the earth, is a sufficient proof of his determined bravery.

"Samuel Bradley was a citizen of this town [Concord] and the father of the Hon. John Bradley, who died in 1815. He was a most amiable and promising young man; and his wife, who afterwards married Richard Calfe of Chester, and survived both, in the latter years of her life, used to speak with great affection of the husband of her youth, and of his tragical end."*

---

* The accounts of the settlement of Concord, of Capt. Ebenezer Eastman, and of the Bradley's, were taken principally from Moore's "Annals of Concord," and Rev. Nathaniel Bouton's two discourses in "commemoration of the organizing of the first Church in Concord."

1721.

It was voted on the 6th of March, "that there shall be a committee chosen to prefer a petition to the General Court for redress, in behalf of the damage that the town sustained, by the town-books being part of them cut and torn out." The book referred to is certainly in a very damaged state, and tradition says that it was so unfortunate as to get a ducking in a *swill-tub*.

19th March. A tract of land beyond Hogg-hill, was ordered to be laid out "to those men who have been out in long marches in the time of the war," and to such other of the inhabitants as would make a speedy settlement upon it. The land was laid out into lots of fifty acres each.

A company of about one hundred persons, from Portsmouth, Exeter, and Haverhill, petitioned the General Court for liberty to settle in the northerly part of Nutfield. In the following year, four townships were granted, Chester, Nottingham, Barrington, and Rochester,* and a few families removed from this place to Chester.

1722.

10th Aug. The Selectmen were ordered "to build a good fort round Rev. Mr. Brown's house with what speed they could."

The town seems to have awakened in some measure, from its apathy respecting schools. Two school-houses were ordered to be built, one in the west part of the town, and the other in the north part. On the 20th November, the Selectmen were ordered to procure a "school-master on the town's cost, who was to keep in the east part of the town, near Widow Mary Whittier, or the next house."

---

* Belknap's Hist. of N. H.

1723.

19th March. A watch-house was ordered to be built.

The following petition was read before the town on the 8th of April:—" Whereas your petitioners having their habitations so distant from the meeting-house, that, at any time being belated, we cannot get into any seat; but are obliged to sit squeased on the stairs where we cannot hear the minister and so get little good by his preaching, though we endeavour to ever so much; and there being a vacant place betwixt the front pew and the pew on the side gallery over the head of the stairs, we humbly request liberty to erect a seat over the same." The petition was granted.

Considerable difficulty existed concerning town affairs. Five meetings were held in succession, and not a vote was passed. The marginal reference to one of them says, that it was " precious time spent for nought."

1724.

30th July. Capt. John White was chosen to attend the General Court, and oppose the petition of Stephen Barker and others, for a township above Hawk's-meadow-Brook. It was, however, granted the following year, and incorporated by the name of Methuen. The boundary marks were not regularly established till the 16th of May, 1738, when the Selectmen of both towns met and established them. They were principally trees and heaps of stone. The trees were marked, on the north-east side with the letter **H**, and on the opposite side with the letter **M**.

1725.

There was great dissention in the town this year, which was rather derogatory to its character, and was memorable on account of the interference of the General Court. It arose in consequence of the commoners endeavoring to extend their jurisdiction over the town. Two parties met on the same day to hold town-meeting. One is represented in the Town Records, as a "small party," which was composed principally of the Commoners. Two sets of town-officers were chosen. The Town party, so called, chose a Committee to prosecute the "faction to a final issue." In the midst of the difficulties, the House of Representatives passed the following resolve in substance:—

"Whereas at the anniversary of the town-meeting in the town of Haverhill, in March last, there happened to be two contending parties who assembled at the meeting-house, and did there and then choose two sets of town-officers, whereby great difficulties arose in the said town, and considerable expense occasioned in the law; and it is feared that no good goverment can be supported unless some speedy care be taken to prevent these disorders. For preventing whereof, and to put an end to said strife, it is ordered by this General Court, that Joshua Swan and Nathaniel Peasley, Constables for the town in 1724, be, and are hereby required to warn the freeholders and other inhabitants to assemble at the meeting-house in Haverhill, on the ninth of June, at ten o'clock, A. M., and then and there to choose all the town-officers which the law requires to be chosen in the month of March annually; and that Richard Kent, Esq.[*] be desired to be present at the said meeting; and he is empowered to moderate the affairs, and no other person be allowed to vote but such as are lawfully qualified; and that the proceedings of both parties at the aforesaid meeting of March 2d are declared null and void, and the charge to be borne as this Court shall order.

        Sent up for concurrence.
In Council 4th JUNE, 1725,
      WM. DUDLEY, Speaker.
    Read and concurred in.
J. WILLARD, Secr'y.
      Consented to, WM. DUMMER.

---

[*] Of Newbury.

A meeting was accordingly held on the ninth of June, and Richard Kent, Esq. presided. The opening of the meeting was followed by some discussion concerning the town affairs, but no vote was taken. The meeting was adjourned till the afternoon, when the Moderator ordered the votes to be brought in for a town Clerk. But few, however, were cast, and no Clerk was declared to be chosen, and the meeting was dissolved. The votes cast were principally for John Eaton. Another order from the General Court, dated June 15, directed that Mr. Eaton should be sworn as the Town Clerk, and that the inhabitants should assemble on the 23d of the same month and choose the remainder of their officers. They met according to the order and succeeded in choosing them.

This interference of the Legislature was nothing less than an exercise of despotic power. They exceeded the authority with which they were clothed by the people; and should such a case happen at this period, probably those concerned would not rest satisfied, until the Legislature gave sufficient reasons for so doing. If such difficulties in a town are to be settled by a higher power, it appears to us that the Legislative body is not the proper umpire. They should be decided in all cases by the Judicial Courts—they are the only suitable and lawful arbitrators. One of the reasons which the General Court gave for interposing its authority, was—*that considerable expense was occasioned in the law*, which amounts to the same as an acknowledgement of the jurisdiction of the Judiciary. This usurpation of power was salutary in this instance, but it should not have been willingly allowed of by the people; for such examples have a tendency to undermine the bulwark of liberty, and if they are frequently followed, they will gradually prepare the people for the reception of a monarchical, or some other government equally repulsive.

A new pound was ordered to be built.

12th Dec. Mary Pearsons was warned out of town, " she having nothing to live upon," says the Recorder. From 1724 to 1770, thirty persons of this description were ordered out of town.

1726.

A petition, signed by ten persons living in the east part of the town, was read in town-meeting on the 2d March, praying that they might have liberty to assemble for worship at the Amesbury meeting-house. The petition was granted.

1727.

Many families lived at so great a distance from the meeting-house, that they found it inconvenient to attend public worship in the winter. At the request of the inhabitants in the northern and western part of the town, they were permitted to hold meetings for worship in each of those places, during the winter of this year.

1728.

It was voted in town-meeting, on the 18th of June, that the northerly part of the town should be set off into a distinct Precinct, or Parish. The conditions annexed, were, that the inhabitants should determine within one month where their meeting-house should be erected, and settle an orthodox minister as soon as possible. Their meeting-house was built and partly finished this year. This parish then included a part of Hampstead, Plaistow, and Atkinson.

At the same meeting, it was thought that two taverns were " sufficient for the town's benefit;" and Lieut. Ebenezer Eastman and John Swett were appointed to keep them.*

Dr. Joshua Bailey, it is believed, was the only Physician in the town at this time.

Silver was valued at 20s. per oz.

---

* Lieut. E. Eastman kept near the house now owned by Mr. Jonathan Rowell. John Swett kept at Holt's Rocks.

1729.

The House of Representatives called upon the town to assist in defraying the expenses of their agents to Great Britain, "to defend their inestimable rights." At a meeting called for that purpose, the town voted to raise fifty pounds, to be delivered to Col. Richard Saltonstall, the representative, and by him to the Committee of the General Court. This was surely a large sum when it is considered that it was a voluntary thing.

On the 26th October, twenty-nine members of the first church, residents in Methuen, now Salem, N. H., had permission granted them to embody themselves into a church in that place.

1730.

The North Parish gave Mr. Haynes an invitation to settle, but he did not accept. Soon after they extended an invitation to Mr. James Cushing, who accepted, and was ordained in October. On the 1st of November, forty-six persons, members of the first church, requested a dismission, "for the purpose of uniting in a church state in the North Precinct," which was granted.

1731.

Newbury granted to John Swett their interest in the ferry at Holt's Rocks, for £3 per year.

About this time an affair happened which was rather derogatory to the characters of those concerned. The Commoners had fenced a certain part of the ox-common with split rails. This was very much disliked by the non-commoners living in the north part of the town, and they determined to be revenged. They soon concerted a plot, and a small party assembled near flaggy meadow, on the night appointed to execute it, carried the rails into large piles, and set them on fire. The loss of the rails was but trifling when compared with the other damage done by the fire. The earth was dry, and it run through the woods, and continued to burn for many days.

1733.

A new bridge was ordered to be built over Little River, near the present site of Hale's Factory.

The Selectmen of this town were prosecuted by the Selectmen of Amesbury, "for not perambulating the line" between that town and this.

The winter of this year was the coldest ever known in New-England. Scarcely a well afforded a supply of water.

An earthquake was felt on the 12th of March.

1734.

Early in the spring, a few caterpillars, a very large and uncommon species, were seen in the woods, clinging to the red and black oak, just as they began to bud. Their number was so small that they did not create any alarm. In the succeeding year, they again made their appearance, but with a numerous levy of a hundred to one, and commenced depredations on the trees. In 1736, they again appeared, but with such an astonishing increase that they seemed to equal in number the locusts of Egypt. Wherever they went, they devoured every green thing. Nearly all the woods in this town, Chester, a part of Methuen, Bradford and Andover, were covered with them. The leaves and tender twigs of one year's growth were entirely destroyed; and in some places they ate large limbs. Many trees died, and if Providence, says our journalist, had continued them to the fourth year, not a tree would have been left. They were so destructive that a traveller might journey onward for miles, without being cheered with the sight of a green leaf in all the forests which he passed. In mid-summer they were as naked and cheerless as in mid-winter. The caterpillars relished the leaves of the red and black oak best, but when they had devoured those, they destroyed every thing before and around them; and, proceeds our journalist, "they would travel from tree to tree—no river nor pond would stop them, for they would swim like dogs and travel in great armies; and I have seen houses so covered with them, that little or no part of the building could be seen." They did not build nests on the trees, like the common caterpillar, were considerably larger, though they resembled them in shape and color.*

The North Parish burying-ground was laid out.

The west part of the town was set off into a distinct parish, and was called West Parish. The inhabitants went immediately to work and completed a meeting house sometime in the fall.

1735.

Mr. Samuel Bachellor was ordained in the West Parish in July. Seventy-seven persons requested a dismission from the parent church, to embody themselves in the West Parish, which was granted.

The town granted to John Swett their interest in the Rock's ferry, for 13s. 6d.

1736.

The throat distemper, as it was called, made dreadful ravages throughout the town. Its victims were principally children, and it is supposed to have swept into the grave nearly one-fourth of the population under fifteen years of age. Almost every house was turned into

---

* This account is taken from the journal which was left by Hon. Bailey Bartlett.

a habitation of mourning, and almost every day had its funeral procession. Many arose in the morning, their cheeks glowing with perfect health, and when the sun went down, they were cold and silent in the winding sheet of the dead. Some parents lost all of their children. 58 families lost 1 each; 34 families lost 2 each; 11 families lost 3 each; 5 families lost 4 each, and 4 families lost 5 each. Only one person died with this disease who was over forty years of age.

This fatal distemper was attended with a sore throat, white or ash-colored specks, an efflorescence on the skin, great debility of the whole system, and a strong tendency to putridity. It first appeared in Kingston, N. H., in 1735; and in 14 months, 113 persons died.*

1737.

This town and Salisbury were deeply interested in the controversy which existed between the provinces of Massachusetts and New-Hampshire, concerning the boundary line; and which was this year settled, by commissioners appointed by the crown. The second charter granted to this province, reads thus:—" extending from the great river, commonly called Monomack, alias Merrimack, on the north and from three miles northward of the said river, to the Atlantic or Western sea or ocean." But when Haverhill and Salisbury were first granted by Massachusetts, they " were made to extend more than three miles north from the river;" and that part beyond the three miles remained under the jurisdiction of Massachusetts.† Of this, New-Hampshire complained, and wished to have the division line placed three miles north of the river. If this was done, it would divide Haverhill nearly in the centre, and make it only three miles in breadth, instead of six. On the 17th of May, the town appointed a committee, consisting of

---

* Rev. John Brown, minister of the First Parish, published a particular account of this distemper, in a large pamphlet.

† Hutchinson.

Col. Richard Saltonstall, Mr. Richard Hazzen, and Deacon James Ayer, to wait upon the Commissioners.

This dispute created great interest in both provinces. The Assembly of New-Hampshire met on the 4th of August, and the Secretary, by the Governor's order, prorogued it to the tenth, then to meet at Hampton Falls. The Assembly of Massachusetts met at Boston on the same day, and also adjourned to the tenth, then to meet at Salisbury;—thus the two Assemblies met within 5 miles of each other. On the tenth a large cavalcade was formed at Boston, and the Governor rode in state, escorted by a troop of horse. He was met at Newbury ferry by another troop, and at the supposed divisional line by three more, who conducted him in all the pomp of power to the George tavern, at Hampton Falls, where he held a council and made a speech to the Assembly of New-Hampshire. The Governor's cavalcade produced the following pasquinade:

> Dear paddy, you never did behold such a sight,
> As yesterday morning was seen before night.
> You in all your born days saw, nor I did'nt neither,
> So many fine horses and men ride together.
> At the head, the lower horse trotted two in a row,
> Then all the higher house pranced after the low,
> Then the Governor's coach galloped on like the wind,
> And the last that came foremost were troopers behind;
> But I fear it means no good to your neck, nor mine,
> For they say 'tis to fix a right place for the line.*

The divisional line was, at length, established three miles north of Merrimack River.

An alms-house was built by the town, but the inhabitants were dissatisfied with the experiment, and it was sold in 1746. The poor were supported in families.

1738.

About this time a ferry was established on the Merrimack, about a mile and a half below the present chain ferry. It was soon after removed a mile up the river,

---
* Belknap's Hist. of N. H.

to the house of Joseph Mulliken, who lived on the Bradford shore.

James M'Hard, had liberty to build a rum-distillery. This was the first establishment of the kind in town; it stood on the stream, near the house now owned by Mr. William White.

The old burial-ground in West Parish, was laid out.

1739.

Silver was extremely scarce, and was valued at 29s. per oz.

Square-toed shoes went out of fashion, and the gentry began to wear silver knee-buckles.

About this time, the sycamore-trees, now standing before Wid. Samuel W. Duncan's mansion, were set out. The work was done by one Hugh Talent, a wanderer from the green fields of Erin, and who was a famous fiddler. He lived with Col. Richard Saltonstall, in the capacity of a servant; and tradition says that he frequently made harmonious sounds with his cat-gut and rosin for the gratification of the village swains and lasses.

1742.

Rev. John Brown, minister of the First Parish, died on the 2d of December. After his death, the parish voted to raise £100, old tenor, to defray the expenses of his funeral, which was to be delivered to "Madam Brown, to be used at her discretion."

1743.

The house of Dr. H. Brown, at Holt's Rocks, was destroyed by fire on the 22d of January, and his daughter, aged 23 years, and a young man who was then living with him, a son of D. Currier, were burnt to death. Their remains were interred in a field, now overgrown with trees, owned by John Johnson, Esq., and grave-stones were erected to their memory. But they are thrown down and so broken and defaced, that the letters are nearly illegible. With the assistance of Mr. Johnson, we found them, lying flat on the ground, and nearly concealed from view. It is in a very romantic situation, on the side of a hill covered with young sycamores, and which slopes gently until it reaches the Merrimack. This gentleman also informed us that other persons, principally infants, were buried in the same place; but no monuments were erected to their memory, and the mounds have totally disappeared.

The little village at the Rocks, increased very slowly. We were informed by Mr. Phineas Nichols, a venerable gentleman, 94 years of age, that there were but four houses in 1750, and that he could distinctly remember them. They were owned and occupied by Dr. Brown, John Swett, Joseph Burrill, and Mr. Nichols' father. Dr. Brown moved to Fryeburg, Maine, soon after.

Mr. Edward Barnard was ordained over the First Parish, the 27th of April.

1744.

The boundary line of the East Parish was run last year, and their meeting-house was completed this fall. On the 19th of November, 17 persons requested dismission from the parent church, to embody themselves in a church at this place; and in the same month, Mr. Benjamin Parker was ordained. His salary was £100 per year; seventy in "provision pay," and thirty in money; but it was soon after cut down to £53. 6s. 8d.*

* East Parish Records.

1745.

A "grammar-school" was commenced in the First Parish.

Thomas Cottle petitioned the town to grant him a ferry on the Merrimack. Mr. Cottle says " the ferry may be sarviceable to the town and other travailers." His petition was granted, and he was to ferry the people of Haverhill one-fourth cheaper than strangers. The place is now known as " Cottle's ferry."

1746.

On the 21st and 22d of August, there was a heavy frost.

The First Parish frequently collected the minister tax in the following manner:—A contribution, as it was called, was taken every sabbath afternoon, when any person who wished to pay his tax in this manner, had liberty to pay such a sum as he pleased. Each person was ordered to fold his money in a paper, and write his name and the amount within. A person was yearly appointed to receive these monies, and pass the amount to the credit of the name within written. If no name was written within the paper, it was considered as a free gift to the minister, and was disposed of as such.

1748.

Col. Richard Saltonstall, and others, remonstrated in the General Court against the proceedings of the March meeting, principally because some of the inhabitants voted who were not duly qualified. The General Court took it in hand and passed a resolve, dated 3d November, 1748, "that the meeting be set aside and all the proceedings consequent thereon be null and void," and directed the Selectmen for 1747 to issue a warrant for another meeting, to be held sometime in November, and that John Choate, Esq.* be appointed Moderator. Accordingly a meeting was holden on the 22d November, when Mr. Choate presided, and the town officers were again chosen.

6th June. The First Parish voted to raise £65. 1s. 6d. old tenor to purchase a bell. This was the first bell in town. Nathaniel Knowlton was chosen bellman, and was ordered to ring it at 1 o'clock, at 9 in the evening, and on the sabbath and lecture days. It was first hung on two pieces of timber placed crosswise at the top, on Main-street, near the parsonage house. Soon after a belfry was built on the ridge of the meeting-house, where it was hung, and the rope descended to the broad aisle.

1751.

30th May. Fifteen persons requested dismission from the parent church, that they might be incorporated in a church then forming in Hampstead, N. H.

1752.

The inhabitants were considerably alarmed by the appearance of the small-pox in the neighboring towns, and John Cogswell and Samuel White were appointed to assist the Selectmen to use every method to prevent its entrance into the town. A set of Constables were chosen to serve such warrants as should be issued for that purpose.

13th April. Nathaniel Peaslee, Esq., was chosen to appear at Salem Court, to answer to two presentments against the town, for not being provided with a "grammar-school master," and for not keeping "Hawk's river bridge in repair."

---

* Mr. Choate was of Ipswich, and a member of the General Court.

1753.

The First Parish voted, 26th March, "that Benjamin Harrod should take down the old bell and dispose of it to the best advantage, and provide a new one not exceeding 500 lbs., or thereabouts."

1755.

A few persons died with the small-pox, in this and the following year, among whom was the father and mother of Edmund Black. In 1758, he petitioned the town to pay the charges of the Doctor and nurse. Mr. Black was a poor, but industrious man, and the town voted to cancel the charges caused by the sickness of his parents.

Serious difficulties commenced in the West Parish. Though many were dissatisfied at the settlement of Mr. Bachellor, still no great disturbance was created till this year, when his enemies, led by Joseph Haynes, a shrewd and fearless man, seized upon certain sentiments uttered in the pulpit, from the text, "It is finished." These sentiments they denounced as downright heresy, and made them the ground-work of a sharply contested controversy, which raged with unabated violence for a number of years, and finally ended in the removal of Mr. Bachellor, 9th October, 1761, upon terms that day recommended by a Council. The subject was considered by the Haverhill Association, and two Councils called for that purpose, who upheld Mr. Bachellor, and published several pamphlets defending his conduct from the aspersions of his enemies. These drew from Joseph Haynes, a large pamphlet, called "A Discourse in order to confute the Heresy, delivered, and much contended for, in the West-Parish, in Haverhill, and countenanced by many of the ministers of the neighboring parishes, viz: That the blood and water which came from Christ when the soldier pierced his side, his laying in his grave, and his resurrection, was no part of the work of redemption, and that his laying in the grave was no part of his humiliation." It was printed in 1757. This drew a pamphlet in the following year, from the Association and Councils, vindicating the measures they had taken, to which Mr. Haynes soon after replied. A Council of nine churches convened by adjournment on the 19th September, 1758, when twenty charges against Mr. Bachellor were laid before it, condemning his conduct and doctrines. The Council sat four days, and decided that they were not sufficiently supported. Col. John Choate of Ipswich, one of their members, differed from this decision and published his "reasons of dissent." The same Council again met in the following year, when Mr. Haynes gave them some "friendly remarks," which were afterwards published; but this second examination of the charges only confirmed them in their former decision.

These two parties were as bitter and violent towards each other as they could well be. Both were in the wrong.

Soon after the struggle commenced, his enemies gained the ascendancy, and between April 1760, and July 1761, they held eight parish meetings, and voted, at various times, "to take the parsonage from Mr. B. and let it to the best advantage—to request him to ask a dismission—that the meeting-house should not be opened to him and his friends—to choose a person to keep the key—to put themselves under the Boston Presbytery—and to choose a Committee to prosecute any person who should be found preaching in the meeting-house without leave from the Parish Committee." These proceedings were, however, protested against by a large portion of the parishioners, whose names were recorded in the Parish Records. The Parish has been agitated by religious controversies most of the time since.

1756.

9th March. The town voted that the soldiers who went in the first expedition to Lake George, and were in the battle of 1755, "should be abated of their polls." Some of them had not returned in 1760, when a similar vote was passed in favor of those who were absent.

1757.

About this time, says tradition, a party of gentlemen arrived from Boston and put up at Lieut. Ebenezer Eastman's tavern. They brought their coffee with them, and requested the landlady to cook it. The good lady, not being particularly acquainted with the article, nor the manner of cooking it, hardly knew what to do. But having a little self-confidence with her other good qualities, she scorned to ask advice, and proceeded to cook it in her best manner. Accordingly she took her bean-pot, put the coffee into it, filled it with water, and boiled it as she would beans. At length, the refreshment was ready, and when the gentlemen sat down, they were not a little surprised to see their coffee set before them, well boiled, in the kernel. They, however, took it very good-naturedly, and afterwards instructed her in the mystery of cooking coffee. This tavern was torn down in 1775.

There is a similar tradition concerning the first use of tea in this town. A Mr. Gile had a present sent to him, from Boston, of one pound of tea. His good wife knew not exactly how to make it, but she concluded to hang on her dinner-pot, and cook it in that. The dinner-pot was hung over the fire, partly filled with water, and the whole pound was put into it. But to make it more luscious, the good lady put in a large piece of beef, for she intended to have a *real dish of tea;*—we presume that she had heard of the old proverb, "the more good things the better." After it had boiled sufficiently, the pot was taken off, "but the liquor was so *despot* strong," said our informant, that they could not drink it, and besides it had made a complete jelly of the meat. For the correctness of these two traditions, we will not undertake to vouch.

Stephen Cross was chosen " to take care of the boys, and the young on the sabbaths, that they profane not the day between meetings."

1759.

Pot and pearl ash works were erected by Samuel Blodget, on the stream, now occupied by Col. John Woodman. It was among the first in the country, and continued in successful operation for some years.

1763.

The throat distemper again generally prevailed in the town, but it was not so fatal as that which prevailed in 1736, and but few persons died. The disorder was of a milder nature, or better understood by the physicians.

1764.

Rev. James Cushing, pastor of the church in the North Parish, died on the 13th of May. During his life he gained the warm affections of his people, and they testified that " he was a solid and fervent preacher, in conduct upright, prudent and steady, and recommended the amiable religion of his master by meekness and patience, condescension and candor, a tender sympathy with his flock, and a studious endeavour to maintain and promote the things of peace."

The Selectmen were ordered to build a pest-house " in case the small pox should again appear."

21st Nov. The First Parish voted that, " the version of Psalms, Tate and Brady, with the largest impression of Dr. Watts Hymns, be sung in public."

1765.

Rev. Gyles Merrill was ordained in the North Parish, on the 6th of March.

The First Baptist Church was gathered, and a meeting-house was immediately erected for its convenience.

This year the Parliament of England passed an act, called the "Stamp Act," which required the people of the American Colonies, in all their legal and mercantile transactions, to use papers stamped with the Royal Seal. It was spiritedly opposed, however, by the Colonies, especially in Boston, where the inhabitants collected and assaulted the house of Lieut. Governor Hutchinson, who was a warm friend of the act. In other places, the bells were tolled and effigies of the stamp-officers were burnt.

The following instructions to Col. Saltonstall, the Representative, will evince the spirit with which it was received in this town.

"Whereas, some matters of great importance to this town and province, are likely to come under consideration at the next Great and General Court; therefore, it is thought proper to draw up and give our Representative some special instructions. As the time prefixed by act of Parliament is near, when their much disputed and *oppressive stamped-papers* were required—when our navigation, Courts of Justice, &c. may not be carried on without them, and the offenders subject to a Court of Admiralty, unless it be repealed. It is resolved that we esteem it our indispensable duty to *pay a due regard to all the legal injunctions* of our King and Parliament, and to duly *resent all arbitrary impositions*, and to declare that we think the 'Stamp Act' *unconstitutional*. And we recommend our Representative to exert himself to the utmost of his power for the *preservation of our just liberties*. Also resolved, that our Representative use his influence that there be no excise on tea, coffee, &c. for the future; and that the duty be taken off from the private consumption of liquors, and that it be not more than four pence on the gallon to licensed persons."

1766.

The second meeting-house in the First Parish had become decayed and too small to accommodate the people. It was last year voted to raise £300, to be paid in lumber, to defray the expenses of building a new house, the dimensions of which were ordered not to exceed 66 feet in length, and 48 feet in breadth. The present meeting-house was accordingly erected and mostly finished, in the autumn of this year.

Rev. Hezekiah Smith was installed over the First Baptist Church, on the 12th of November.

1767.

A powder-house was erected.

The first fire-wardens were chosen. They were Cornelius Mansise, Enoch Bartlett, Samuel White, Esq., and Isaac Osgood.

The West Parish extended an invitation to Mr. Joseph Willard to settle among them, and he accepted; but he was never ordained, nor are there any reasons given on the records, why he was not. Probably the late disturbances had not sufficiently subsided.

1768.

21st March. The thanks of the town were voted to the "Gentlemen of the house of Representatives for their firmness in defending the liberties of the people."

Samuel Bachellor was chosen a delegate on the 20th September, to attend a Convention holden at Boston on the 22d, "to consult, advise and act as his majesty's service, and the peace and safety of his subjects in this province may require." As a principal instruction to Mr. B., says the Recorder, "it was voted that the King's troops should not be hindered their landing in this province by force of arms."

A Society was organized, called the "Fire Club," designed for mutual assistance and protection in case of fire; and also for other purposes, which are thus explained:—
"The articles provide that half the members shall draw tickets at the quarterly meetings, upon which shall be the different routes to be pursued in case of theft; that those who draw tickets, upon the first information of theft upon the property of any member, shall repair to the place where the theft was committed, or to his usual place of abode, and pursue the roads they have drawn, unless the Committee of advice shall prescribe different routes; and it is their duty to use the utmost exertions to apprehend the thieves and recover the stolen property. All extra expenses to be paid by the Club."*

1769.

James Hudson established "Salt-works" on the stream now occupied by Col. John Woodman; and on the 21st September the town gave him £13. 6s. 8d. to encourage him. But he found the enterprise unprofitable, and it was soon abandoned.

1770.

The West Parish extended an invitation to Rev. Phineas Adams, who accepted, and was ordained this year; the precise time cannot be ascertained.

At a meeting of the Boston merchants, it was resolved to use all lawful means to prevent the importation of British goods. On the 9th of April, this town voted that, "We will, by all lawful ways and means, exert ourselves to expose to shame and contempt, all persons who shall offer to make sale of British Goods imported contrary to the agreement of Merchants, or that shall purchase such goods in this town, or be aiding and

---

* Sketch of Haverhill.

assisting to bring them into it; and that all persons who shall violate this vote, shall be rendered incapable of being chosen into any office of profit in this Town." Thanks were also voted to those Boston merchants who endeavored to prevent the importation of British goods.

1773.

A violent whirlwind passed over a part of this town, on the 13th of August. About 8 o'clock in the morning, a large black cloud arose in the South-west, charged with wind and rain. The wind came in a vein of only a few rods in breadth, and sweeping over Silver's Hill, struck the house of Mr. Bradley, now owned by Hon. Moses Wingate. Mr. Bradley immediately ran to the door and attempted to hold it, while the family was thrown into the greatest confusion, running hither and thither, amid the falling bricks, broken glass, and splinters of wood. The roof was instantly blown off, and a bundle of wool was taken from the garret and carried to Great Pond. Not a pane of glass was left in the house. The barn, which stood within a few rods of the house, was totally demolished, and a valuable horse which was then in it, escaped unharmed.

1774.

Rev. Edward Barnard, minister of the First Parish, died on the 26th January, aged 54. He was a bright ornament to the New-England clergy. His father and grandfather were, in succession, the ministers of the First Parish in Andover; and he was the brother of Rev. Thomas Barnard, of Salem, who, says Dr. Eliot, in his New-England Biography, was respected as one of the most profound, liberal and excellent men of his profession. The same author thus remarks of Rev. Edward Barnard: " He was a most accomplished preacher; his popular talents were not eminent, but his discourses were correct and excellent compositions, and highly relished by scholars and men of taste. He was a fine classical scholar, and excellent in poetry as well as prose." Four of his sermons and one poem, were published; a sermon delivered at the ordination of Rev. Henry True, at Hampstead, 24th June, 1752; a fast sermon; a sermon delivered at the ordination of Rev. Gyles Merrill, in the North Parish, 6th March, 1765; and a sermon delivered at the ordination of Rev. Thomas Cary, over the First Parish in Newburyport, 11th March, 1768.

A few years before this, the Baptists made their appearance, and caused a division in Mr. Barnard's Society; they accused him of being unconverted and of not preaching the gospel. He was an Arminian, as were the most of his contemporaries on the Merrimack. In a sermon preached thirty years after his ordination, he says:—" Nothing has been delivered by me that I would not venture my own soul upon. The fallen state of man, which gave rise to the gospel dispensation, the fulness and freeness of divine grace in Christ as the foundation of all our hopes, the influence of the spirit, the necessity of regeneration, implying repentance towards God and faith towards Jesus Christ, the necessity of practical religion, originating from evangelical principles are some of the many things which have been urged, and which will appear of the greatest importance at death and the day of judgement."

Proposals were issued to publish a volume of his sermons, but the Revolution broke out, and the design of his friends was abandoned. The author of the " Sketch of Haverhill," says that he has perused some of them, and remarks, that they were "indeed correct and excellent compositions, and would rank among the best American sermons." The day after his death, the town met and chose a Committee to conduct the funeral, and procure a monument to be erected over his grave.

Rev. Benjamin Parker, of the East Parish, preached as one of his bearers, and the Salem Gazette thus notices it:—" We have just heard from Haverhill, that the Rev. Mr. Parker, having preached as a bearer to the Rev. Mr. Barnard, deceased, the people of Mr. B's parish requested a copy of his sermon for the press; and a number of gentlemen therein were pleased, at the same time, to make him a present of a very handsome suit of clothes. The promoter and encourager of said affair has also presented him with a new wig. We should think that this kindness, extended to a needy minister, in connexion with their repeated generosity and respect shown to Mr. B's bereaved family, would be one powerful inducement for some of our promising and ingenious young preachers to settle in the work of the ministry with such a people."

The principles of Col. Richard Saltonstall, who was a Tory, were very repugnant to the Whig party, which composed a majority of the voters. A party from the West Parish, and Salem, New-Hampshire, collected before his house, armed with clubs and other instruments, to mob him; but he made them rather ashamed of their conduct. He came to the door, and with much dignity, told them his reasons for pursuing a different course from that which they had adopted. He ordered refreshments for them, and requested them to go to the tavern and call for entertainment at his expense. They accepted of his invitation, and huzzaed to his praise. He soon after went to England, to escape the resentment of the Whigs, where he was well received by his connexions. Before the causes appeared which determined the Colonies to strike for their Independence, he was quite popular, was beloved by his townsmen, and possessed considerable influence. He died at Kensington, Great Britain, 6th October, 1785.

After the repeal of the Stamp Act, in 1767, the British Parliament passed another, in October, 1770, equally offensive, imposing duties on teas, glass, paints and paper, which again aroused the spirit of the Colonies. Seven armed vessels were sent to Boston, from Halifax, by the British Government, to awe the people into obedience. The inhabitants of this town met on 28th July, and passed nine resolves, expressing their disapprobation of the proceedings of the British Parliament. They voted not to " import, purchase, vend or consume, any East India tea, until the duty [which was three pence per lb.] imposed upon its importation into the Colonies should be taken off, and the Port of Boston opened."

800 lbs. of powder were ordered to be purchased, and a proportionable quantity of balls and flints.

1775.

On the 3d January, the town voted to relieve the poor of Boston by subscription. On the 12th, Nathaniel Peaslee Sargent, Esq., and Jonathan Webster, jr., were chosen delegates to attend the Provincial Congress. It was voted to defend its resolves, and to sign a covenant similar to theirs. 63 minute men were raised, who were to be disciplined one day every week, and the town allowed them 2s. per day until they were called into active service, or disbanded. $30 were raised to employ a person to drill and instruct the militia, of whom James Sawyer was Capt., Timothy Johnson, Lieut., and Samuel Eaton, Ensign.

A manufactory of Salt Petre was established by Nathaniel Marsh and Israel Bartlett, and the town voted them £50, for their encouragement. But owing to the unsettled state of the times, it became unprofitable, and was soon discontinued.

On Sunday, 16th of April, a destructive fire broke out in Main-street, and all the west side of it, from the house now occupied by Mrs. Harrod, to the corner, and a barn behind the house now occupied by Mr. Peter Osgood, was burnt. 17 buildings were destroyed, including a large brick tavern, owned by Mr. John White, the store of Dea. Joseph Dodge, the store of James Duncan, Esq., a house occupied by Mrs. Alley, and a distillery. The earth was parched with a drought, and every thing was combustible. The meeting-house was frequently on fire, and there being but one engine, it was difficult to subdue the raging element.

Soon as the news of Lexington Battle, which happened on the 19th of April, reached this place, a company started for Boston, to join the brave patriots who were gathering in that quarter. It was in the battle of Bunker Hill, and two of its members, John Eaton and Simeon Pike were killed.

Capt. Nehemiah Emerson enlisted in the continental army in December, and continued in service till 1783. He marched to New-York, and was there when Independence was declared; he was one of the number who retreated from Ticonderoga, was at the taking of Burgoyne, 1777, and wintered at Valley Forge. He was promoted to the rank of Captain in 1780.

1776.

On the 25th June, the town voted that, "if the Hon. Congress, for the safety of the United Colonies, should declare them independent of the Kingdom of Great Britain, *this town does engage with their lives and fortunes to support them in the measure.*"

1777.

Considerable dissention had existed in the East Parish for the last three or four years, between Rev. Benjamin Parker and a part of his people. It was occasioned by the refusal of Mr. Parker to relinquish a part of his salary. In 1775, after they had vainly endeavored to allay the difficulties, the people called upon the neighboring ministers for council, and sent a committee to request Mr. Parker to meet with them; but he refused, and desired that the parish "would not trouble him with any more Committees hereafter, for he would not hear them."* At length, a mutual council was holden this year, on the 21st January, when a compromise was effected, and the connexion between him and the parish was dissolved. Mr. Parker graduated at

---

* East Parish Records.

Cambridge, in 1737. He preached an excellent sermon at the funeral of Rev. Edward Barnard, which was published.

A person was chosen by the town "to collect evidences against those who were deemed inimical to their country." A Committee was chosen to supply the families of the soldiers in the continental army with food and clothing.

The General Court resolved to raise 1300 men to fortify the passes on North River, and passed an act granting a bounty of £90 to such as would enlist for 8 months. Zebediah Parker, James Pecker, Robert Griffin, and Daniel Merrill, of this town, enlisted.

Rev. John Shaw was ordained in the First Parish, 12th March, with a salary of £100. Great dissentions existed before his settlement. Repeated trials had been made to procure a minister, but none had succeeded until now. No less than five candidates had preached in the vacant pulpit, and some of them were men of sterling worth, fervent piety, and conspicuous talents; but the strong excitement which existed, biased the better judgment of the voters.

Dea. David Marsh, grandson of Onesiphorus Marsh, jr., died on the 2d of November, in the eightieth year of his age. He married Mary Moody, in 1722, who died 12th August, 1794. They had 12 children, all of whom lived to an advanced age; perhaps there is no family in the vicinity so remarkable for its longevity. Elizabeth, born 29th June, 1723, died in Oct., 1807, aged 83; Mary, born 12th March, 1725, died 1813, aged 88; Judith, born 5th May, 1727, died 1816, aged 89; Cutting, born 20th March, 1729, died 1809, aged 80; David, born 27th March, 1731, died 23d Oct., 1812, aged 81; Moses, born 9th Feb., 1733, died 20th Oct., 1820, aged 86; Jonathan, born 25th May, 1735, died 7th March, 1825, aged 89; Enoch, born 3d Aug., 1737, died 4th Feb., 1806, aged 68; Nathaniel, born 31st Dec., 1739, died 14th July, 1815, aged 75; John, born 2d Nov., 1742, died 13th Sept., 1821, aged 78; Lydia, born 5th Feb., 1745, died 12th July, 1828, aged 83; Abigail, born 3d April, 1747, died 17th Feb., 1831, aged 84. The descendants of Onesiphorus Marsh, sen., the first of that name who settled in this town, are exceedingly numerous, and are scattered in every direction over the New-England States.

1778.

On the 12th January, it was voted in a full meeting, "that an Union of the 13 Independent States is a matter of the greatest importance." The "plan of Union" being read; they voted that "it was generally agreeable, though, in some respects we could wish it altered."

This year the town exerted every nerve to raise men and money for the continental army, and for the service of the State. Fifteen soldiers were raised, and the Town Treasurer was ordered to hire money to pay them. £60 were paid to four men, who served "as guards at Cambridge." £120 were paid to eight soldiers who "served about Boston." £7. 11s. were paid to two men for "going to Boston." Nine soldiers enlisted in the militia, and were paid by the town. Two men served on Winter Hill 5 months, to whom the town paid £50. Eight men served in the militia three months, and six men marched to Providence, who were paid by the town. On the 30th of June, the town raised £2600 to defray the charges "it had been at in procuring soldiers for the continental army and for the service of the state." It was also voted "to raise £500 to hire the soldiers this town is now obliged to raise." On the 19th July, six soldiers were hired, to be stationed at Cambridge, to whom the town paid £110.

The Treasurer was ordered to supply the militia officers with such sums of money as were necessary for the "hire of soldiers, and if there is no money in the Treasury, then the Treasurer is to hire money until it can be raised by the town."

1779.

A Committee of "correspondence and safety" was chosen, consisting of six persons, of whom Gen. James Brickett was Chairman.

On the 7th of September, the enormous sum of £6000 was raised to defray the town charges.

Hannah Belknap, daughter of Nathaniel Ayer, died in November, aged 106 years and 11 months.

1780.

An immense quantity of snow fell this winter; it was so deeply drifted, that in breaking the road over the Common, a large hole was dug through a drift, through which a company of men rode on horseback.*

18th May. The remarkable dark day and night.

1781.

On the 15th January, the town raised the enormous quantity of 32,256 lbs. of Beef for the continental army. Twenty-eight soldiers were likewise raised, whose charges were paid by the town. 3d July. Four men were drafted for Rhode-Island, and paid by the town.

1783.

The Selectmen received a circular letter from Boston, " concerning the return into this State, of certain persons called Refugees." A town-meeting was called purposely to act on the subject, when it was voted that the " Representative be instructed that whenever the affair respecting the return of the Refugees should be laid before the General Court, that he do use his influence in said Court to prevent their return."

On the 3d September, a treaty of peace was signed, and the 13 United States became an independent nation. The object for which the inhabitants of the Colo-

---

* Bartlett's Journal.

nies fought and bled, was now obtained; and there were but few towns, if any, which made greater exertions to forward the cause of freedom than this; no effort was spared; no sacrifice was thought too great. The courage of the inhabitants never flagged, even at the darkest period; 'they had nailed the flag to the mast,' to use the expression of a veteran of that period, 'and they determined to see it wave in the winds of freedom, or fall nobly fighting.' They were willing to spend their treasures and shed their blood; and when there was scarcely room to hope, the votes which were passed in their town-meetings, show a spirit of coolness, determination and patriotism which is truly astonishing;—they evinced a chivalry far nobler than that of olden time; they were actuated by a principle from which death only could separate them.

The following lists of men who were in the army at different periods, were furnished us by Hon. Israel Bartlett. They were drafted from the company which belonged to the village, and of which Mr. Bartlett was Lieut. in 1777, and afterwards Capt. We did not insert them in their regular order, because it was thought best to give them in a body. These were drafted from the Artillery Company for the continental service in 1775 and 1776:—Thomas Cogswell, Capt.; Samuel Kimball, 1st Lieut.; William Lemont, 2d Lieut.; Samuel Walker, Ensign; John White, Quarter-Master; John Dow, James Pecker, Theodore Tyler, Joseph Whiting, John Eaton, Stephen Dustin, Jonathan Sargent, Moses Harriman, Nathan Ayer, James Townsend, Joseph Johnson, Stephen Jackson, David Harris, Jonathan Harris, Nehemiah Emerson, Jonathan Dustin, jr., Samuel Middleton, Samuel Middleton, jr., William Baker, John Stickney, John Tyler, Job Gage, David Perley, John Downing, Nathaniel Kimball, Samuel Woodman, Ephraim Dodge, Samuel Buck, Daniel Tyler, William Greenleaf, David Moores, Stephen Runnels, William Gage, Daniel Remich, Moses Keezar, Samuel Lecount, Joshua Moores, Joseph Wakefield, James Rix, John Whittier, Bart Pecker, John Alley, and Philip Bagley, privates.

The following is a list of those who served six weeks at Roxbury. They were commanded by Capt. Eaton, and marched in December, 1775. Obadiah Ayer, Daniel Hill, jr., Moses Willcomb, Amos Clement, John Whiting, Nehemiah Emerson, jr., Peter Middleton, Ebenezer Ballard, Moses Whittier, Samuel Greenleaf.

It frequently happened that, when an order came to draft soldiers, two, three and four men were classed, and were obliged to hire one man to serve in their room. This was done so as to make each man bear an equal portion of the burthen. The following is a list of those who served two months in 1776, or hired. Samuel Appleton, John Cogswell, jr., Isaac Reddington, John Green, Theodore Tyler, Amos Gile, William Wingate. David Marsh, Enoch Marsh, and Nathaniel Marsh, were classed, and hired one man; James Duncan, Samuel Duncan, and Jonathan Barker, were classed, and hired one man; Israel Bartlett and Phineas Carlton, were classed, and hired one man.

On the 29th June, 1776, an order arrived from the General Court to raise 43 men in this town. The quota of the Artillery company was eleven. They were destined for Ticonderoga, and were paid £9 per month, by the Government. Those who hired, paid a bounty of $30. Those who marched, were James Brickett, Brig. General; John Wingate, Abraham Swett, Ensign, James Rix, Nathan Ayer, Benjamin Mooers, jr., John Gage, Peter Middleton, Dudley Dustin, Joshua Moores, James Clement, and ——— Pecker.

On the 18th July, 1776, another order was received from Col. Whittier, to draft every 25th man, destined for Ticonderoga. John Bailey, Thomas Hopkins and Nathaniel Bodge, were drafted from the Artillery, and marched on the 17th of August. On the 25th of the same month, every 25th man was raised, and marched for Dorchester. On the 22d September an order was received, to raise every 5th man in the town, under fifty years of age, destined for New-York. The quota of the Artillery Company was twelve. And it was so classed that three men were to furnish one soldier each, and twenty-two were to furnish nine. In December, another was received, to raise every fifth man in the town, to march to New-Jersey. The quota of the Artillery Company was again twelve; three of whom marched, and the others employed substitutes.

In January, 1777, says Mr. Bartlett's Record, "orders were received to raise every seventh man in the town, from 16 years old and upward that had a being." Every town in the Commonwealth received the same order. The object was to raise a continental army for three years from the 1st of January. The quota of the Artillery Company was found to be 30; and the following men, exclusive of officers, were raised, principally by a tax on the company: James Rix, Jacob Rowe, Moses Downing, William Harriman, Samuel Back, John Thomas, Samuel Remich, John Shaw, John Shaw, jr., Moses Moores, William Baker, David Peasley, Moses Keezar, William Greenleaf, John Lee, Robert Martin, Job Gage, Oliver Page, William Pecker, James Clement, James Clement, jr., William Huston, Thomas Thornton, John Tyler, Moses Lecount, Samuel Middleton, jr., John Graham, Robert Hopkins, John Dow, Jacob Back. In July, eleven men were drafted from the Company to reinforce the Northern army till the 1st January, 1778. They were raised in the following manner:—Nine men furnished one soldier; twenty-four furnished four; and thirteen furnished two. It appears by the record, that the detachment wanted two of being complete. In September, an invitation was received from the General Court, for half of this regiment to turn out as volunteers, to reinforce the Northern army, then at Saratoga; and to remain in service thirty days after their arrival at Head Quarters. The following men turned out from the Artillery Company. Nathaniel Marsh, Capt.; Israel Bartlett, Lieut.; James Ayer, Benjamin Mooers, jr., Nathan Ayer, Jonathan Barker, Edmund Chase, Ebenezer Dustin, Moses Emerson, Ebenezer Greenough, John Gage, Jacob George, David Green, James Haseltine, Samuel Walker, Thomas Haynes, Cotton Kimball, Dudley Ladd, jr., Samuel Souther, John Souther, Jeremiah Stickney, Benjamin Baker, Ebenezer Foster, Joshua Moores, Jonathan Harris, Mark Witham, John Cook, Enoch Cordwell, and James Pell. These men were accompanied by Brig. General James Brickett. They marched on the 4th of October, arrived at Head Quarters just after a cessation of arms had been declared, and were absent five weeks.

In March, 1778, two men were detached to serve as guards at Cambridge. In April, an order was received to raise fifteen men in this town, to complete the fifteen batallions which were raising for the continental army. The town voted a bounty of £100 to each soldier who would enlist. They were to serve nine months after their arrival at Fishkill. Those who were detached from the Artillery, were Nathan Kimball, Thomas Sargent, William Appleton, Moses Harriman, Gilbert Bond, Ephraim H. Brown, Samuel Eames, Francis Smiley, Jeremiah Davis, and Edward Barker, jr. In the same month, another order was received for a detachment of ten men, to serve eight months after their arrival at Peekskill. The town voted a bounty of £90 to each soldier that would enlist. In June, twelve men were detached for Rhode-Island, to serve eight months; and the following were detached from the Artillery. John Whittier, Peter Middleton, Mark Witham, John Gage, Joshua Moores, and Theodore Tyler. In the same month, six men marched to Cambridge, and were paid by the town. In July, six men were detached from the Artillery, to serve six weeks at Rhode-Island. In September, nine men marched from this town, three from the Artillery Company, to serve at Boston till the 1st of January, 1779.

The foregoing items were principally taken from the records of the Artillery Company. There were then but two Companies in the town, sometimes called the 1st and 2d. We are sorry to say that the records of the latter have never been found, and it is believed that they have been destroyed.

1784.

29th June. John Sawyer, who had been in a state of partial delirium for some years, leaped from the belfry of the First Parish meeting-house. Mr. Bradford, the bell-man, who had but one leg, was ascending to the bell, when Sawyer went past him, and arrived at it first. Without any previous disclosure of his design, he suddenly leaped from the fearful height, and landed on the side-walk. Dr. Daniel Brickett was the first physician called to his assistance. Soon as he arrived, Sawyer cried out in intense agony, "Doctor, Doctor! do kill me!" His back was broken, and he survived but a few hours.

1786.

In September, a letter was addressed by the town of Boston to every town in the State, "concerning the common interest of the country." A Committee was chosen to reply to it, of which Gen. James Brickett was Chairman. It breathes the purest and loftiest patriotism. With grateful hearts they acknowledge the divine aid in the darkest period of the Revolution, and express the highest confidence in the constitution of the United States. We extract the following:—" If at any time we are aggrieved, when we apply for redress, the doors are not closed against us, nor guarded by a military power to overawe us. We have a right to apply for relief, and the constitution has pointed out an easy, cheap and expeditious mode to procure it. The late riotous proceedings * in some Counties in this Commonwealth, in interrupting the Courts of Justice, from which Government derives so much energy and support, are so repugnant to the Constitution, and so abhorrent to every idea of peace and good order, that we think it our indispensable duty to bear this public testimony against them, as subversive of government, and tending to introduce a state of anarchy which may terminate in the establishment of despotism and arbitrary power This town has borne its full share of all the burdens, losses, and expenses of the late war, and its subsequent proportion of expenses since the peace. The present form of Government we *deliberately adopted and wish not*

---

* Probably referring to Shays' rebellion, which broke out in the fall of this year, when large bodies of the insurgents collected under him at Wilbraham, and under Day, at West Springfield.

to see it sacrificed. We are ready, therefore, to join you in a firm and vigorous support of our Constitution in the redress of grievances, and in promoting industry, economy, and every other virtue which can exalt and render a nation respectable.

    Signed, JAMES BRICKETT, Chairman."

1790.

There was a ship-yard at Rocks' Village, and a few vessels were built. None, however, have been built since the year 1800.

Four distilleries were in full operation; three in the village, and one at the Rocks. In some productive seasons, several thousand barrels of cider were distilled. The West India trade, at this time, was considerable, and many vessels were owned in town, built for that purpose. Large quantities of lumber were exported thence, and exchanged for molasses.

1791.

A duck manufactory was established by Samuel Blodget, Esq., but it did not succeed.

The town had hitherto chosen but one representative. This year it was voted to choose a second, "*if he would not be of any expense to the town,*"—and Samuel Blodget, Esq. was chosen second Representative.

Nathaniel Peasley Sargent, better known as Judge Sargent, died in October. He was the son of Rev. Christopher Sargent, of Methuen, and his mother was the daughter of Col. Nathaniel Peasley, of Haverhill. Mr. Sargent graduated at Cambridge, in 1750, and soon after commenced the practice of law in this town. He was never distinguished at the bar as an advocate, yet he possessed sound learning, and there were but few men more respected for integrity, and uniformity of conduct. We have heard much in his praise from the lips of the aged. In 1776, he was appointed Judge of the Superior Court of Judicature, and in 1790, immediately after the resignation of Chief Justice Cushing, he was appointed to the highest seat on the bench; and he is spoken of as an able and impartial Judge.

1793.

The first paper published in this town, was issued in September. It was styled the "Guardian of Freedom," and was edited by Benjamin Edes, jr. The next year it was transferred to the possession of Samuel Aiken. It advocated federal politics.

1794.

Haverhill Bridge was completed in the fall. It was erected on three arches of 180 feet each, supported by three handsome stone piers, 40 feet square. It had as many defensive piers, or sterlings, extending 50 feet above, and a draw of 30 feet over the channel. Soon as it was passable, Judith Whiting, the grandmother of Joseph Whiting, then in her hundredth year, walked over it unaided. The old lady died soon after, wanting twelve days to complete a century.

In 1796 there were seven bridges over the Merrimack; the Essex, three miles from Newburyport; Merrimack, eight; Haverhill, fifteen; Andover, twenty-four; Dracut, at Pawtucket Falls, thirty-four; McGregor's, at Amoskeag Falls, forty-two; and Concord, fifty-six. They were all private property, and were arched, excepting Dracut and McGregor's, which were horizontal. A Mr. Palmer was the proprietor of the arched bridge in this country.

Rev. John Shaw died suddenly, on Monday the 29th of September, aged 48. The day before, he was in usual health, and preached through the day. His character was unspotted, and he was a "bright example of meekness, patience and charity." He was so loved and respected by the inhabitants, that they voted to adjourn the town-meeting, which was convened on the day of his funeral. Mrs. Shaw, who was greatly respected for her piety and domestic virtues, was afterwards married to Rev. Stephen Peabody, of Atkinson. She was the sister of the wife of John Adams. Mr. Shaw left only one son, the late William S. Shaw, Esq. of Boston, and two daughters.

1795.

Rev. Abiel Abbot was the first candidate who preached, after the decease of Mr. Shaw, and the parish gave him an unanimous call to settle. He was ordained on the 8th of June.

Merrimack Bridge was completed in the fall; it was built a few rods above Holt's Rocks. It was 1,000 feet in length, and was the longest bridge over the Merrimack. It had four arches, a draw, and was supported by five piers and two abutments. There was but little travel over the bridge, and the proprietors suffered it to fall to decay. It was swept away by the ice in the spring of 1818.

1796.

The town began to reckon its monies in Dollars, Cents, etc.

A malignant fever broke out in some of the neighboring towns, and a Committee of thirteen was chosen to adopt measures to prevent its introduction into this.

21st Sept. It was voted to build a pound with stones. It is now standing on the south end of the Common.

1797.

Rev. Isaac Tompkins was ordained in the East Parish, on the 7th of January. His salary was voted yearly. The contract between him and the Society, ran thus:—" The salary was not to exceed $266 66, nor be less than $183 33; and if the Parish did not allow him a satisfactory support, a committee was to be mutually chosen who should fix it between the above sums."

1798.

The Guardian of Freedom was discontinued, and the " Impartial Herald" was soon after issued.

The affairs of the nation were discussed at a town-meeting, and it was voted to send the President, John Adams, the following address:—

" While we disapprove of an interference of the people with the administration of our National Government, we consider it our duty, at this time, to assure you that the measures you have adopted and pursued as first Magistrate of the Union, have uniformly met our hearty concurrence. In full confidence that those measures have been dictated by wisdom, and the purest principles of patriotism, we cannot withhold the expression of our grateful thanks for your undeviating firmness in their execution—your late exertions to redress our wrongs—to accommodate differences unhappily existing between this country and the French Republic—to conciliate the affections of our Allies—to preserve our neutrality—to establish our peace and happiness—and above all to support the independence, dignity and freedom of the United States, afford the highest evidence of the justice and wisdom of your administration; and demands, in an eminent degree, the gratitude of every patriotic citizen.

" We humbly deprecate the calamities of war—but when the safety, the independence, the freedom of our country require, under the directions of the Government of our choice, imploring a blessing from heaven, we are prepared, with our property and at the hazard of our lives, to support our Government, to vindicate our rights, and to defend our country."

This letter was transmitted to Hon. Bailey Bartlett, then Representative to Congress, and by him to the President. The following is the President's reply:—

"To the inhabitants of the town of Haverhill in the State of Massachusetts.

"*Gentlemen:*—I thank you for a respectable and affectionate address, which has been presented to me by Mr. Bartlett, your Representative in Congress.

"The interference of the people with the administration of the National Government, in ordinary cases, would be, not only useless and unnecessary, but very inconvenient and expensive to them, if not calculated to disturb the public councils with prejudices, passions, local views, and partial interests, which would better be at rest. But there are some great conjunctions in which it is proper, and in such a government as ours, perhaps necessary. If ever such an occasion can occur, the present is one.

"Your assurance to me that the measures I have adopted as first Magistrate of the Union, have uniformly met your hearty concurrence; and your declaration that you are prepared with your property, and at the hazard of your lives, to support your Government, vindicate your rights, and defend your country, are to me a great consolation.   JOHN ADAMS.

PHILADELPHIA, June 6, '98.

1800.

The Impartial Herald was discontinued, and "The Observer" was issued by Galen H. Fay.

An eulogy on the death of Gen. Washington was delivered, by Rev. Abiel Abbot, on the 22d of February, and the General's address on leaving the Presidential chair, was also read. The town ordered it to be printed, and one copy to be given to every family.

A steeple was built to the Baptist meeting-house.

1801.

Rev. Gyles Merrill, minister of the North Parish, died on the 27th of April. His memory is still fresh in the minds of those who have survived him, and they testify to his amiable disposition, and devotedness as a christian. There was nothing theatrical in Mr. Merrill's manner, while in the desk;—he made but few gestures—yet he exhibited a meekness and simplicity which made him an interesting preacher. He had the welfare of his people much at heart, and he constantly studied how he might best serve them. He left three sons; Moses Merrill, Esq., of this town, James C. Merrill, Esq., Counsellor at Law, Boston, and Samuel Merrill, Esq., Counsellor at Law, Andover.

Rev. Phineas Adams, minister of the West Parish, also died on the 27th of November. He graduated at Cambridge, in 1762. The West Parish was very fortunate to procure such a man as Mr. Adams, for he was well calculated to heal the difficulties that existed. He possessed an amiable disposition, bland and conciliatory manners, and sound sense. He experienced many trials, though no serious division happened while he was among them. Since his death, the pulpit has been alternately occupied by different ministers until the settlement of Mr. Grosvenor.

1802.

On the 24th of Jan., the weather was so warm that the ice in the river moved with the tide, and there was but little snow till the 22d of February, when a large quantity seems to have fallen; for the Hon. Bailey Bartlett, Ichabod Tucker, Esq., and some others, rode to Ipswich on the snow-crust, over the fences, in a large double sleigh.*

Catharine Emerson died 14th June, aged 100.

The Merrimack Lodge was organized on the 15th of June, and has ever since been in successful operation.

---

* Bartlett's Journal.

1803.

The happy connexion which had heretofore existed between Rev. Abiel Abbot and his people, became dissolved on the 13th of June. The inadequateness of his salary was the cause of the controversy, which commenced early in the year. Mr. Abbot requested the Parish to make an addition of $200, and informed it that nothing less would be considered a "competent support." The parish would not comply with this request, and Mr. Abbot immediately asked a dismission. He was again settled over the first Church and Society in Beverly, on the 13th of December. He died on quarantine-ground, at New-York, 8th June, 1828, and was buried on Staten Island. The following is a list of publications which were kindly furnished us by Rev. David Oliphant, of Beverly:—

Memorial of Divine Benefits—a sermon preached at Exeter, on the 15th, and at Haverhill on the 29th of November, 1798, the days of public Thanksgiving in New-Hampshire and Massachusetts.

Traits of resemblance in the People of the United States of America to Ancient Israel—a sermon preached at Haverhill, November 28, 1799, on the Anniversary Thanksgiving.

Eulogy on the Life and Character of Washington—delivered by request, on the 22d of Feb., 1800, before the inhabitants of Haverhill.

The Duty of Youth—a sermon occasioned by the death of Miss Sarah Ayer, April 7, 1802, at Haverhill.

The Mariner's Manual—a sermon preached in Beverly, March 4, 1804.

A Discourse before the Portsmouth Female Asylum, August 9, 1807.

A Discourse, delivered at Plymouth, December 22, 1809, at the celebration of the 188th Anniversary of the landing of our Forefathers.

Sermons to Mariners—(a duodecimo vol.) published in 1812.

An Address before the Massachusetts Society for suppressing Intemperance, June 2, 1815.

Discourse before the Missionary Society of Salem and vicinity, and the Essex South Musical Society, October 2, 1816.

Discourses on Baptism.

The Parent's Assistant and Sunday School Book, published in 1822.

Charge at the Ordination of *Rev. Bernard Whitman*, February 15, 1826.

Address before the Berry Street Conference, May 31, 1826.

Ecclesiastical Peace Recommended—a Discourse before the Annual Convention of the Congregational Ministers of Massachusetts, May 13, 1827.

The Example of the first Preachers of the Gospel considered—a sermon preached at the Installation of Rev. Abiel Abbot, in the Congregational Church in Peterborough, N. H., June 27, 1827.

Letters written in the interior of Cuba, between the Mountains of Arcana, to the East, and of Cusco, to the West, in the months of February, March, April, and May, 1828.—Boston, 1829.

A posthumous vol., entitled *Sermons by the late Rev. Abiel Abbot, D. D. of Beverly, Mass.; with a Memoir of his life*, by *S. Everett*—Boston, 1831.

1804.

The citizens celebrated the 4th of July. A dinner was provided by Mr. Harrod, and some of the citizens sat down to a cold collation on the parade-ground.

20th July. Daniel Webb, an Englishman, was found suspended from the limb of a tree. He was immediately taken down, and means were used to resuscitate life, but without effect.

A code of By-Laws was reported and accepted by the town.

1805.

Rev. Hezekiah Smith, minister of the First Baptist Society, died on the 24th of January. He was born on

Long Island, 21st April, 1737, and received a public education at Princeton College, where he took the degree of A. M. in 1765. After he left College, he travelled over a great part of the United States, a distance of 4000 miles, and preached about two hundred times. On his arrival at Charleston, South-Carolina, he was ordained as an Evangelist. In the spring of 1766, he came to New-England, but with the intention of returning in the fall; he was, however, prevailed upon to accept the invitation of this Church, and was installed on the 12th of November, of the same year. Soon after his installation, Congress appointed him a Chaplain in the Army; and in this situation he remained till 1780, when he was honorably discharged. While in that station he was highly esteemed, both by officers and men; and he often exposed himself in the time of battle, to encourage the soldiers and comfort the wounded and dying. Upon his return, the Society voted him a salary of £100 in silver. Brown University is greatly indebted to his exertions. He travelled through various parts of the country, collecting monies for its benefit, a service for which he was eminently qualified. At an early period, that Seminary, sensible of his talents and great worth, chose him one of its Fellows; and in 1797, conferred on him the degree of D. D. But few excelled him as a preacher; his discourses were plain and evangelical, and his voice was strong and impressive. "In the family, no man exceeded him; there the softer affections were blended with just authority. The law of love and kindness was in his mouth. As a friend he was constant and sincere. The last sermon he preached, he was uncommonly engaged and persuasive. The Thursday following, he was suddenly seized with a paralytic shock, and spoke no more."*

8th March. The ice broke up and went out of the river with tremendous force, moved two ships on the stocks, and did other damage.

Rev. William Bachelder was ordained over the First Baptist Society, in November.

---

* His funeral sermon, preached by Samuel Stillman, D. D., Pastor of the First Baptist Church in Boston.

1807.

On the 25th of May, a party of eleven men, who were employed in the ship-yard, accompanied a vessel which had been launched a few days before, some distance down the Merrimack. The wind blew violently, and it rained hard. They started on their return with their sails unfurled, and the boat moved lightly over the waters. When a little this side of the Rocks, the boat capsized, and all were precipitated into the river. Six of the party, who were stout, and athletic men, were drowned. Their names were Matthew Pettingill, Samuel Blanchard, John Foss, William Hoyt, Benjamin Cole, and Joshua Weed, and all were heads of families.* Mr. Cole was found the same day; four were found the next Saturday, and on the Sunday following, Mr Weed arose and was taken up. They were all brought into the village and buried on the Sabbath, the first four in the forenoon and Mr. Weed in the afternoon. It was surely a solemn day. A deep gloom clothed the countenances of all, and it will long be remembered by the surviving connexions.

Samuel Blodget, better known to our elderly citizens as Judge Blodget, died in August. He was a native of Woburn, though he lived many years in this town. He was at the taking of Louisburg, in 1745, and before the Revolution he was the Judge of an Inferior Court in the County of Hillsborough, New-Hampshire.

Judge Blodget was an active, enterprising man, and possessed great mechanical ingenuity. In 1759, he established a pot and pearl ash works in this town, which were among the first in the Country, and a duck manufactory in 1791. In 1783, he raised a valuable cargo from a ship that was sunk near Plymouth, with a machine of his own invention. Encouraged with this success, he went to Europe for the purpose of raising money from a rich Spanish ship, but was not permitted to make the attempt. He then went to England for the

---

* Those who escaped, were Nicholas Colby, Moses Kimball, Joseph Kimball, Nathaniel Soley, and Joseph Wells.

purpose of weighing the Royal George, one of the largest ships in the British Navy, but met with no better success, and was looked upon as an enthusiast. In 1793, he began Blodget's canal, so called, at Amoskeag Falls. He labored several years on this work, and expended all his property on that, and in attempting to lock the falls; but without succeeding to his wishes. He attempted many works, but almost always failed in the execution. He was eccentric in his manners, though he possessed such a genius as would, if properly cultivated and accompanied with application, have immortalized his name.

The Judge intended to live one hundred years, and often told his friends that such was his calculation. His elixir vitæ was rigid temperance, activity, and to sleep, in all weathers, with open doors and windows. He did not, however, live so long as he expected, though he enjoyed uninterrupted health and cheerfulness until his sickness. He died in the 85th year of his age, of consumption, in consequence of exposing himself while travelling from Boston to Haverhill, in a cold night.

1808.

A Committee was chosen to present a petition to the President of the United States, " praying him to suspend a part or the whole of the Embargo Act."

Owing to the strong excitement and other causes which existed, after Rev. Mr. Abbot was dismissed, the First Parish was destitute of a regular minister until the 21st of December, when Rev. Joshua Dodge was ordained.

This year Haverhill Bridge was rebuilt. It is a noble structure, having four arches, supported by three stone piers, the stones of which are firmly fastened with iron. The draw, which should have been over the channel, is on the Haverhill shore, and is about 28 feet in width; much inconvenience is suffered on account of its narrowness. There is no bridge over the Merrimack, and but few in the New-England States, more durable, or of greater strength. The immense quantities of ice that are borne down the river with tremendous force, have no other effect upon it than a slight tremulous motion.

1810.

The Haverhill Light Infantry was organized on the 26th of May, and Jesse Harding was elected Captain. One of the articles of its constitution directs that, if any of its members should be removed by death, his body shall be consigned to the grave with military honors. On the 6th of May, 1823, an elegant standard was presented to the Company, by the Ladies of this village, through the hands of Miss Polly Dow, accompanied with a pertinent address. The ceremony of delivering and receiving it, was executed in an intelligent and graceful manner, and was spoken of at the time as being highly creditable to the parties. The Company is now commanded by Capt. Chauncey Hastings, who was elected in 1831, and there are but few independent Companies in the Commonwealth whose military conduct is more praiseworthy, and whose evolutions are more correct. The Company is furnished with tents and every other necessary requisite for a fatigue-march. In 1831, it established an armory, at an expense of over five hundred dollars; and the accoutrements are there kept in the neatest and most perfect order.

1812.

Some cakes of ice were seen passing in the river so late as the 24th of May.

The United States declared war against Great Britain on the 18th of June.

The town voted to give the soldiers, while in actual service, ten dollars per month, including the wages allowed by the General Government.

1814.

The spotted fever made its appearance in February, and a considerable number died with it in the course of the season.

10th Sept. The Militia Company of this town was ordered to appoint an "alarm post" and to hold themselves in readiness to march at a moment's warning. About the same time, the Light Infantry, commanded by Capt. Samuel W. Duncan, was ordered out by Governor Strong for the defence of the sea coast. They obeyed the summons with alacrity, and were highly spoken of for the correctness of their evolutions, and good conduct while engaged in the fatiguing duties of the camp.

The Merrimack Bank was incorporated 14th June, and began operations with a capital of $100,000. The capital was increased $50,000, February 2d, 1818.

1815.

23d Sept. This day will long be remembered for the violence of a gale, since called the "September Gale." It commenced about 9 o'clock in the morning, in this town, and continued till 2 in the afternoon. The air was filled with the limbs of trees, leaves, and a salt-spray blown from the Ocean, which encrusted on the east side of the buildings, and there remained for some days. The water in the river tasted extremely brackish; and the east side of many trees which withstood the fury of the gale, were killed, as is supposed, with the salt spray.

1816.

About this time the attention of the citizens of Haverhill and Newburyport was called to a subject very important to them, the removal of the obstructions to boat navigation on the Merrimack, between the former place and Pawtucket Falls. A Company was incorporated at the May Session for that purpose; but we believe that nothing of any consequence was done. In July, 1825, we find that a Committee was chosen "to survey the Merrimack above Haverhill, to ascertain the practicability of canalling the falls."

The summer of this year was extremely cold; and the hopes of the farmer were almost wholly destroyed.

In the fall a violent wind passed over some of the neighboring towns, and over the westerly part of this. The house of Mr. Ladd Haseltine was demolished, and his son, Jonathan, was killed by the falling chimney. Some other buildings were also blown down, and fences and trees were prostrated."

1817.

Phineas Woodbury, M. D., a native of New-London, New-Hampshire, died on the 1st of March. In 1813 he was appointed Surgeon in the U. S. Army; but finding his health gradually declining, he set out to return to his friends in New-Hampshire, and arrived at Haverhill on the 19th of February. He was a member of the Masonic Institution, and his brethren in this town, with true benevolence, attended him in his last sickness, and reared a handsome monument over his grave, on which is engraved a suitable inscription.

1818.

The Haverhill Female Benevolent Society was organized on the 13th of January. This Society is now in full operation, and the object of its benevolent members is to relieve such as are in needy circumstances. It now consists of sixty-five members, and any female may become a member by paying fifty cents annually. In

1827, it passed the following resolve:—"Resolved unanimously, that no wine, or cordial be admitted into the future meetings of this Society, and that every proper effort be made to promote temperance among its beneficiaries."

The present Stage Company went into operation in March, with a Capital of $4,200. In 1831 the capital had increased to $28,900.

Rev. William Bachelder, minister of the First Baptist Society, died on the 8th of April. He was born in Boston, on the 25th of March, 1768, and died in the twenty-sixth year of his ministry. But few men have passed from among us whose memories are more ardently cherished by the living, than is that of Mr. Bachelder. He adorned every relation in life, the civil, social and domestic. He was unwearied in the discharge of his duties, both temporal and spiritual, and made zealous efforts to promote the education of candidates for the ministry. The Maine Literary and Theological Institution, will long cherish his memory as one of its earliest patrons and warmest advocates. An ardent but humble piety shone in his daily conduct, and the patience and resignation which brightened his dying moments, accorded with his character as a minister and christian.

Brigadier General James Brickett died on the 10th of December. He practised Physic successfully for many years, in this town, and at an early period of the dispute between the Colonies and Great Britain, he ranked himself with the Whigs, and became a firm and devoted patriot. Soon after the war commenced, he enlisted in the Army, where he held the rank of a Brigadier General. In 1777, he went as a volunteer with the Company which marched from this town to the Plains of Stillwater, under the command of Capt. Nathaniel Marsh, and arrived just after a cessation of arms had been declared. He was appointed by General Gates to command the troops which escorted General Burgoyne and his suite to Albany. In this expedition he incurred considerable expense, and when he laid his account before Congress, that body refused to remunerate him, because he was not then an officer of the Army.

1819.

Miss Hannah Chase, a beautiful and amiable young lady, aged 22, committed suicide by drowning, on the 13th June. The verdict of the jury was thus:—"Her death, for aught that appears to us, was by sane suicide, unless insanity came suddenly upon her, of which it is impossible for us, under existing circumstances, to have knowledge."

1821.

Moses B. Moody presented two elegant stoves to the First Parish.

The Merrimack Society for improvement in the Arts and Sciences, was organized, October 2d.

The West Parish voted $10 to Rev. Joshua Dodge, "for past services." An invitation was extended to Mr. Thaddeus Pomeroy to settle, but he did not accept.

A clock was put up in the First Parish meeting-house, on the 1st December.

1822.

On the 16th of December, the First Parish raised $500 to purchase a new bell.

The Second Baptist Society was organized, and a meeting-house was completed in the fall. Rev. William Bowen was ordained. In the year following, a steeple was added to the house, and it is now a very convenient and handsome building.

1824.

A brick meeting-house was completed in October, for the Christian Society. The Church was gathered in 1806, and was supplied with Itinerant Preachers until the 2d of August, 1826, when Elder Henry Plummer was ordained. Elder Frederick Plummer was among the first who endeavored to promulgate the tenets of the Christians in this town. He embraced religion in early youth, and when about nineteen years of age, began to preach. He was ordained in the grove situated on the east bank of Little River, a few rods above the bridge; and he delivered a number of discourses from a large rock, which stood near the spot now occupied by the druggist-store of Dr. Moses Nichols.

1826.

The new brick meeting-house, erected in 1825, by the Universalist Society, was dedicated 12th April; and on the same day, Rev. Thomas G. Farnsworth was installed. This Society was incorporated 12th June, 1824.

25th May. A house belonging to Mr. Benjamin Bradley, with all the contents of the occupant, was destroyed by fire.

On the 14th of July, Andrew Frink disappeared in a sudden and mysterious manner. Immediately on the knowledge of his elopement, his friends and neighbors turned out *en masse* to discover him, but returned unsuccessful. About three weeks after, his body was found nearly two miles north of the village lying in a brook, in a loathsome and putrid state. Before his body was discovered, a strange, unknown man was seen by some people in the adjacent woods. When the people in the village heard of it, a party went in pursuit of the person, supposing him to be Mr. Frink. At length, with great difficulty, they succeeded in catching him, and found that it was not Mr. Frink, but literally a wild man of the woods. From the answers he gave to their questions, it was judged that he had been unfortunate in his intercourse with the world; and he refused to mingle with society.

Rev. Isaac Tompkins, minister of the East Parish, died on the 26th of November.

A donation of $300 was received by the First Parish, from a person unknown.

2d Aug. There was a violent hail storm in the East Parish. Eight days after, Mr. Daniel Johnson, brought a peck of hail into the village, which he collected from a heap then two and a half feet high. The heap was beside a fence at the foot of a hill.

Rev. Moses Welch was ordained in the North Parish, on the 26th of December, and on the following day, Rev. Moses G. Grosvenor was ordained in the West Parish.

1827.

An elegant brick building was completed for an Academy. It is two stories high, 62 feet in length, 33 feet in breadth, has a cupola, and is furnished with a bell. The Institution was opened on the 30th of April, when an oration was delivered by Hon. Leverett Saltonstall, of Salem, an Ode was sung, composed for the occasion, by John G. Whittier, of this town, and a Hymn, by Dea. Robert Dinsmoor, of Windham, New-Hampshire. Oliver Carlton, A. M., was the first instructer. The land on which the building stands, was presented to the proprietors by two aged ladies, Lydia and Abigail Marsh, both of whom have since died. It is sincerely hoped that this Institution will soon become as eminent for its literary, moral and religious character, as any other of the kind in the State.

Agreeably with the request of Rev. Joshua Dodge, the connexion between him and the First Parish, was dissolved on the 18th of June.

4th July. The citizens celebrated the day in a splendid manner. An Oration was delivered by Nathan W. Hazen, Esq., and the meeting-house was tastefully decorated by the ladies.

9th Oct. The house and barn of Daniel Appleton, and the barn of Hon. James H. Duncan, with its contents and some cattle, were destroyed by fire. The loss was computed at 7 or 8,000 dollars. On the 22d of November, a new house belonging to Benjamin Godkin, was destroyed by the same element; and on the 14th of December, the barn of Jonathan K. Smith. These fires, excepting that of Mr. Godkin, were supposed to have been the work of an incendiary.

The town raised $600 to build Engine-houses, and procure fire apparatus.

1828.

Rev. Dudley Phelps was ordained in the First Parish on the 9th of January, and is the present pastor.

5th Feb. The Haverhill Temperance Society was organized, on the principle of total abstinence.

The West Parish gave Rev. Moses G. Grosvenor notice that his service was no longer wanted.

The Merrimack Bridge, connecting the Rocks' Village with West-Newbury, was completed in the fall of this year. It is built on Towne's system. It is 900 feet in length, is supported by four stone piers, and two abutments, each extending some distance from the shore. It has four defensive piers, or sterlings, extending some distance above, and a draw.

Serious difficulties made their appearance in the West Parish Society. They were not allayed in the onset as they should have been, but were permitted to ripen, and the [consequence was, a separation of the parties. One of them now occupies the old meeting-house, and on the 26th of October, Rev. Daniel D. Smith was ordained. In 1831, he left, according to the articles of agreement. The party which left the first meeting-house, erected a handsome brick edifice, about a mile west of it.

1830.

Haverhill Lyceum was established on the 25th of February.

In March an elegant organ was put up in the meeting-house of the First Parish. A few of our worthy citizens who felt desirous of improving the church music, stepped forward, bought an organ, and loaned it to the parish.

The late venerable High Sheriff of Essex County, Hon. Bailey Bartlett, died on the 9th of September, aged 80. Mr. Bartlett received only a common school education, and kept an English goods store, as did his father, till 1789; yet a great taste for reading marked every period of his life. He had also a taste for agriculture and mechanism, and was an early member of the Agricultural Society of the State and of the County. His mechanical genius, he turned toward the art of constructing bridges, and suggested many improvements.

Mr. Bartlett lived at the period of our Revolution, and was a firm friend of John Adams, and a fellow boarder with him and Samuel Adams on the memorable 4th of July, 1776. When the declaration of Independence was proclaimed in the yard of Congress Hall, he was present, and has often said that it was received with murmurs by the crowd. On the 1st of July, 1789, he was appointed Sheriff. Gov. Hancock presented him with the commission in person, and stated to him that he did it with peculiar pleasure, as it was the only nomination which met the unanimous concurrence of his council. He held the office until the day of his death, with the exception of only six months, when he was elected Treasurer of the County.

In 1797, he succeeded Judge Bradbury as Representative of Essex North District, in the Congress of the United States, of which he was a member four years. He was a member of that body during the contest between Thomas Jefferson and Aaron Burr; and was the chamber companion of the late Chief Justice Parker, between whom a cordial friendship existed until the death of the latter. Judge Parker, in a letter to a friend, thus bears testimony to his worth; he says:—"he is the last man whose feelings I would intentionally wound, having, for more than thirty years, known the purity and integrity of his character, both public and private." Nineteen days before his death, he attended

Court, when sentence of death was pronounced on the unhappy Knapp. He returned the same day to Haverhill, when it took several persons to lift him from his chaise.

Mr. Bartlett was the oldest officer in Massachusetts, except the Clerk of the County of Middlesex, and probably held the office of Sheriff longer than any other person. He was generally beloved by the citizens, and whenever they met him, they did homage, not only to his gray hairs, but to his virtues. On the day of his funeral, many of the shops were closed, and his neighbors generally attended to pay him their last tribute of respect—to mourn over the remains of one who had been long among them, and to take a last look of the man they respected.

His virtues were not wholly of a private nature. While he held the office of Sheriff, he was kind and indulgent, almost to a fault, to the unfortunate victims of the law; and it is said that he often paid the exaction of the creditor out of his own purse, rather than to imprison the poor debtor. His kind treatment of a political libeller estranged some of his political friends, but added a bright gem to his character. In the last war an attempt was made to tax Marshal Prince, of this State, with barbarous treatment of the British prisoners; but the Sheriff immediately stepped forward, fearlessly vindicated the character of the Marshal, and bore testimony to his humanity.

1831.

Rev. Samuel H. Peckham was ordained in the North Parish, on the 18th of February, and the same council dismissed Rev. Moses Welch.

Rev. Abijah Cross was ordained over the Society attending the new brick meeting-house in the West Parish, on the 18th of May.

The Youth's Temperance Association was organized, on the principle of total abstinence.

TOPOGRAPHY.

Haverhill is pleasantly situated on the Merrimack, a large and noble river, and, following its channel, is about eighteen miles from its mouth. It is about twenty-nine miles from Boston, twenty-two from Salem, twelve from Newburyport, and thirty from Portsmouth, the most populous town in New-Hampshire. It is bounded on the North, by the southern line of New-Hampshire; on the South, by Bradford and West Newbury; on the East, by Amesbury, and on the West, by Methuen. The Merrimack and its islands, belong to this town, as will be seen by the deed, which conveys to the inhabitants of Pentucket "the river and the islands in the river." We have been informed that this subject—the claim of Haverhill to the river and its islands—has heretofore excited some controversy among individuals; but, if they will take the pains to examine the deed critically, it will be seen, that the claim of Haverhill is indisputable.

This is an ancient town; and since its settlement, in 1640, eight towns, now containing a large population, have been settled wholly, or in part, by its inhabitants. The names of these towns are, Methuen, Salem, Atkinson, Plaistow, Hampstead, Chester, Concord and Haverhill; all except Methuen are in New-Hampshire. The town, when it was purchased of the original proprietors, was twelve miles in length, and six in breadth, with the river and its islands. In 1725, Methuen was incorporated, and about two miles were taken from the west end and added to that town. In 1737, Commissioners were appointed by the Crown of England, to establish the long disputed boundary line between the Colonies of Massachusetts and New-Hampshire. This line was run through the centre of Haverhill—hence three miles has, ever since, been under the jurisdiction of New-Hampshire. The town is now about ten miles in length, and three in breadth, besides the river. It contains fifteen thousand acres, and the soil is generally very productive. In the West and North Parishes, there are a few farms under a very high state of cultivation. Perhaps it will not be amiss, as we have just alluded to the farming interest, to mention the name of David How, Esq., who, it is believed, has owned more land, and carried on the farming business to a greater extent than any other person in Massachusetts. He delights to till the earth, and has spared no pains to enrich and cultivate it. He has retrieved many acres of worn-out land, and brought many lots of barren and unprofitable soil to a high state of cultivation.

There are three small streams in the town, besides the Merrimack, called Little River, Creek Brook, and Country Brook. Little River takes its rise in Plaistow, N. H., and empties into the Merrimack at the western part of the village. A few rods from its mouth, there is a flannel manufactory, a saw-mill, and grain-mill, owned by Mr. Ezekiel Hale. Large quantities of alewives are caught in this stream. Creek Brook is in the West Parish, and takes its rise from Creek Pond. It carries two grain-mills; one of which is owned by Mr. Aaron Chapman, and the other by Mr. Enoch Bradley, jr. Country Brook runs through the East Parish, and empties into the Merrimack. It carries two saw-mills, one carding-machine, one fulling-mill, and one grain-mill. One of the saw-mills is owned by Mr. Joab Peasley, and the other by Mr. Cyrus Noyes; the carding-machine is also owned by Mr. Noyes; the clothing-mill is owned by Mr. John Chase, and the grain-mill by Mr. Leonard Johnson.

There are four Ponds within the limits of the town, and three of them are situated within a mile of the village, and within half a mile of each other.

Creek Pond is in the West Parish, near Mr. Aaron Chapman's mills. The shores are irregular, the waters clear almost to transparency, and it has, for the most part, an even and sandy bottom. There are many fine farms in the neighborhood, and the surrounding scenery is exceedingly beautiful.

Plug Pond is situated a short distance north of the village. In the months of July and August, the water presents a greenish and disagreeable appearance. It is better known to many of our elderly people by the name of Ayer's Pond; it was so called, because the Ayers settled near it, and owned most of the adjoining land.

Round Pond is but a short distance from Plug pond. It is wholly fed by springs issuing from the bottom, and from this circumstance the water is exceedingly cold. The village is supplied with pure, good water, by an aqueduct from this pond. Pickerel and perch are caught in its waters. This pond is also better known to our elderly people, by the name of Belknap's Pond, from a man of that name who settled near it.

Great Pond is situated only a few rods from Round Pond. Perhaps there is not a more beautiful body of water in New-England; the scenery which surrounds it is delightful. The southern and eastern shores exhibit a succession of hills of various heights, thickly wooded with tall pines and oaks, which fling their deep shadows over the transparent waters below. In these woods the coy partridge is found, and various other kinds of game, which affords a pleasant amusement and healthy exercise to those who are skilled in gunnery. Its northern shores rise more gradually, affording a beautiful prospect of cultivated farms, large orchards, and neat and commodious dwelling-houses. The water covers about 250 acres, and is, in some places, fifty feet in depth. Its surface is 150 feet from the bed of the Merrimack; it abounds with white and red perch, and pickerel of the largest size have frequently been caught there. This pond has become a fashionable resort for parties from the village.

There are some eminences in the town, but none which can be dignified with the title of mountains; among them are Golden Hill, Silver's Hill, Turkey Hill, and Brandy Brow. Golden Hill is situated about a mile east of Haverhill bridge, and its base is only a few rods from the Merrimack. It is in full view of the village, and was, a few years since, brought under a high state of cultivation, by the exertions of David How, Esq. The prospect from its brow is extensive and picturesqe; the Merrimack flows majestically at its base, where boats of almost every description, from the heavy gondola to the light and trembling skiff, are seen gliding along its surface. And now and then a larger craft, with its shrouds and white masts lifted high in the air, and its broad sails overshadowing the water.

Silver's Hill is situated about three fourths of a mile west of Haverhill bridge, and is also plainly seen from that place. The Merrimack runs at its base; it is now owned by David How, Esq., and is, of course, in a high state of cultivation. It took its name from a former owner.

Turkey Hill is composed of a long, irregular range of elevated land, situated in the East Parish. It rises considerably above the East Parish meeting-house, which stands at its base.

Brandy Brow is situated in the northerly part of the town. A part of it is composed of a stone which presents a reddish appearance, and, perhaps, from this circumstance it took its name. Upon the brow of this hill, there is a large rock which stands at the corner of four towns—Haverhill, Plaistow, Amesbury, and Newtown.

There are no extensive forests, and most of the wood used is brought from the neighboring towns. We have noticed many kinds of trees in the various parts of the town, and it may be said that the oak predominates. There is, also, the walnut, sycamore, elm, locust, hemlock, spruce, ash, white and black birch, willow, alder, wild black cherry, plum, white and pitch pine, and a few white and rock maple. There are many others of a smaller kind, but which would more properly rank with the shrub. The sycamore, or buttonwood, as it is more frequently called, attains to the greatest size. About twenty of them are now standing on the bank of the Merrimack, before the mansion of Wid. Samuel W. Duncan; and, together with the willows which adorn the bank of the river for some distance, make a delightful shade. This appears to be a favorite retreat of the citizens of all classes, and on the pleasant evenings of summer, it is frequently thronged.

Our fields abound with various kinds of delicious fruit, which grow spontaneously, and some of them in great abundance—among which, are the whortleberry, blueberry, strawberry, raspberry, and vine and bush blackberry. Many gardens are enriched with peaches, rareripes, and plums of every description; and a few fine growing orchards are almost in the heart of the village. Considerable attention is paid, especially by the ladies, to the culture of exotic flowers and plants.

The location of Haverhill Village is exceedingly beautiful. Golden Hill rises abruptly on the East, and Silver's Hill rises more gradually on the West. The noble Merrimack runs on the South, and winds around it in the form of a crescent. The village is built on the south side of a gentle acclivity, which rises gradually from the river, the houses appearing one above another, affording a delightful view. The two principal streets, Water and Main-streets, are somewhat irregular; and this, together with the irregular structure of some of the buildings, are almost the only things which mar the prospect. Water-street is a mile or more in length, and is thickly lined on both sides with buildings of every description; it runs parallel with the river. Main-street intersects with Water-street opposite Haverhill bridge, and runs north. This is a very pleasant street, and is adorned on each side with a number of elegant buildings. The early settlers calculated that a village would, at some period, rise on the site of the present one, for in 1643, when the accommodation grant, spoken of in that year, was surveyed, these two streets were reserved. A few years since, Summer-street was opened on the brow of the hill, intersecting with Main-street, and the north side is adorned with elegant dwelling-houses. This is the pleasantest street in the village. No buildings are erected on the south side of it, which leaves a charming prospect of the green hills of Bradford, on the opposite side of the river, and of the picturesque village which lies beneath it. A number of other streets have been opened within a few years, which add much to the beauty of the town.

There are eight houses for public worship within the limits of the town; four of which are in the village, two in the West Parish, and two in the East Parish. The denominations which worship in them, are, one Christian, one Universalist, two Baptists, and four Congregationalists. The meeting-house in Plaistow, stands but a few rods from the line of Haverhill, and is principally owned by the inhabitants of the North Parish. There are a few Friends in town, but they have no house for worship.

In the easterly part of the town, there is another village, called the "Rocks Village," which is now in a very flourishing condition. It has three stores, one tavern, a house for public worship, and is celebrated for its manufactory of horn combs. It is connected with West-Newbury by Merrimack bridge, which affords a safe and easy communication, and will doubtless increase the trade of the village. It was owing to the enterprise and energy of a few individuals of that place, that this bridge was erected. This village has grown up within a few years, and most of the buildings have the appearance of being new. Before 1800, there was a ship-yard in this place, and a few vessels were built.

There is another small village in the North Parish, consisting of fifteen or twenty houses, principally situated on the main road to Concord, New-Hampshire. The people are principally tillers of the soil, and the most of them are, what is called, "forehanded farmers." Their meeting-house, which is situated in Plaistow, was erected before the boundary line was established between the two provinces. Soon after this was effected, a few of the inhabitants petitioned the General Court for liberty to hold meetings and act, in all respects, as a "distinct and separate Precinct." This liberty was granted, and they have, ever since, enjoyed all immunities commonly allowed to Parishes—though they have generally, since 1737, united with Plaistow to procure a minister. We have been thus particular in making these statements, because many people have thought that they did not enjoy the privilege of raising and appropriating monies, and other immunities of a parish, without the concurring voice of Plaistow.

Haverhill is a place of considerable business, and has, of late become quite a manufacturing town; its importance, however, is not so great as its central situation deserves. It has an extensive back country, and is a good market for most kinds of country produce. The farmer can sell his articles here nearly or quite as advantageously as at any other market, and foreign and domestic goods can generally be purchased as cheap as in Boston. There are about forty stores, and many of them are well filled with every description of goods.

The article of shoes, is now extensively manufactured. It is impossible to state the exact number of pairs that are annually made, or the stock invested in the trade. A few houses have been so obliging as to furnish us with a statement of their manufactures, for the past year, and the aggregate is over 1,000,000. If this business increases as rapidly for a few years to come as it has the three last years, no town in the State will exceed this in the number of shoes manufactured, or the amount of capital invested in the trade. Some of our most worthy and enterprising young men are engaged in the business.

Large quantities of hats are manufactured, which are exported to the southern States, and other places. The most extensive establishment is owned by Mr. Nathan Webster; there is another in the village, owned by Mr. David Webster, four in the West Parish, owned by Messrs Isaac How, Phineas How, Jonathan Crowell, and Gilman Haynes; one in the North Parish, owned by Mr. Samuel Whittaker. These establishments employ a great number of workmen. Hats are manufactured to the amount of $100,000 annually.

The manufacture of horn combs is very extensive. This business is confined wholly to the East Parish. We were informed by a number of intelligent gentlemen, who carry on the business, that the amount of combs manufactured in the year 1831, would exceed $30,000. It gives employment to about a hundred persons of both sexes; and no doubt, will be a source of profit to the enterprising gentlemen engaged in the business.

The tanning of leather is carried on to a considerable extent, though not so extensively as is desirable—for a large portion of the leather manufactured, is purchased in other places. The currying business is also considerable, and there are a few extensive establishments of this description.

A few years since, the manufacture of leather gloves was carried on extensively; and about thirty men were constantly employed in manufacturing plated ware for saddles, harnesses, and other articles, before the tax was laid upon it. This business, however, begins to revive, and a number of establishments are now in the West Parish in full operation.

Ship-building, we are sorry to say, is not so extensive as it was before 1800. At that period, and even before the revolution, it was considered a very important branch of business. Many ships were built and a large quantity of shipping was owned, for so small a place, which was principally employed in the West India trade. Ships of four hundred tons can be safely launched in the Merrimack at high tide. In 1810, vessels were built, amounting to 1800 tons; both ship-yards were occupied, and about sixty men were constantly employed in them. This business was seriously interrupted by the restrictive measures of Government previous to the last war, but it began to revive with the revival of commerce, and so late as 1816, it was deemed profitable and important. It is hoped that the business will be pursued with energy, as considerable quantities of fine timber are now growing in the vicinity, the average price of which is five dollars per ton.

Perhaps it will not be amiss before this work is closed, to make a few remarks on the character of the early inhabitants. It has already been said that the settlement was projected and headed by a minister, who was a worthy and upright man. His people mostly followed his example, and prided themselves on the purity of their moral conduct, and extreme exactness of their religious devotions. We are bold to assert that there was no settlement in the vicinity, containing a less number of idle and vicious persons, in proportion to the population, than this. The Court Files are a good criterion to judge by in this matter; and, while examining them, we were surprised to find so small a number of prosecutions for immoral conduct. This state of things continued until the commencement of the Indian wars, when the moral and religious feeling of the inhabitants began sensibly to deteriorate. This was natural; for war, of whatever description, has a powerful tendency to lessen the regard of the parties for religious devotions—to undermine the moral feelings, however firmly they may be established, and indeed, to blunt all the finer sensibilities of the heart. Religious and moral admonitions were then less frequently given; the father had other things to employ his thoughts—the life of the mother was one of continued fear for herself and for those she loved, and while fear predominates in the breast, it is surely a poor time to administer religious instruction. The person then, who possessed vicious inclinations and an ill-natured disposition, had greater liberty to indulge them, and consequently more power to corrupt companions.

After the close of the wars, the inhabitants did not return to the primitive simplicity which characterized them before their commencement. A new generation was on the stage—new opinions and new desires had become popular, and the primeval ones were laid aside. Ignorance, with his cloven foot and beastly shape, stalked among them; for nearly all thoughts of schools, in the time of the wars, were, of course, relinquished. It may be truly called an age of darkness; immorality and vice fearlessly erected their standards, and battled too successfully with the advocates of opposite principles.

This state of things continued, with but little deviation, until the great reformation in 1740, which affected the greater part of New-England. Public morals and the religious feelings of the inhabitants, then met with a great and radical change. They have ever since been gradually ripening, and at no period since the settlement, have the public morals been elevated to so high and noble a standard as at the present day. This is, perhaps, contrary to the settled opinions of many; but, while developing the morals of the early inhabitants, we endeavored to compare them impartially with those of the present age, and became satisfied that what we have now asserted is substantially correct.

We do not wish to be understood, that the moral and religious opinions and deportment of the early settlers exercised no influence over the succeeding generations. On the contrary, they did exercise influence of a most salutary nature; which was not confined to that generation, but is felt and acknowledged, even when the last of its number has long mouldered in the dust. And even at this day, there is a living power among us which was established by the early settlers, nearly two centuries ago. It lived through the darkest age of immorality and has descended to us, not in its primordial shape, but in a purer and less bigoted form.

Our history is now finished. We have narrated—and have endeavored to do it impartially—the principal events which have transpired since the settlement. The work was commenced with a knowledge of the high and responsible duty which every historian owes to the public, and with a full determination to discharge it as faithfully as our humble abilities would permit. If we have related incidents which injure the feelings of those who are proud of ancestral honor—if we have spoken of by-gone characters in a manner which wounds the pride of some of the present generation, we are free to say, that our opinions were not biassed by fear, or the promise of reward—that the fault, if any exists, is not with us, but with their ancestors. On a few subjects, we have differed materially from some of our friends, but we have not ventured to utter our opinions until they had been closely investigated. We may have erred—we would not be considered infallible—and if we have, the reader may be assured that it was not intentionally.

APPENDIX.

Succession of Ministers.

FIRST PARISH.

Names.	Time of Ordination.	Deceased.	Age.
Rev. John Ward,	———— 1641,	Dec. 27, 1693,	88.
" Benjamin Rolfe,	Jan. 7, 1694,	Aug. 29, 1708,	46.
" Joshua Gardner,	Jan. 10, 1711,	March 21, 1715,	28.
" John Brown,	May 13, 1719,	Dec. 2, 1742,	46.
" Edward Barnard,	April 27, 1743,	Jan. 26, 1774,	54.
" John Shaw,	March 12, 1777,	Sept. 29, 1794,	48.
" Abiel Abbot,	June 8, 1795,	June 13, 1803.*	
" Joshua Dodge,	Dec. 21, 1808,	June 18, 1827.*	
" Dudley Phelps,	Jan. 9, 1828.		

NORTH PARISH.

Rev. James Cushing,	Oct. —, 1730,	May 13, 1764,	59.
" Gyles Merrill,	March 6, 1765,	April 27, 1801,	62.
" Moses Welch,	Dec. 26, 1826,	Feb. 17, 1831.*	
" Sam'l H. Peckham,	Feb. 18, 1831.		

WEST PARISH—FIRST SOCIETY.

Rev. Samuel Bachellor,	July —, 1735,	Oct. 9, 1761.*	
" Phineas Adams,	————, 1770,	Nov. 17, 1801,	60.
" Moses G. Grosvenor,	Dec. 27, 1826,	————, 1828.*	
" Daniel D. Smith,	Oct. 26, 1828.		

EAST PARISH.

Rev. Benjamin Parker,	Nov. —, 1744,	Jan. 21, 1777,*	72.
" Isaac Tompkins,	Jan. 7, 1797,	Nov. 21, 1826,	65.
" John H. Stevens,	————, 1829.		

FIRST BAPTIST SOCIETY.

Rev. Hezekiah Smith,	Nov. 12, 1766,	Jan. 24, 1805,	67.
" William Batchelder,	Nov. —, 1805,	April 8, 1818,	51.
" George Keely,	Oct. 7, 1818.		

SECOND BAPTIST SOCIETY.

Rev. William Bowen,	————, 1825.	
" Otis Wing.		

FIRST UNIVERSALIST SOCIETY.

Rev. T. G. Farnsworth,	April 12, 1826.	

CHRISTIAN SOCIETY.

Elder Henry Plummer,	Aug. 2, 1826.	

WEST PARISH—SECOND SOCIETY.

Rev. Abijah Cross,	May 18, 1831.	

* Time dismissed.

CATALOGUE
Of the natives of Haverhill, who have received a College Education.

HARVARD COLLEGE.

1684—*Gurdonus Saltonstall, Mr., V. D. M.,
[Connec. Colon. Gub.
1695—*Nathanael Saltonstall, Mr., Tutor.
1695—*Richardus Saltonstall, Mr.
1709—*Johannes Wainwright, Mr.
1710—*Obadias Ayer, Mr.
1717—*Richardus Hazzen, Mr.
1720—*Timotheus White, Mr.
1722—*Richardus Saltonstall, Mr., Mass.
[Prov. Cur. Sup. Jurid.
1727—*Nathanael Saltonstall, Mr.
1737—*Moses Emerson, Mr.
1741—*Johannes Brown, Mr.
1743—*Jacobus Pecker, Mr., M. M. S. V. Præses.
1743—*Cotton Brown, Mr.
1748—*Ward Brown
1751—*Richardus Saltonstall, Mr.
1751—*Johannes White, Mr.
1752—*Thomas Brown, Mr.
1757—*Jeremias Pecker, Mr., 1761
1759—*Johannes Whittier, Mr.
1761—*Moses Badger, Mr.
1761—*Johannes Marsh, Mr., S. T. D. Tut.
1766—*Nathanael Saltonstall, Mr., M. M. S. Soc.
1771—*Johannes White, Mr.
1772—*Josua-Bailey Osgood, Mr.
1773—*Daniel Parker, Mr., 1782
1774—*Edvardus Barnard, Mr.
1775—*Isaacus Osgood, Mr.
1787—Leonard White, Mr.
1787—Petrus Eaton, Mr., S. T. D.
1792—Stephanus-Peabody Webster, Mr.
1793—Phineas Adams, Mr.
1795—Josua Wingate, Mr.
1798—*Gulielmus-Smith Shaw, Mr., A. A. et. S. H. S.
1802—Leverett Saltonstall, Mr., A. A. et. S. H. S.
1804—Ebenezer Greenough

1804—Moses Webster, Mr.
1806—*Thomas Tracy*, Mr., 1816
1807—Jacobus-Cushing Merrill, Mr., S. H. Soc.
1807—Samuel Merrill, Mr.
1810—*Samuel-White Duncan, Mr.
1810—Isaacus-Reddington How, Mr.
1812—Jacobus-Henricus Duncan, Mr.
1813—Richardus Saltonstall, Mr.
1828—Carolus Minot, Mr.

YALE COLLEGE.

1809—Theodore Eames, Mr.
1814—Johannes-Mulliken Atwood
1821—Carolus Atwood, Mr.

DARTMOUTH COLLEGE.

1798—Gulielmus Moody
1802—*Samuel Walker*
1810—Moses S. Moody
1813—Benjamin Greenleaf, Mr.

UNION COLLEGE.

1831—Nathanael Hills

LIST
of the Representatives of Haverhill.
[Copied principally from the Legislative Files.]

1648 to 1654, Robert [Clement
1654, John Clement
1655 to 1660, none
1660, John Davis--2d Session
1661 to 1666, none
1666, Nath'l Saltonstall
1667, Henry Palmer
1668, William Davis
1669 to 1672, Nathaniel [Saltonstall
1672, George Brown
1673, Humphrey Davy--2d Session
1674, Henry Palmer
1675, George Brown
1676 to 1680, Henry [Palmer
1680, George Brown
1681, Daniel Hendrick
1682, none
1683, Peter Ayer
1684, Robert Swan
1685 and 1686, Peter Ayer
1687 to 1689, none
1689 and 1690, Peter Ayer
1691, John Johnson
1692, { George Brown / Samuel Hutchins

1693, { Daniel Ladd / Thomas Hart
1694, Daniel Ladd
1695 and 1696, Peter Ayer
1697, John Page
1698, Peter Ayer
1699, Richard Saltonstall
1700, John White
1701, Samuel Ayer
1702, John White
1703, { John White, 1st Session--John Haseltine, 2d Session
1704 and 1705, Samuel [Watts
1706 and 1707, James [Saunders
1708, John White
1709, James Saunders
1710 to 1713, John Ha- [seltine
1713, John White
1714, John Haseltine
1715 and 1716, John [White
1717, Amos Singletary
1718, John Saunders
1719, John White
1720 to 1726, John Saun- [ders
1726 and 1727, James [Saunders
1728 and 1729, Richard [Saltonstall
1730 to 1733, Nathan [Webster
1733 and 1734, William [White
1735 and 1736, Richard [Saltonstall
1737, Nathaniel Peasley
1738, Richard Saltonstall
1739 to 1742, Nathaniel [Peasley
1742, Richard Hazzen
1743, Richard Saltonstall
1744 and 1745, Philip [Haseltine
1746 to 1749, Nathaniel [Peasley
1749 and 1750, Nathaniel [Saunders
1751, John Haseltine
1752 and 1753, Nathaniel [Peasley
1754, Richard Saltonstall
1755 to 1761, David Marsh
1761 to 1769, Richard [Saltonstall
1769 and 1770, Samuel [Bachellor
1771 to 1776, Jonathan [Webster, jr.
1776, { Jona. Webster / Nath'l P. Sargent
1777 to 1781, Jonathan [Webster
1781 to 1784, Bailey [Bartlett
1784 and 1785, Samuel [White
1786, Nathaniel Marsh
1787, Isaac Osgood
1788, { Bailey Bartlett / Nathaniel Marsh
1789 and 1790, Nathaniel [Marsh
1791, { Francis Carr / Samuel Blodget
1792, to 1796, Francis Carr
1796, none
1797 and 1798, Nathaniel [Marsh
1799, Benjamin Willis

1800, Benjamin Willis
1801, none
1802 and 1803, Francis [Carr
1804 to 1807, David How
1807 and 1808, James [Smiley
1809, Leonard White
1810 and 1811, Ebenezer [Gage
1812 to 1819, David How
1819, Charles White
1820, to 1823, Moses Wingate
1823 and 1824, Enoch [Foot
1825, Stephen Minot
1826, none

1827, { Moses Wingate / James H. Duncan
1828, { Charles White / John Brickett, jr.
1829, { Thomas Harding / John Brickett, jr. / William Bachellor
1830, { Thomas Harding / William Bachellor / John Brickett, jr.
1831, Caleb B. LeBosquet
1832, Caleb B. LeBosquet
" Thos. G. Farnsworth
" Ephraim Corliss
" James Davis, chosen 2d Monday in November, 1831.

CENSUS OF HAVERHILL---1830.

MALES.

Under 5	5 to 10	10 to 15	15 to 20	20 to 30	30 to 40	40 to 50	50 to 60	60 to 70	70 to 80	80 to 90	90 to 100
257	233	206	221	426	265	141	90	75	33	12	1

FEMALES.

Under 5	5 to 10	10 to 15	15 to 20	20 to 30	30 to 40	40 to 50	50 to 60	60 to 70	70 to 80	80 to 90	90 to 100
244	188	193	187	416	258	175	127	96	45	19	4

Males, - - - - 1960
Females, - - - 1952

Total, - - - - 3912
Population in 1820, - - 3070

Gain, - - - - 842

The population at present is about 4200. More than half of the inhabitants reside within half a mile of Haverhill Bridge.

DIRECTORY.

Professional Gentlemen.
Brickett, Daniel *Physician.*
Cross, Abijah *Clergyman.*
Duncan, James H. *Lawyer.*
Farnsworth, Thomas G. *Clergyman.*
Howe, Isaac R. *Lawyer.*
Keely, George *Clergyman.*
Kinnison, Timothy *Physician.*
Longley, Rufus *Physician.*
Minot, Charles *Lawyer.*
Minot, Stephen *Lawyer.*
Parker, Gilman *Lawyer.*
Peckham, Samuel H. *Clergyman.*
Phelps, Dudley *Clergyman.*
Plummer, Henry *Clergyman.*
Stevens, John H. *Clergyman.*
Whiting, Augustus *Physician.*
Wing, Otis *Clergyman.*

Merchants, Manufacturers, Mechanics, &c. &c.
Alley, Joseph A. *Tailor*, Osgood's Building.
Ames, Ezra C. *Merchant*, No. 5, Main-street.
Appleton, J. A. & G. & Co. *Merchants*, Water-st.
Appleton, John *Tailor*, No. 2, Mechanics' Row.
Ayer, George W. *Shipwright*, Water-st.
Ayer, James 2d *Joiner*, Green-st.
Ayer, Richard *Tanner*, West Parish.
Ayer, Samuel W. *Grocer*, Water-st.

Bailey, Benjamin *Wheelwright*, West Parish.
Bailey, Phineas *Wheelwright*, " "
Balch, J. & M. P. *Watchmakers & Jewellers*, Main-st.
Bartlett, Charles L. *Deputy Sheriff*, Water-st.
Bartlett, Israel *Silversmith*, Water-st.
Brickett, John *Blacksmith*, North Parish.
Brickett, John jr, " "
Brown, William *Tavern and Livery Stable*, Main-st.
Burr, Harriet *Milliner*, Water-st.

Caldwell, Jacob *Shoe Manufacturer*, East Parish.
Caldwell, William *Distiller*, Water-st.
Caldwell & Pierce, *Merchants & Shoe Manufacturers*, [Water-st.
Carleton, Charles *Mason*, West Parish.
Carleton, Israel jr. *Tanner & Currier*, near Plug Pond.
Carleton, I. jr. & J. *Stove Manufacturers*, "
Carleton, Michael *Clock & Watch-maker*, Water-st.
Carleton & Newcomb, *Merchants & Silversmiths*, Water-st.
Chamberlain, John *Chaise-maker*, Water-st.
Chapman, Aaron *Miller*, West Parish.
Chase, Abigail *Milliner*, No. 9, Main-st.
Chase, Anthony *Shoe Manufacturer*, East Parish.
Chase, John *Clothier*, "
Chase, Moody *Taverner*, Washington-st.
Chase, Samuel *Merchant & Shoe Manufacturer*, Water-st.
Chase, Tappan *Grocer & Shoe Manufac'r*, East Parish.
Chase, Thomas G. *Comb Manufacturer*, Rocks' Village.
Cochrane & Brown, *Merchants*, Water-st.
Colby, Stephen *Joiner*, River-st.
Colby, William " "
Corliss, John jr. *Silversmith*, West Parish.
Corliss, Phineas *Cigar Manufacturer*, No. 11, **Main-st**.
Crowell, Jonathan *Hat Manufacturer*, West Parish.
Currier, Hugh M. *Mason*, Water-st.
Currier, Nathaniel jr, *Currier*, Main-st.

Davis, Charles *Shoe Manufacturer*, Water-st.
Davis, James *Comb Manufacturer*, Rocks' Village.
Davis, John *Chaise & Harness-maker*, Main-st.
Dole & Kimball, *Chaise-makers*, River-st.
Dole, Paul *Grocer*, "
Dow, Charles W. *Carpenter*, East Parish.
Dow, John *Merchant*, No. 3 Main-st.
Dunbar, Charles H. *Cabinet & Chair-maker*, Water-st.

Easterbrook, Joseph, *Joiner*, Rocks' Village.
Easterbrook, Samuel, *Mason*, "
Eaton, Jeremiah B. *Chaise-maker*, Water-st.
Eaton, Job *Cabinet-maker*, "
Eaton, Timothy *Plater*, West Parish.
Eaton, Ward *Grocer*, Hale's Mills.

Edwards & Harding, *Curriers*, Water-st.
Edwards, John *Constable*, Pecker-st.
Emerson, B. & M. E. *Butchers*, Main-st.
Emerson, Benjamin 2d, *Shoe Manufacturer*, Main-st.
Emerson, Ithamar *Plough Manufacturer*, North Parish.
Emerson, Jesse *Shoe Manufacturer*, West Parish.
Emerson, Moses 3d, *Merchant*, Water-st.
Emerson, Nathan *Joiner*, West Parish.

Farnum, Roswell *Shoe & Boot-maker*, Main-st.
Fitts, Jeremiah *Joiner*, River-st.
Foot, Enoch *Merchant*, Rocks' Village.
Foot, Samuel C. *Comb Manufacturer*, Rocks' Village.
Foss, William *Currier*, Water-st.

Gale, James *Bookseller & Stationer*, Water-st.
Gale, Moses *Merchant*,   "
Galley, James *Barber*,   "
George, Samuel *Shoe Manufacturer*, "
George, William *Carpenter*, East Parish.
Gilman, Frederick *Barber*, Water-st.
Goodridge, Barnard *Shipwright*, Water-st.
Goodridge, Ezekiel   "   "
Gould, William A. *Harness-maker*, Stage-st.
Greely, Joseph *Shoe Manufacturer*, Water-st.
Gubtal & Haseltine, *Shoe Manufacturers*, Water-st.

Harriman & Sargent, *Printers*, Main-st.
Hale, Ezekiel *Woollen Manufacturer*, Hale's Mills.
Hammond, Andrew W. *Chaise-maker*, Water-st.
Harding, Thomas *Tanner*,   "
Harmon & Kimball, *Merchants & Shoe Manufacturers*,
                                                     [Water-st.
Harriman, Nathan B. *Blacksmith*, West Parish.
Haseltine, Abigail W. *Mantuamaker*, Water-st.
Hasselton, Ladd *Chaise-maker*, West Parish.
Hasselton, Leonard   "   "
Hasselton, Samuel *Plater*,   "
Hasselton, Stephen *Blacksmith*, North Parish.
Hasselton, Ward *Chaise-maker*, West "
Hastings, Chauncey *Silversmith*, Water-st.
Hayes, Thomas M. *Morocco Dresser*, "
Haynes, Gilman *Hat Manufacturer*, West Parish.

Haynes, Moses *Shoe Manufacturer*, West Parish.
Heath, Dustin *Joiner*, Winter-st.
Heath, William   "   "
Hersey, Caleb *Merchant & Shoe Manufacturer*, Water-st.
Hills, Nathaniel *Druggist*,   "
Hills, Elisha D. *Joiner*, West Parish.
How, Isaac *Hat Manufacturer*,   "
How, Jacob *Merchant*, Water-st.
How, Phineas *Hat Manufacturer*, West Parish.
Hutchinson, Elisha *Morocco Dresser*, Water-st.

Insurance Agency of the Commonwealth In. Co. Bos-
    [ton, *Moses Nichols*, Main & Water-sts.
Insurance Agency of the Manufacturers' In. Co., Bos-
    [ton, *James Gale*, Water-st.

Johnson, Andrew *Blacksmith*, Stage-st.
Johnson, Thomas *Miller*, East Parish.
Johnson, John & Samuel *Blacksmiths*, Water-st.
Johnson & M'Questen, *Merchants & Taverners*, Rocks'
    [Village.
Jordan, Thomas *Pump-maker*, Main-st.

Keely & Chase, *Merchants & Shoe Manufacturers*, No.
    [2, Main-st.
Kinrick & Eaton, *Painters & Glaziers*, Water-st.
Kimball, Alfred *Joiner*, Kent-st.
Kimball, Benjamin jr. *Merchant*, Water-st.
Kimball, Moses *Joiner*, Washington-st.
Kimball, James B. "   "
Kimball, Richard *Shoe Manufacturer*, Main-st.
Kimball, Richard *Mason*, Water-st.
Kimball, William *Grocer*,   "
Knight, Samuel *Joiner*, Pecker-st.
Knowles, Rufus K. *Tanner & Currier*, Rocks' Village.

Ladd, John *Comb Manufacturer*, Rocks' Village.
Ladd, Nathaniel *Blacksmith*,   "
Ladd, William H. *Chaise & Harness-maker*, Water-st.
Lake, Oliver P. *Shoe Manufacturer*, East Parish.
Le Bosquet, J. H. & Co. *Hard Ware Merchants & Lamp*
    [*Manufacturers*, No. 7, Main-st.

Marble, Leonard *Chaise-maker,* How-st.
Marsh, D. & J. *Merchants & Card Manuf'rs,* Water-st.
Marshall & Fletcher, *Coopers,* "
Meady, Thomas *Merchant & Shoe Manufacturer,* "
Merrill, David *Baker,* "
Merrill, Ebenezer *Blacksmith,* "
Moody, Edward S. *Comb Manufacturer,* Rocks' Village.
Morse, Edmund *Joiner,* Main-st.
Mulliken, Stephen *Shoe-maker,* Water-st.

Nichols, Abel *Whitesmith,* Pleasant Point.
Nichols, Moses *Druggist,* Main & Water-sts.
Noyes, Cyrus *Miller,* East Parish.
Noyes, James *Merchant & Shoe Manufacturer,* No. 6,
[Main-st.
Noyes, Samuel *Comb Manufacturer,* Rocks' Village.

Orne, Ephraim B. *Comb-maker,* Rocks' Village.
Osgood, Peter *Druggist & Shoe Manufacturer,* Main-st.

Page & Kimball, *Merchants & Shoe Manufacturers,*
[Main-st.
Palmer, Daniel *Mason,* Water-st.
Palmer, James *Whitesmith,* Pecker-st.
Palmer, Moses S. *Blacksmith,* "
Perley, Daniel S. *Shoe Manufacturer,* Water-st.
Peterson, James *Joiner,* How-st.
Pettengill, David *Shipwright,* River-st.
Pingree, Benjamin P. *Taverner,* North Parish.
Plummer, John *Gilder & Sign Painter,* Stage-st.
Plummer, Thomas *Wheelwright,* River-st.
Porter, Dudley *Merchant,* Water-st.
Post-Office, *James Gale, P. M.* "
Post-Office, *John Johnson, jr. P. M.* Rocks' Village.

Quimby, Philip *Joiner,* Water-st.
Quimby, Philip jr. " "

Rollins, John I. *Comb Manufacturer,* Rocks' Village.
Ross, Moses *Grocer,* Mechanics' Row and Water-st.
Runnels, Thomas *Blacksmith,* River-st.
Russell, Samuel *Shoe Manufacturer,* near Great Pond.

Sargent, Amos *Brick-maker*, West Parish.
Sargent, Phineas *Grocer and Boatman*, River-st.
Sargent, Robert *Brick-maker*, Hale's Mills.
Savary, William *Livery Stable*, Water-st.
Sawyer, James *Wheelwright*, North Parish.
Sawyer, Leonard   "   "
Slocomb, Rufus *Taverner & Wagoner*, Water-st.
Smiley, Amos *Grocer*,   "
Smiley, James *Grocer*, North Parish.
Smiley, M. *Mantuamaker*, How-st.
Smiley, William *Grocer*, No. 3, Mechanics' Row.
Smith, R. & J. *Milliners*, Main & Water-sts.
Stickney, Jeremiah *Taverner*,   "
Steel, M. *Confectioner*,   "
Swan, Daniel *Hatter*, Rocks' Village.

Thayer, A. W. *Printer*, Water-st.
Trow, Ephraim S. *Clock & Watch-maker*, Water-st.
Trow, John *Shoemaker*,   "
Tyler, Job *Morocco Dresser & Shoe Manufacturer*, No's.
          [4, 5, & 6, Mechanic's Row.

Webb, William *Shoemaker*,   Water-st.
Webster, David *Hat Manufacturer*,   "
Webster, Isaiah *Shoe Manufacturer*, West Parish.
Webster, Jonathan 3d, *Blacksmith*, North Parish.
Webster, Joseph *Joiner*, West Parish.
Webster, Nathan *Hat Manufacturer*, Green-st.
West, Charles *Mason*, Water-st.
West, Edwin   "   "
West, Hazen *Wagoner*,   "
West, Thomas 3d, *Mason*, Hale's Mills.
Whitaker, John *Hatter*, North Parish.
Whitaker, David *Shoe Manufacturer*, North Parish.
Whittier & George, *Merchants & Shoe Manufacturers*,
                                    [Water-st.
Whittier, Warner *Merchant*,   "
Williams, Nancy *Mantuamaker*,   "
Wingate, James *Clock & Watchmaker*, "
Wingate, P. & M *Dressmakers*,   "
Woodman, John *Shoe Manufacturer, Tanner & Currier*,
                                    [Water-st.
Woodward, Caleb *Merchant Tailor*, No. 8, Main-st.

SOCIETIES.

Fire Club.
Organized 1768.
MOSES NICHOLS, Clerk & Treasurer.

Haverhill Bridge.
Incorporated 1793.
JAMES H. DUNCAN, President; BENJAMIN WILLIS, Vice President; LEONARD WHITE, Treasurer; CHARLES WHITE, Clerk.

Merrimack Bridge.
Incorporated 1794.
RICHARD STUART, President; MOSES NEWELL, Vice Pres.; ENOCH FOOT, Treas.; GEORGE FOOT, Clerk.

Social Library.
Organized 1796—740 *Volumes.*
GILMAN PARKER, Librarian, Treasurer, & Clerk.

Aqueduct Company.
Incorporated 1802.
DAVID HOW, JAMES H. DUNCAN, JESSE HARDING, Directors; CHARLES WHITE, Treas. & Clerk.

Merrimack Bank.
Incorporated 1814.
DAVID MARSH, jr., Pres.; LEONARD WHITE, Cashier.

Female Benevolent Society.
Organized 1818.
Mrs. JESSE HARDING, Mrs. MOSES GALE, Mrs. ISAAC R. HOWE, Mrs. AUGUSTUS WHITING, Managers; Miss ELIZABETH MARSH, Secretary & Treasurer.

Stage Company.
Organized 1818.
THOMAS NEWCOMB, JOHN DOW, CHARLES WHITE, Directors; HIRAM PLUMMER, Treas. & Agent.

Fragment Society.
Organized 1825.
Mrs. A. W. THAYER, Mrs. OLIVER BROWN, Mrs. ABEL PAGE, Mrs. SARAH WHITTIER, Managers; Miss LYDIA WHITE, Secretary & Treasurer.

Haverhill Academy.
Incorporated 1827.
Rev. GEORGE KEELY, Pres.; NATHAN WEBSTER, Treas.; JAMES H. DUNCAN, Sec'ry.

Temperance Society.
Organized 1828.
Rev. GARDNER B. PERRY, President; Rev. DUDLEY PHELPS, Vice Pres.; ABIJAH W. THAYER, Sec'ry and Treasurer.

Savings Bank.
Incorporated 1829.
JAMES H. DUNCAN, Pres.; ISAAC R. HOWE, BENJAMIN GREENLEAF, Vice Pres.; JAMES GALE, Secretary and Treasurer.

Haverhill Lyceum.
Organized 1830.
RUFUS LONGLEY, Pres.; ISAAC R. HOWE, Vice-Pres.; JAMES H. DUNCAN, Cor. Sec'y; JAMES GALE, Rec. Sec.; GILMAN PARKER, Treasurer.

Mutual Fire Insurance Company.
Incorporated 1830.—Not yet organized.

East Haverhill Temperance Society.
Organized 1830.
Rev. OTIS WING, Pres.; TIMOTHY KINNISON, Vice-Pres.; ANDREW KINNISON, Sec'y.

Mechanics' Library Association.
Organized 1831.—200 *Volumes.*
ELBRIDGE G. EATON, Pres.; FREDERICK GILMAN, Vice-Pres.; THOMAS M. HAYES, Sec'y.

Youth's Temperance Association.
Organized 1831.
ELIAS T. INGALLS, Pres.; THOMAS M. HAYES, Vice-Pres.; MOSES H. WHITTIER, Sec'y and Treasurer.

INDEX

----, George 28 Israel Jr 68
ABBOT, 122 Abiel 84 109 110 121 185 187 189 190 215 Rev Mr 193
ADAMS, Eliphalet 116 John 185-187 202 Mrs John 185 Phineas 169 188 215 216 Samuel 202
AIKEN, Samuel 184
ALLEY, John 178 Joseph A 220 Mrs 173
AMES, Ezra C 220
ANDROSS, Edmund 113 Gov 114
APPLETON, Daniel 200 G 220 J A 220 John 78 220 Samuel 179 Thomas R 13 William 181
ATKINSON, Theodore 144
ATWOOD, Carolus 217 Johannes-Mulliken 217
AYER, 145 207 Capt 128 130 George W 220 Hannah 177 James 67 68 158 180 James 2nd 220 John 29 32 146 John 2nd 29 68 130 John Jr 26 John Sr 26 29 Nathan 178-180 Nathaniel 177 Obadiah 179 Obadias 216 Peter 28 29 52 54 59 62 217 218 Richard 220 Robert 29 54 Ruth 126 Samuel 97 104 125 126 146 218 Samuel W 33 220 Sarah 189 Thomas 28 29 67 126 Thomas Jr 54

BACHELDER, William 191 197
BACHELLOR, Mr 163 164 Samuel 156 168 215 218 William 219
BACK, Jacob 180 Samuel 180
BADGER, Moses 216
BAGLEY, Philip 178

BAILEY, Benjamin 220 John 179 Joshua 153 Phineas 220
BAKER, Benjamin 180 William 178 180
BALCH, J 220 M P 220
BALLARD, Ebenezer 179
BARKER, Edward Jr 181 Jonathan 179 180 Stephen 150
BARNARD, Edvardus 216 Edward 160 170 175 215 John 46 Mr 137 171 Mrs John 46 Rev Mr 172 Thomas 170
BARNSBY, Henry 65
BARTLETT, 177 188 Bailey 7 41 122 156 187 188 202 218 Charles L 220 Enoch 168 Israel 173 178-180 220 Joseph 127-129 Mr 203
BATCHELDER, William 215
BAYSE, Matthew 15
BELKNAP, 78 141 149 158 207 Hannah 177
BENTLEY, Mr 114
BETTE, Widow 60
BLACK, Edmund 163
BLANCHARD, Samuel 192
BLODGET, Judge 192 Samuel 166 183 192 218
BODGE, Nathaniel 179
BOND, Gilbert 181 Joseph 67
BOSWORTH, Hanniel 52 Miss 52
BOUTON, Nathaniel 17 148
BOWEN, William 198 215
BOZMAN, Mr 79
BRADBURY, Judge 202 Tho 18
BRADFORD, Mr 181
BRADLEY, Benjamin 199 Daniel 65 95 137 Enoch 206 Hannah 95 Isaac 78-81 83 84 John 148

229

BRADLEY (continued)
  Jonathan 147 148 Joseph 68 70
  78 95 97 107 108 112 125
  Martha 95 Mary 95 Mr 170
  Mrs 107-110 112 Mrs Samuel
  148 Samuel 147 148 Sarah 95
BRADLY, Daniel 65 Joseph 65
BRATTLE, Mr 114 Rev Mr 138
BRICKETT, Daniel 182 220 James
  176 179 180 182 183 197 John
  220 John Jr 219 220
BROOKS, Edward 141 Mrs
  Edward 141
BROWN, 221 Cotton 141 216 Dr
  160 Ephraim H 181 George 28
  34 46 217 H 159 Joanna 141
  Johannes 216 John 30 141 146
  157 159 215 Madam 159 Miss
  141 159 Mrs John 30 Mrs
  Oliver 227 Nicholas 67 Peter 41
  54 Rev Mr 149 Richard 135
  Thomas 141 216 Ward 141 216
  William 220
BRUMIDGO, Edward 21 68
BUCK, Samuel 178
BURGOYNE, 174 Gen 197
BURNS, 98
BURR, Aaron 202 Harriet 220
BURRILL, Joseph 160
BUTLER, William 26
BUTTON, Hannah 52 Matthias 28
  39 49 Old 49

CALDWELL, Jacob 221 William
  221
CALFE, Mrs Richard 148 Richard
  148
CANADA, Governor Of 110
CARLETON, Charles 221 I Jr 221
  Israel Jr 221 J 221 Michael 221
CARLTON, Christopher 146
  Edward 30 John 45 46 Oliver
  200 Phineas 179
CARR, Francis 218 219
CARTIER, 79
CHADWICK, James 60
CHAMBERLAIN, John 221
CHAPMAN, Aaron 206 221
CHARLES, Ii 114
CHARLEVOIX, 63

CHASE, 223 Abigail 221 Anthony
  221 Edmund 180 Hannah 198
  John 206 221 Moody 22 Samuel
  221 Tappan 221 Thomas G 221
CHECKLEY, Mrs Samuel Sr 121
  Samuel 139 Samuel Sr 121
CHENARIE, John 28 33
CHILD, Samuel 72
CHIPMAN, John 141 Mrs John
  141
CHOATE, John 162 164
CLARK, Edward 28 36 146
CLEMENT, Amos 179 Elizabeth 19
  James 179 180 James Jr 180
  Job 11 24 25 30 32 43 John 26
  33 42 43 217 Margaret 25 Mr
  42 Mrs John 43 Nathaniel 146
  Robert 19 26 42 43 217 Robert
  Jr 28 Robert Sr 29
CLEMENTS, Job 24 John 39 43
  Robert 18 24 43
COBBETT, Rev Mr 49
COCHRANE, 221
COFFIN, 32 36 71 111 Dionis 20
  Enoch 145 Isaac 21 Joan 20
  John 20 Joshua 8 Mary 20 Mrs
  19 Mrs Tristram 19 Robert 117
  Sarah 129 Tristram 18 19 21
  26 145 William 129
COGSWELL, John 162 John Jr
  179 Thomas 178
COLBY, Nicholas 192 Stephen 221
  William 221
COLE, Benjamin 192
COOK, John 180
COOPER, Dr 141
CORDWELL, Enoch 180
CORLISS, Ephraim 26 33 219
  George 26 30 87 John Jr 221
  Mary 87 Phineas 221
COTTLE, Thomas 161
COTTON, Elizabeth 113 Joanna
  141 Rowland 113 141
COUSINS, Isaac 28 34 36
CROSS, Abijah 203 215 220 Peter
  51 Stephen 166
CROSSE, John 15
CROWELL, Jonathan 211 221
CURRIER, D 160 Hugh M 221
  Nathaniel Jr 221

CUSHING, Chief Justice 184
  James 154 166 215 Jeremiah 57
  Jonathan 138
CUTLER, Timothy 115

DALTON, John 126
DANA, Mr 141 Mrs 141
DAVIS, Charles 221 Christian 21
  Ephraim 146 George 30 James
  10 28 43 219 221 James Jr 26
  32 James Sr 26 32 Jeremiah
  181 John 26 33 217 221
  Joseph 146 Mr 124 125 Mrs
  George 30 Samuel 146 Thomas
  18 19 21 26 28 31 38 39 54
  William 217
DAVY, Humphrey 217
DAY, 182
DECHAILLONS, 117
DELUDE, 129
DENIZEN, Elizabeth 113 Maj Gen
  43 Mr 113
DEROUVILLE, Hertel 117
DINSMOOR, Robert 200
DODGE, Ephraim 178 Joseph 173
  Joshua 193 198 200 215
DOLE, Paul 221
DOW, Charles W 221 John 68 178
  180 221 226 Martha 95 Polly
  194 Stephen 69 95 Stephen 3rd
  72 Stephen Jr 68 69 Stephen Sr
  68
DOWNING, John 178 Moses 180
DRAKE, Mr 86 95 Samuel G 79
DUDLEY, Gov 117 Joseph 126
  Thomas 25 Wm 151
DUMMER, Margaret 25 Richard 30
  Wm 151
DUNBAR, Charles H 221
DUNCAN, Jacobus-Henricus 217
  James 173 179 James H 200
  219 220 226 227 Samuel 179
  Samuel W 68 195 208 Samuel-
  White 217 Wid Samuel W 68
  113 159
DUNSTAN, Thomas 86
DUSTAN, Thomas 86
DUSTIN, Abigail 93 Dudley 179
  Ebenezer 180 Elizabeth 93
  Hannah 7 63 93 John 93
  Jonathan 93 Jonathan Jr 178

DUSTIN (continued)
  Joshua 96 97 Lydia 93 Martha
  93 95 Mary 93 Mehitable 93 Mr
  87 88 95 Mrs 88-93 119 Mrs
  Thomas 87 Mrs Thomas 3rd 93
  Nathaniel 93 Sarah 93 Stephen
  178 Thomas 86 93 96 97
  Thomas 3rd 93 Timothy 93
DUSTON, Thomas 86

EAIRES, Capt 128
EAMES, Samuel 181 Theodore 217
EASTERBROOK, Joseph 221
  Samuel 221
EASTMAN, Ebenezer 142 145-148
  153 165 Sarah 95
EATON, 223 Capt 178 Elbridge G
  227 Jeremiah B 221 Job 221
  John 26 152 174 178 Petrus
  216 Samuel 173 Thomas 54 76
  95 Timothy 86 221 Ward 221
EDES, Benjamin Jr 184
EDMUNDS, Alice 19
EDWARDS, John 222
ELA, Daniel 52-54 56-59 Mrs
  Daniel 57-59
ELIOT, Dr 170
ELIZABETH, Queen Of England 25
EMERSON, Ann 139 B 222
  Benjamin 2nd 222 Capt 123
  Catharine 188 Dorothy 60
  Elizabeth 60 95 Hannah 93
  Ithamar 222 Jesse 222 Jona-
  than 67 105 124 Joseph 54 M E
  222 Michael 40 44 51 54 93
  Miss 93 Moses 180 216 Moses
  3rd 222 Mrs Robert 49 Nathan
  222 Nathaniel 51 Nehemiah 40
  67 68 123 124 131 174 178
  Nehemiah Jr 179 Robert 49 54
  139 Sarah 95 Stephen 146
  Thomas 95 Timothy 95
EMERY, John Sr 36 Mrs John Sr
  36
EVERETT, S 190

FAIRFIELD, 95 101 M D 91 92
FANE, Elizabeth 19
FARMER, 78 113 141 John 8 127
FARNSWORTH, T G 215 Thomas G
  199 219 220

FARNUM, Roswell 222
FAY, Galen H 187
FIRMIN, Giles 9
FISKE, James 26 29 32 33 Mr 139
FITTS, Jeremiah 222
FLETCHER, 224
FOOT, Enoch 219 222 226 George 226 Samuel C 222
FORD, Mary 70 Robert 54 67 Samuel 67
FOSS, John 192 William 222
FOSTER, Ebenezer 180
FRANKLIN, Jonathan 73
FRINK, Andrew 199
FYRMIN, Gyles 10

GAGE, Ebenezer 219 Job 178 180 John 179-181 Josiah 59 William 178
GALE, James 222-224 227 Moses 222 Mrs Moses 226
GALLEY, James 222
GARDNER, Capt 117 Joshua 135 137 215 Mr 138
GARY, Thomas 171
GATES, Gen 197
GEORGE, 225 Jacob 180 James 37 Samuel 222 William 222
GIBBS, William 8
GIDDINGS, George 15
GILE, Amos 179 Mr 165 Mrs 165 Samuel 10 26 54
GILMAN, Frederick 222 227
GODKIN, Benjamin 200 Mr 201
GOODRIDGE, 71 Barnard 222 Ezekiel 222
GOULD, William A 222
GRAHAM, John 180
GREELY, Andrew Sr 48 Joseph 73 222
GREEN, David 180 John 179 Richard 30
GREENLEAF, Benjamin 8 217 227 Samuel 179 William 178 180
GREENOUGH, Ebenezer 180 216
GREGORY, Jonas 51
GRIFFIN, John 47 Robert 175
GROSVENOR, Moses G 200 201 215 Mr 188
GUBTAL, 222

HAINES, Elizabeth 84 85 Jonathan 84 Joseph 84 85 Mary 84 Mr 17 Ruth 84 85
HALE, Ezekiel 11 34 206 222 Moses 139 Mr 30 Sarah J 93 Thomas 26 28 31 33 39
HAMMOND, Andrew W 222
HANCOCK, Gov 202
HANSON, Elizabeth 63
HARDING, 222 Jesse 194 226 Mrs Jesse 226 Thomas 219 222
HARMON, 222
HARRIMAN, 222 Moses 178 181 Nathan B 222 William 180
HARRIS, David 178 Jonathan 178 180
HARROD, Benjamin 163 Mr 190 Mrs 173
HART, Thomas 218
HARTSHORNE, Mrs Thomas 122 Ruth 70 Thomas 122 126
HASELTINE, Abigail W 222 James 180 John 32 49 67 68 100 218 Jonathan 196 Ladd 196 Nathaniel 67 76 136 Philip 218 Robert 32 39
HASSELTON, Ladd 222 Leonard 222 Samuel 222 Stephen 222 Ward 222
HASTINGS, Chauncey 194 222
HATCH, Col 121 Mrs Col 121
HAWKE, 46
HAYES, Thomas M 222 227
HAYNES, 103 Gilman 211 222 Jonathan 101 Joseph 85 86 101 163 164 Moses 223 Mr 102 154 Thomas 180 Young 102
HAYWARD, John 55
HAZEN, Nathan W 200
HAZZEN, Moses 146 Richard 158 218 Richard Jr 146 Richardus 216
HEATH, Bartholomew 26 29 33 54 111 Dustin 223 John 97 Josiah Jr 97 Josiah Sr 97 Nehemiah 146 William 223
HENDRICK, Abraham 70 Daniel 26 29 34 54 217 Israel 68
HERSEY, Caleb 223
HILL, Daniel Jr 179

HILLS, Elisha D 223 Nathanael 21 / Nathaniel 223
HOIT, John 33
HOLDRIGE, William 28
HOLT, Joseph 67 Nicholas 46
HOPKINS, Robert 180 Thomas 179
HOW, David 36 206-208 219 226 Isaac 211 223 Isaacus-Reddington 217 Phineas 211 223
HOWE, Isaac R 220 227 Mrs Isaac R 226
HOWLET, Thomas 30
HOYT, John 84 William 192
HUBBARD, 17 24
HUDSON, James 169
HUGHES, Christopher 28
HUSSEY, Christopher 11 26
HUSTON, William 180
HUTCHINS, John 28 37 46 56 Mrs John 37 Samuel 135 217 Thomas 40
HUTCHINSON, 22 89 92 103 110 118 119 157 Elisha 223 Lt Gov 167 Mr 71 126

INCE, Jonathan 130
INDIAN, Cutshamakin 16 Miantonamoh 17 Pasaquor 13 Passaconnamy 16 17 Passaconnaway 18 Passaquo 18 Passaquoi 19 Saggahew 13 18 19 Samuel 49 Simon 49 53 Wonolanset 17
INGALLS, Elias T 227 Samuel 70

JACKSON, Stephen 178
JAMES, King Of England 141
JEFFERSON, Thomas 202
JENKS, Joseph 35
JEWETT, Mr 41
JOHNSON, 26 Andrew 223 Catharine 126 Daniel 200 Edward 130 John 41 122 126 160 217 223 John Jr 224 Jonathan 107 108 Joseph 178 Leonard 206 Lt 130 Mrs John 122 Ruth 126 Samuel 223 Thomas 126 223 Timothy 146 173
JORDAN, Thomas 223

KEELY, 223 George 215 220 227
KEEZAR, George 95 John 58 72 73

KEEZAR (continued) John (continued) 95 119 Moses 178 180 Mr 78 101
KENT, Richard 151 152 Stephen 28 33 35 37 39
KIMBALL, 221 222 224 Alfred 223 Benjamin Jr 223 Cotton 180 Hannah 95 James B 223 Joanna 53 John 53 95 Joseph 53 192 Mary 53 54 Moses 192 223 Nathan 181 Nathaniel 178 Priscilla 53 Richard 223 Samuel 178 Thomas 53 William 223
KINGSBURY, 95 Ephraim 53 62 Henry 54 Joseph 97 Methitable 95 Sergeant 112 Thomas 67 95 97
KINNISON, Andrew 227 Timothy 220 227
KINRICK, 223
KNAPP, 203
KNIGHT, Samuel 223
KNOWLES, Rufus K 223
KNOWLTON, Nathaniel 162

LADD, Capt 148 Daniel 10 26 29 42 44 52 101 218 Daniel Jr 72 Dudley Jr 180 John 223 Mr 102 Nathaniel 71 223 Samuel 60 101 William H 223
LAKE, Oliver P 223
LAPERRIERE, 118
LEBOSQUET, Caleb B 219 J H 223
LECOUNT, Moses 180 Samuel 178
LEE, John 180
LEMONT, William 178
LENNARDSON, Samuel 89-91
LEVERETT, Rev Mr 138
LEWIS, 13 14 35
LINDALL, 128
LITTLEFIELD, 128
LITTLEHALE, John 49-51 Richard 11 23 26 30
LONG, Richard 77
LONGLEY, Rufus 220 227
LORD, Robert 18

M'HARD, James 159
M'QUESTEN, 223
MACCLARY, John 39

MANSISE, Cornelius 168
MARBLE, Leonard 224
MARSH, Abigail 175 200 Cutting 175 D 224 David 175 179 218 David Jr 226 Elizabeth 175 226 Enoch 175 179 J 224 Johannes 216 John 67 175 Jonathan 67 76 175 Judith 175 Lydia 175 200 March 175 Mary 175 Moses 175 Nathaniel 173 175 179 180 197 218 Onesiphorus Jr 67 175 Onesiphorus Sr 67 175 Thomas 70
MARSHALL, 224
MARTIN, Robert 180
MASH, 67
MATHER, 79 Cotton 11 74
MEADY, Thomas 224
MERCIER, Hannah 49 Richard 49
MERRIE, Joseph 10 24 26
MERRILL, Daniel 175 David 224 Ebenezer 224 Gyles 167 171 188 215 Jacobus-Cushing 217 James C 188 John 104 Moses 188 Nathaniel 137 Samuel 188 217
MIDDLETON, Peter 179 181 Samuel 178 Samuel Jr 178 180
MINOT, Carolus 217 Charles 8 220 Stephen 219 220
MOODY, Edward S 224 Gulielmus 217 Mary 175 Moses B 198 Moses S 217
MOORE, 148
MOORES, Benjamin Jr 179 180 David 178 Joshua 178-181 Moses 180
MORSE, Edmund 224
MULLIKEN, Joseph 159 Stephen 224

NEFF, Mary 87 Mrs 91 William 87
NELSON, Mr 11
NEWCOMB, 221 Jesse 68 Thomas 226
NEWELL, Moses 226
NEWMARSH, 128
NICHOLS, Abel 224 Moses 199 223 224 226 Mr 160 Phineas 160
NICHOLSON, Col 92

NORTON, Rev Mr 39
NOYES, Cyrus 206 224 James 224 Samuel 224

OLIPHANT, David 189
ORMSBIE, Goodman 28
ORNE, Ephraim B 224
OSGOOD, Isaac 168 218 Isaacus 216 John 30 Josua-Bailey 216 Peter 173 224

PAGE, 224 Benjamin 55 Ebenezer 116 John 28 57 218 John Jr 54 Joseph 111 116 Mrs Abel 227 Nathaniel 146 Oliver 180
PAINE, Mr 11
PALMER, Daniel 224 Henry 10 26 28 30 31 217 James 224 Moses S 224 Mr 184
PARKER, Benjamin 160 171 174 215 Chief Justice 202 Daniel 216 Gilman 220 226 227 Judge 202 Mr 70 Samuel 55 69 Zebediah 175
PAYSON, Edward 139
PEABODY, Mrs Stephen 185 Stephen 185
PEALSEY, Joseph 73
PEARSON, Joseph 139
PEARSONS, Mary 152
PEASLEE, Joseph 26 33 68 Nathaniel 68 146 162 Robert 146
PEASLEY, David 180 Joab 206 Miss 183 Nathaniel 151 183 218
PEASLY, Joseph 41 103 105
PECKER, 179 Bart 178 Jacobus 216 James 28 175 178 Jeremias 216 Samuel 67 76 William 180
PECKHAM, Samuel H 203 215 220
PELL, James 180
PENHALLOW, 108-111
PERLEY, Daniel S 224 David 178
PERRY, Gardner 53 Gardner B 227 Goodman 28
PETERS, Mr 84 Obadiah 147 148
PETERSON, James 224
PETTE, Mrs Peter 55 Peter 55
PETTEE, Peter 86

PETTENGILL, David 224
PETTINGILL, Matthew 192
PHELPS, Dudley 201 215 220 227
PIERCE, 221
PIKE, 107 111 112 John 77 84 Joseph 77 Mr 108 126 129 134 Simeon 174
PINGREE, Benjamin P 224 Mr 106
PLUMMER, Frederick 199 Henry 199 215 220 Hiram 226 John 224 Thomas 224
POMEROY, Thaddeus 198
PORTER, Dudley 224
PRICE, Capt 117
PRINCE, Marshal 203
PROVINCE, Governor Of 110

QUIMBY, Philip 224 Philip Jr 224

RANDOLPH, 114 Edward 113
REDDINGTON, Isaac 179
REMICH, Daniel 178 Samuel 180
RICHARDSON, John 20
RIX, James 178-180
ROBIE, Ichabod 71 John 71
ROBINSON, John 10 16 26
ROLFE, Benjamin 66 76 120 126 130 215 Ezra 65 Henry 30 Mehitable 121 Miss 121 Mr 67 73 75 76 105 111 121 122 124 125 129 131 Mrs 121 129 Mrs Benjamin 126
ROLLINS, John I 224
ROSS, Moses 224
ROWE, Jacob 180
ROWELL, Jonathan 153
ROWLANDSON, Mary 63 Rev Mr 89
RUNNELS, Stephen 178 Thomas 224
RUSSELL, Samuel 224

ST DUNSTAN, 86
SALTONSTALL, Col 167 Elizabeth 75 113 Guerdon 113 115 John 113 Leverett 200 216 Major 66 Mr 114 116 Mrs Richard 134 135 N 114 Nathanael 216 Nathaniel 19 46 47 60 65 68 72 75 104 112 113 115 134 217 Richard 104 111-113 134 135

SALTONSTALL (continued) Richard (continued) 154 158 159 161 172 218 Richardus 216 217
SANDERS, John 145
SARGENT, 222 Amos 225 Christopher 183 Jonathan 178 Judge 183 Mrs Christopher 183 Nath'l P 218 Nathaniel Peaslee 173 Nathaniel Peasley 183 Phineas 225 Robert 225 Thomas 181 Zebulon 68
SAUNDERS, 106 James 218 John 218 Nathaniel 218
SAVAGE, Henry 24 26
SAVARY, William 225
SAWYER, Henry 28 James 173 225 John 181 182 Leonard 225 Nathan 68
SEAVER, Nicholas 134
SEWALL, 20 59 60 86 89 90 104 106
SHATSWELL, Mary 36 Theophilus 28 34 36 42 43
SHAW, Gulielmus-Smith 216 John 175 180 184 215 John Jr 180 Mr 185 Mrs 185 William S 185
SHAY, 182
SHERMAN, John 130
SHERRAT, Hugh 54
SHERRATT, Hugh 18 24
SHERRIT, Elizabeth 46 Hugh 21 26 31 33 45 54
SHUTE, Jacob 145
SILVER, Mr 123
SIMONS, Goodman 40 Widow 48 William 45
SINGLETARY, Amos 218 Benjamin 65 Nathaniel 65 Richard 28 61
SLAVE, Hagar 121
SLOCOMB, Rufus 225
SMILEY, Amos 225 Francis 181 James 219 225 M 225 William 225
SMITH, Daniel D 201 215 Hezekiah 168 190 215 J 225 Jonathan K 67 200 Mrs 120 126 Mrs Nathaniel 71 72 Nathaniel 71 72 R 225
SOLEY, Nathaniel 192
SOUTHER, John 180 Samuel 180

STANTON, Robert 138
STARBUCK, Mary 20 Nathaniel 20
STARLING, Josiah 70
STEEL, M 225
STEVENS, Benjamin 142 John H 215 220
STICKNEY, Jeremiah 180 225 John 178
STILLMAN, Samuel 191
STOCKBRIDGE, John 70
STRONG, Gov 195
STUART, Richard 106 226
SWAN, Daniel 225 Joshua 65 66 151 Mr 123 124 Mrs 123 124 Robert 28 46 51 59 217 Robert Jr 70 Robert Sr 65 66 70 Samuel 65 66 70 111 Timothy 41
SWETT, Abraham 179 John 136 140 153 154 156 160 Joseph 37 Mrs Joseph 37
SYMES, Mr 48
SYMMES, Thomas 139 141
SYMONDS, Samuel 43

TALENT, Hugh 159
THAYER, A W 225 Abijah W 227 Mrs A W 227
THOMAS, John 180
THORNTON, Thomas 180
TOMPKINS, Isaac 186 199 215
TOWNSEND, James 178
TRACY, Thomas 217
TROW, Ephraim S 225 John 225
TRUE, Henry 171
TRUMBULL, 112
TUCKER, Ichabod 188
TURNER, Major 117 125
TYLER, Abraham 10 Daniel 178 Job 225 John 178 180 Theodore 178 179 181
TYLOR, Abraham 24 26 35 36

VAUDREUIL, M Gov 118

WAINWRIGHT, Capt 127 130 131 Col 146 Francis 131 Johannes 216 John 131 144 Mary 126 127 Miss 128 Mrs 128 Mrs Simon 123 Simon 59 65 66 68 70 123 126

WAKEFIELD, Joseph 178
WALDRON, Richard 144
WALKER, Admiral 146 Nathaniel 141 Samuel 178 180 217 Timothy 146
WARD, 9 Alice 19 Elizabeth 19 75 113 John 10 18 19 22 25 26 74 76 112 215 Mary 19 75 Mr 11 15 24 27 28 35 39-41 43 45-47 56 57 66 67 73 74 N 74 Nathaniel 22 74 Rev Mr 21 27 Saltonstall 66 75
WARE, Nathaniel 144
WASHINGTON, Gen 187
WASSE, Thomas 43
WATTS, Dr 166 Samuel 67 218
WEBB, Daniel 190 William 225
WEBSTER, Benjamin 55 David 211 225 Eben 67 Isaiah 225 Israel 36 John 36 67 Jona 218 Jonathan 218 Jonathan 3rd 225 Jonathan Jr 218 Joseph 225 Mary 36 Moses 217 Nathan 36 211 218 225 227 Stephanus-Peabody 216 Stephen 36 67
WEED, Joshua 192
WELCH, Moses 200 203 215
WELLS, Joseph 192
WEST, Charles 225 Edwin 225 Hazen 225 Thomas 49 Thomas 3rd 225
WHITAKER, David 225 Hannah 72 Jacob 67 John 225
WHITE, Charles 8 18 219 226 Johannes 216 John 21 68 69 76 135 150 173 178 218 Leonard 216 219 226 Lydia 227 Mary 21 Nicholas 146 Samuel 142 162 168 218 Timotheus 216 William 10 18 19 21 26 28 34 40 44 57 58 68 76 141 142 146 159 218 Zechariah 95
WHITING, Augustus 220 John 179 Joseph 178 184 Judith 110 121 184 Mrs Augustus 226
WHITMAN, Bernard 190
WHITTAKER, Abraham 59 Anna 121 Joseph 78 80 81 83 97-100 Mary 98-100 Mrs Abraham 59 Samuel 211

WHITTIER, Col 179 Johannes 216 John 178 181 John G 200 Mary 149 Moses 179 Moses H 227 Sarah 227 Thomas 30 52 54 57 106 Warner 225 Widow Nathaniel 67 William 146
WIER, Nathaniel 26
WILD, William 32
WILLARD, J 151 Joseph 168
WILLCOMB, Moses 179
WILLIAMS, John 11 26 Nancy 225 Samuel 117
WILLIS, Benjamin 218 219 226
WILSON, Mr 20
WING, Otis 215 220 227
WINGATE, James 225 John 179 Josua 216 M 225 Moses 170 219 P 225 William 179
WINTER, Jonathan Jr 173
WINTHROP, 17 Fitz-John 115 Gov 9 Mr 10 25
WITHAM, Mark 180 181
WOOD, Susannah 95 Thomas 95
WOODBRIDGE, Benja 75 John 15 25 Mary 75
WOODBURY, Phineas 196
WOODIN, John 28
WOODMAN, Edward 11 John 24 31 95 166 169 225 Samuel 178 Susannah 95
WOODWARD, Caleb 225

www.ingramcontent.com/pod-product-compliance
Lightning Source LLC
Chambersburg PA
CBHW070311230426
43663CB00011B/2086